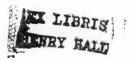

Continental Philosophy and Modern Theology

Continental Philosophy and Modern Theology

An Engagement

DAVID BROWN

Basil Blackwell

First published 1987

Basil Blackwell Ltd
108 Cowley Road, Oxford, OX4 1JF, UK

Basil Blackwell Inc.
432 Park Avenue South, Suite 1503
New York, NY 10016, USA

British Library Cataloguing in Publication Data
Brown, David, 1948–
  Continental philosophy and modern theology:
  an engagement.
  1. Philosophy and religion   2. Philosophical
  theology
  I. Title
  230′.01   BR100
  ISBN 0–631–15734–4

Library of Congress Cataloging in Publication Data
Brown, David, 1948 June 1–
  Continental philosophy and modern theology.
  Bibliography: p.
  Includes index.
  1. Theology, Doctrinal—History—19th century
2. Theology, Doctrinal—History—20th century.
3. Philosophy, Modern—19th century.   4. Philosophy,
Modern—20th century.   I. Title.
BT28.B75 1987   230   87–11817
ISBN 0–631–15734–4

Typset in 10½ on 12 pt Times
by Cambrian Typesetters, Frimley, Surrey
Printed in Great Britain by T.J. Press Ltd, Padstow

Contents

I= theologians   II = philosophers

I = theologians   II = philosophers

I = theologians　II = philosophers

Acknowledgements

It has been my good fortune to know well three men, all now retired, each of whom has sought in his own very different way to relate philosophy and theology more closely to each other. I remain deeply grateful for the example which Donald MacKinnon, John MacQuarrie and Basil Mitchell have set, and the encouragement which they have given me over the years, without which this book would never have been written.

More immediately I must thank my own college of Oriel for the happy environment which it has given me to pursue these studies, and in particular Professor Ernest Nicholson who generously took over my duties as Chaplain while they were being completed. Oriel is very fortunate in having a large number of research students not only from Britain and North America but also from the continent of Europe. Here once again I owe a deep debt, particularly to Rüdiger Bender and Paul de Rosa who commented in detail on the manuscript, resulting in numerous alterations and improvements. I was also greatly helped by several discussions with Katya Fiedler and Jörg Disse. The faults that remain are of course my own.

It would be invidious to single out particular individuals, but I am also grateful to many colleagues who commented on sections of the manuscript read at seminars and discussion groups in Oxford and elsewhere.

Professor David Scott and the Reverend Alan Padgett very kindly helped with the proof-reading.

Introduction

This book has a dual aim which means, I hope, that it will prove of use both to the student beginning the study of doctrine and to the professional scholar.

First, the more basic purpose. Several years of teaching undergraduates contemporary issues in doctrine have convinced me that there is a desperate need for the arguments on opposite sides to be set out as clearly and concisely as possible. For so often when one recommends a range of books to be read, the student gets entangled in the details of a particular theologian's argument and is unable to see the wood for the trees. Indeed, for the public at large 'theological' has come to be equated so much with mere assertion that the word has become virtually synonymous with the obscure and dogmatic. So part of my purpose here is an evangelical one of demonstrating that theology is as rational a discipline as any other, with criteria and arguments to be weighed and assessed. To illustrate the disputes I have drawn upon a wide range of theologians (mostly contemporary), so that the students should become familiarized not only with the key points at issue but also the most significant figures in the dispute, as well as a host of lesser scholars who are also mentioned in passing. Given such an overall aim it could perhaps plausibly have been argued that a legitimate excuse existed for not taking sides in various issues. But I think that that would have been the way of cowardice, and so I have always also indicated my own views. A possible advantage in this may be that, rather than sitting back impassively, the reader will also in consequence be challenged to make a positive response of his own to the questions raised.

My second and deeper aim is partly a reflection of my own personal academic interests and partly a desire to make more explicit the wider context in which theology is in fact practised. As is well known, philosophy as an academic discipline is still largely divided between the analytic tradition as it is practised in the English-speaking world and continental philosophy as found in France and Germany. The result is that names that are marginal to English philosophy like Hegel and Husserl bulk largely on the continent, while the reverse is also true, for example in respect of Frege. The historical reasons for this need not be pursued here. What is important is their effect. For, whereas English-speaking philosophy's preoccupation with linguistic analysis has produced a degree of technicality that has prevented any major influence on other disciplines, continental philosophy's turn instead to an analysis of experience (as in the Phenomenology of Husserl or the Existentialism of Heidegger and Sartre which grew from it) has had considerable ramifications on the intellectual climate as a whole, not least in theology. The net result is thus that it is impossible to fully comprehend contemporary theology without also having some knowledge of continental philosophy. It is therefore with this end in view that each section has not only a piece on significant theologians but also one on some relevant aspect of philosophy.

Despite the fact that my own background is in analytic philosophy, I have sought to resist the temptation common among English-speaking philosophers of regarding continental philosophy as 'shallow' simply because it is in general more accessible and less technically argued. For the issues it raises are clearly important ones. Also, unlike Anglo-Saxon philosophy, among its numbers it has philosophers of the first rank who are prepared to speak and comment upon essentially theological issues. Here one thinks of men like Levinas or Ricoeur. This makes all the more regrettable the way in which English-speaking theologians are so often content to let their knowledge of continental philosophy be confined to Existentialism and not explore the considerable developments which have taken place since. At any rate, this book has been written in the conviction that not only do existing influences need to be better known but also that there are within current French and German philosophy many untapped sources of useful illumination. Hence the explanation of my hope that what follows will also be of use to the professional theologian.

Inevitably it has sometimes proved necessary to explore the past in order to understand the present and so occasional discussions like the sections on Neo-Platonism or Luther will be found. But these are incidental to my main aim which has been to ensure that the reader emerges with a good grasp of the current range of positions to be found in contemporary theology and continental philosophy. Naturally if the reader also comes to share at least some of the conclusions I reach on the doctrinal issues in question, that will be a very pleasant bonus![1]

1

Theological Method

In this chapter I shall examine the three most commonly canvassed methods of founding a system of Christian doctrine, appeals to experience, revelation and tradition. Though theologians frequently stress one or other to the virtual or actual exclusion of the rest, I shall maintain that all three need to be held in complementarity. The chapter will then end with a discussion of the implications of Biblical criticism for the use to which the Bible may be put by the systematic theologian.

Reflection on experience

Schleiermacher to Rahner

Schleiermacher (1768–1834) is often described as the father of modern theology. There are a number of ways in which this might be held to be true, for example through the impetus he gave to hermeneutics (of which more later in the chapter). Most fundamental of all is the direction he gave theology towards reflection on experience. In this he can be seen as part of the Romantic reaction to the Enlightenment, the experiental turn displayed by European thought in response to the Enlightenment's exclusive exaltation of reason. Thus it is to typical Romantic notions such as intuition and feeling that Schleiermacher appeals in his first famous work, *On Religion: speeches to its cultured despisers* (1799).

For the typical Enlightenment thinker religious belief had meant no more than deism, belief in a God who, as it were, set the world in motion but then took no further part in it. By contrast, Schleiermacher attempts to place God at the centre of human concerns by insisting that there are certain universal human experiences that cannot help but raise the question of God. Much subsequent theology, particularly what has usurped for itself the name of 'Liberal Theology', would claim that all theology is in fact of this kind, a reflection on universal human experience, and that even the Bible has to be interpreted in this light. The next section on revelation considers what is wrong with this claim, but first we must examine the more limited areas where there would be general agreement that Schleiermacher was right. For unless there are some elements in our experience that raise for at least some of us the question of God, it is hard to see how theology could even begin to engage our interest.

However, specifying these areas and assessing their epistemological status (what they tell us about God) is far from easy. The nature of the problem can perhaps best be illustrated by contrasting two major twentieth-century theologians, the Protestant Paul Tillich (1886–1965) and the Catholic Karl Rahner (1904–84). Both make appeal to experience central to theology but in characteristically different ways, labelled in what follows the 'metaphysical impulse' (Tillich) and the 'sacramental' (Rahner). Though there are in fact elements of each impulse in both theologians, it seems best to stress that impulse for which each is best known. Both are in any case anticipated by Schleiermacher. Of the two I find Tillich's the more difficult to defend but also the more tempting. As it is a common temptation in theology, it will be profitable to locate first its source and identify what is wrong with it before turning to Rahner's rather different approach.

As many find Tillich's existentialist language hard-going on first encounter, let me first illustrate his basic strategy by reference to a much more straightforward book, Keith Ward's *The Concept of God*. He divides human beings between those who 'tend to view reality, from the first, as a whole' and those who see it 'as a wholly contingent collocation of diverse and essentially unrelated elements'.[1] Not surprisingly, it is the former group whom he identifies as those who find in God a concept that can give coherence to their experience: 'he is the ground of the meaning and value in reality, called one because apprehended under a unitary integrating image.'[2] Such an appeal to an holistic desire to integrate all of one's experience in a single unifying concept certainly takes up one strand in Schleiermacher's thought. In the 'Second Speech on Religion' he writes: 'The contemplation of the pious is the immediate consciousness of the universal existence of all finite things, in and through the Infinite, and of all temporal things in and through the Eternal. Religion is to seek this and find it in all that lives and moves, in all growth and change, in all doing and suffering . . . Where this is found religion is satisfied . . . Wherefore it is a life in the infinite nature of the Whole, in the One and in the All.'[3]

Now at one level this must be right. For there is no doubt that a key impulse in religion has been identified, something that helps to explain why even atheistic systems such as Marxism and Theravada Buddhism are sometimes treated as religions. It is because they are all equally concerned to give some overall unity to experience by providing a total, all-encompassing explanation of the way the world is. Moreover, this 'metaphysical' impulse, as we might call it, can also be given some sort of rationale. For, if God is defined as the source of all that exists, then all our experience, deriving as it does from the source, might be expected to reflect something of that original unity. But two qualifications are immediately evident. First, the argument does not work the other way round. That is to say, while, if God exists, we might legitimately expect the world to reflect the divine unity, the mere desire for such unity can of itself provide no reason for believing in the existence of an objective ground to that unity, nor even that that ground would be God. Our desire might be a vain will-o'-the-wisp, and even if it is not, this unity might be explained in another way, for example in the unity of dialectical materialism as Marxists believe. Secondly, and this brings us at last to Tillich, the danger of relying too exclusively on this metaphysical impulse is that it may lead us to oversimplify and thus fail to see difference, where difference should be acknowledged. Think again of the issue from the divine end. What if God has assigned a relative independence to the world? Might that not prevent complete integration, for example of irreconcilable human evil? Again, even in the case of God himself, why should a basic unity be thought to preclude complexity? Would we not be prepared to describe some human beings as totally integrated characters, and yet their complexity remains considerable?

It is a failure to take qustions like this with sufficient seriousness that leads Tillich to some of his strangest pronouncements on the nature of God. In his main work, *Systematic Theology*, he adopts what he calls 'the method of correlation'.[4] We are first to analyse the tensions and questions posed by human existence and, when we find an answer appropriate to them, that answer will be what is meant by God. So, for example, man asks about the ground of his own being and what can resist the threat of non-being. The method of correlation means that God as answer must be the ground of our being, the infinite power which resists non-being. But the argument is not conducted just in general terms. Specific tensions are also identified which are seen as having their ultimate resolution in God. Three such 'polarities' that he mentions[5] are individualization and participation, form and dynamics (cf. what I am and what I might become) and freedom and destiny. The details need not concern us here. What is worrying is the way in which he goes beyond such specific resolutions to assert that since God is the resolution of all such tensions, he must be beyond all potential sources of conflict. So, for example, he denies that God is properly personal since this would be to take sides on the issue of individual versus participant. Instead he is envisaged as 'participating in every life as its ground and aim'.[6] But in response one wants to ask whether in making God 'equally near'[7] both polarities Tillich has not undermined the aseity or independence of God as a distinct agent. Indeed, decisive confirmation of this comes with the implication that Tillich draws from his conviction that God must also be beyond any potential conflict between essence and existence (roughly, the definition of something and its actuality). He writes: 'God does not exist. He is being itself beyond essence and existence. Therefore to argue that God exists is to deny him.'[8]

This conclusion is just silly. Not only is it, as Tillich admits, in conflict with traditional use of the terms, in effect it puts God beyond the possibility of anything significant at all being said about him, such has been the extravagant blossoming of metaphysical compliments. But in this Tillich is by no means alone. It is one of the objections that might be made against Hindu thought, in which Brahman is also put beyond all attributes, even including good and evil. However, this was not what influenced Tillich. Rather, it was the early nineteenth-century German philosopher Hegel whose philosophy is largely built round the resolution of such opposed polarities, though Tillich would no doubt have wished to ascribe the greater influence to Hegel's slightly younger contemporary Schelling, at least to judge by his remarks about the relative status of the two philosophers in his *Perspectives on 19th and 20th Century Protestant Theology* and elsewhere. But for simplicity's sake we shall continue to emphasise the more famous and more widely influential Hegel.

However that may be, the two main dangers in the metaphysical impulse should now be obvious. First, it may preclude us from taking seriously enough the degree of independence accorded the world (and particularly humanity) by God in creating it. Secondly, it tends to equate unity or wholeness and simplicity, but not only is this identification not nearly as straightforward as may initially appear, as we shall see in more detail in chapter 2 there are good grounds for challenging any such assumption.

The other and I think more plausible impulse that has its basis in experience is what we might call the sacramental impulse, meaning thereby the detection of signs of transcendence in our experience, which need not, of course, imply any overall unity inhering all our experience. An influential example of this kind of approach is to be found in the sociologist Peter Berger's *A Rumour of Angels*. He identifies five 'signals of transcendence' in human experience which move 'inductive faith' to make statements about God.[9] These are order, play, hope, damnation and humour. As the list indicates, they are a diverse group. But what they all share is the way in which all such experiences suggest the possibility (but not the proof) of something beyond themselves. This is what makes the use of the label 'sacramental' so appropriate; for like religious sacraments these experiences are seen as pointing to something beyond themselves.

The range of Berger's reference is impressive. Order and hope are a traditional pair. But the other three are less familiar. Play is mentioned because during it time seems suspended and eternity is perhaps glimpsed; damnation because some evils seem so aweful that no purely human condemnation will suffice; and humour because our ability to laugh in any situation, even in a concentration camp, implies that 'the imprisonment of the human spirit . . . is not final but will be overcome.'[10] Inevitably, some of his illustrations will be found more persuasive than others, and many will find more persuasive, experiences that he does not consider. I shall mention some of these in a moment. But Berger's little book is important because he challenges the common view that it is only a fairly explicit religious experience that could raise for us the question of God. Instead, hints of the transcendent, 'a rumour of angels', are all about us in our everyday experience.

Schleiermacher is someone who pursued the sacramental impulse in more obviously religious experience, and thereby set the pattern for much subsequent theology. Thus in his most important work, *The Christian Faith* (1821), he appeals to 'a consciousness of absolute dependence' which he defines as 'the consciousness that the whole of our spontaneous activity comes from a source outside of us'.[11] I must admit to feeling some sympathy with the reaction of his fellow professor at Berlin. Hegel remarked that, if Schleiermacher's account of the religion impulse were true, then a dog would make the best Christian.[12] For while admittedly recognition of dependence is integral to the idea of worship, it is puzzling why Schleiermacher should have placed such exclusive emphasis on this experience, and also why he should have regarded it as absolute.

By contrast, Karl Rahner is much more impressive simply because of the range of experiences to which he points. So, for instance, he draws attention to a common aspect of our experience of love. We find ourselves accepted absolutely and unconditionally by another, or ourselves extend a similar value to others, and yet there seems no satisfactory explanation of this in the person himself. Again, on occasion we experience responsibility as a demand upon us that just cannot be manipulated but instead draws us out beyond ourselves into what can sometimes be seen as an infinite sense of duty. But Rahner is not just content to refer us to what are perhaps the more obvious experiences such as these moral ones, or that are more explicitly

religious like awe before a beautiful landscape. He also claims that such
signs of transcendence are present everywhere, even if their presence is
denied. 'This unfulfilled transcendentality remains, even though it may
be pushed to one side. It is at work behind countless phenomena of
individual and collective life: in boredom, the mists of which swallow
up the variety of real life; in aggressive irritation at the present because
it comes at us with such intolerable incompleteness that we are tempted
to flee it into a kind of utopian dreamworld of the future.'[13] And so on.

Rahner's ideas were pursued with most philosophical rigour in *Spirit
in the World* and its more theological successor, *Hearers of the Word*,
then subsequently mainly through articles which have been usefully
gathered together in the numerous volumes of his *Theological
Investigations*. But even in his only complete 'popular' presentation of
his theology, *Foundations of the Christian Faith*, the implications of this
style of approach are made entirely clear. The question of God is seen
as being raised each time our experience challenges us to go beyond
itself. Indeed, adopting a criticism of Hegel against Kant, he argues
that for man even to impose limits is already to go beyond them. 'In the
fact that he affirms the possibility of a merely finite horizon of
questioning, the possibility is already surpassed, and man shows
himself a being with an infinite horizon . . . The infinite horizon of
human questioning is experienced as a horizon which recedes further
and further the more answers man can discover.'[14] The point he is
making is that to appreciate something as a limit one has already
stepped out to a perspective that is beyond that limit, and so man is
constantly pushing beyond his experience as he reflects upon it. It is
this that makes so appropriate his designation of God as 'the infinite
horizon', 'the unlimited distance' and so forth. It is this too which
explains his description of God as 'the sacred mystery' since, if he is
perceived in this way, he will always be beyond being grasped by any
set limits of description.

Just as Tillich's approach to the use of the metaphysical impulse was
influenced by Hegel, so Rahner's here was influenced by another
philosopher, the Belgian Jesuit, Josef Maréchal. However, lest the
reader be misled by these comments, perhaps I should add that in other
ways they share a major philosophical influence upon them, namely the
Existentialism of Heidegger (discussed in chapter 3). But for the
moment I simply want to highlight one obvious contrast between them,
the way in which Rahner through Maréchal belongs to a very different
tradition of approach to methodology, an approach which has come to
be known as Transcendental Thomism. Both Hegel and Maréchal were
reacting to the greatest philosopher of the Enlightenment, Immanuel
Kant (1734–1804). So it is only proper that we should assess the
significance of what Rahner is saying against his wider background.

Kant to Maréchal

The significance of Kant for theology is perhaps best summed up in what he himself says at the beginning of his most important work, the *Critique of Pure Reason*, that he has abolished knowledge to make room for faith.[15] For it encapsulates his two main contributions: the negative one of 'abolishing' the traditional arguments for the existence of God at least to the extent of showing that they cannot be regarded as demonstrably valid, as conclusive deductive proofs; the positive one of none the less insisting that God is necessary as a 'postulate of practical reason' in the sense that without such an undergirding belief we could have no reason to hope for complete moral fulfilment in the next life.

On one common reading of his philosophy, Hegel's reaction to this banishing of God to a merely transcendent hope was to stress his immanence in the world, such that he could even be seen as in some sense emerging from it. How that is possible we shall consider in the next chapter when we look at the theme of creation. In the meantime suffice it to say that, while Tillich would be unhappy with such a comparison, the method prescribed for locating God (i.e. through the resolution of conflicts or polarities) is clearly common to both him and Process Theology (also examined in the following chapter). So despite Tillich's desire to place God firmly beyond the world and any dependence on it, like Process Theology he can be seen as part of the Hegelian response to the Kantian challenge of the relegation of God to the marginal.

That last remark may seem unfair to Kant, at least in respect of what we have said so far about his views. For does he not still insist on faith? That is true, but one needs to bear in mind that it is a faith that by necessity cannot receive any kind of confirmation in this life. This is because of the thrust of the *Critique* as a whole, in which only knowledge of phenomena, the directly experienced, is admitted, with things-in-themselves remaining beyond our cognition. Admittedly, in the twentieth century thanks to the publication of the *Opus Postumum*, a work unfinished at his death, it is generally agreed that towards the end of his life Kant moved towards a more positive assessment of our ability to speak of God's involvement in the world, with any suggestion of deism firmly rejected. But this is still in marked contrast to his earlier writings, in which it would be true to say that God remains little more than a hope, not someone of whom one can have experience, far less proof. Indeed, the only work published in his lifetime exclusively devoted to the philosophy of religion, his *Religion within the Limits of Reasons Alone* of 1793 clearly reduces religion to little more than a moral creed, though it has one interesting feature which one might not have expected from the optimism of the Enlightenment, namely stress on the propensity of human beings to evil. It was this earlier less sympathetic account that was best-known in the nineteenth century and indeed continues to be the best-known. Thus, despite the modifications of Kant's old age, it is this picture that must be borne in mind when considering the reaction of Hegel and indeed even the response of Maréchal.

Thus just as Hegel represents one possible reaction to the Kantian challenge – relocating God as essentially immanent in this world of experience, so Maréchal represents another – redefining the conditions for such knowledge. It is a response, however, which is more directly related to Kant's argument and indeed even borrows his terminology. Kant in analysing what makes knowledge possible had proposed various 'transcendental' conditions, the intuition of certain concepts such that without them we could not structure our experience at all or render it intelligible. He has in mind such basic notions as space, time and cause, and he calls them 'synthetic a priori' because they must be known in advance of our experience, if we are to make sense of that experience. In other words, for knowledge to exist at all an active structuring of our experience has to take place with these concepts. Where Maréchal comes in is in questioning whether the existence of God is not presupposed as one of the transcendental conditions of every such active structuring of our experience.

Maréchal develops his argument in the process of a five-volumed work, *Le point de départ de la métaphysique*, which began to be published from 1922 onwards, though the fourth volume only appeared after his death in 1944. The first four volumes trace the history of philosophy from its earliest Greek beginnings to the immediate post-Kantian philosophy of Fichte, though in fact most of two volumes are devoted to Kant. This is in itself significant in that it indicates that long before Vatican II (1962–5) the necessary reorientation of Catholic thought away from too narrow a concentration on Aquinas and towards answering modern challenges to faith was already beginning to take place. Indeed, Rahner and the other major Roman Catholic theologian to be influenced by him, Bernard Lonergan,[16] were both exhibiting his effect upon them long before this revolutionary Council, and so themselves added to the pressure for change. Admittedly, the fact that the position of all three is known as Transcendental Thomism might seem to give the lie to any pretence of revolutionary intellectual implications. But, given the official status of Thomas Aquinas at the time, Maréchal had little alternative but to present his position as still that of Aquinas ('entièrement loyale'[17]), even though viewed through the eyes of Kant.

In rough outline, Maréchal's argument might be put as follows. All knowledge involves a structuring of experience, partly by the object and partly by the subject. But to impose structure implies an awareness of bounds and limits, while to impose a limit is already to transcend that limit. Therefore, every act of knowledge has as the transcendental condition of its possibility the transcending of a limit, and thus knowledge as a whole the transcending of all limits. But that is what we mean by God. Therefore God is implied as the transcendental condition of all knowledge or, as he sums it up: 'Objects in our view are intrinsically related to the Absolute. Their transcendental structure points to Infinite Being, of which they constitute so many finite participations.'[18]

Maréchal obviously thought the argument conclusive. However, what it does show is far from clear. Certainly it would be unfair to object that we are not aware of this infinite underlying presence. For, as Rahner points out, the situation might be rather like the way in which we take the existence of light for granted, though we cannot in fact see without it. But even so an infinite beyond limits is hardly necessarily the same thing as God. Yet, to be fair to Maréchal, one reason for his making the identification is the way in which, unlike Kant, he assigns a very active role to the object in structuring the experience. For this in turn might suggest that the ultimate object doing all this structuring is personal.

But there seem just too many contentious steps in the argument for it to be as conclusive as Maréchal would wish. Certainly, writing in the very different tradition of Oxford analytic philosophy, Ralph Walker sees no possibility of assigning any transcendental role to God, though he does maintain that without belief in a divinely 'pre-established harmony' we can have no grounds for trusting that the future pattern of our experience of the world will resemble its present form.[19] (This is not a transcendental condition because we could adapt to very different forms of experience.) But this is not to say that Transcendental Thomism is therefore of no importance. By drawing attention to a wide range of experience where the question of God is raised, it shows that theology is a discipline that is concerned not just with a narrow set of phenomena called 'religious' experience.

Having admitted the success of Kant's critique of the traditional arguments and denied complete success to Maréchal's response, what then are we to say of the role of justificatory arguments for theology? One major trend in England has been to treat the various arguments as 'cumulative', as together amounting to a plausible inductive case, though none conclusive in themselves. In *The Justification of Religious Belief* Basil Mitchell found illustration for this type of approach from disciplines as varied as history and natural sciences. His successor as professor of the philosophy of religion at Oxford in *The Existence of God*[20] gives a detailed argument of this kind for the existence of God.

In so doing Swinburne relies heavily on religious experience and the argument is presented with considerable scientific rigour, making use of, as it does, confirmation theory. For my part I seriously doubt whether such rigour is plausible. There are just too many uncertain quantities. But this should not be taken as discounting either the possibility or the need to show the essential reasonableness of religious belief. Nor should the absence of rigour or absolute conclusiveness make us despair. After all, in the other two main areas of value, in morals and aesthetics, the foundations are equally contentious and equally hard to establish definitively. Above all we need today to learn a rather different lesson from Kant. His contemporaries rightly had their over-confidence in the power of reason to produce conclusive proof deflated. In our case we need constantly to be on our guard against minimalizing, against supposing that where there is room for doubt, no more can be said. The challenge Maréchal offers us is that throughout the whole range of our experience we are being interrogated as to the possibility of whether there may not indeed be much, much more.

The appeal to revelation

Barth and Troeltsch

So far we have been looking at the treatment by theologians of what has been variously labelled 'natural theology' (as opposed to revealed theology), or 'the anthropological method' (because it starts from man's experience), or 'general revelation' (because it considers experiences which, unlike 'special revelation', could theoretically be had by all men). But, however labelled, one thing is clear. Karl Barth's theology is at the opposite extreme both in method and content, and indeed was forged in reaction to it. In assessing how far his enormous influence this century has been justified, it will be helpful first to look at some positive points that can be made in his defence before turning to some of the difficulties raised, in particular Troeltsch's claim that the rules of the historical method preclude belief in such a God.

The more exclusively the antropological method is adopted the more we have what goes under the name of Liberal Theology. To the uninitiated it might seem that no theology could claim to be Christian without assigning some authority to relevation over and above human experience, and in one sense this is of course right. But it is important to be clear about the very limited sense in which much Liberal Theology is prepared to accord a special status to revelation. For in effect all it understands by special revelation is general revelation at its best, man at the maximum point of insight but with the direction remaining entirely from man to God. There is no special divine initiative. The world remains exactly as it always was. So anyone could have acquired the same insight if he had been sufficiently attuned to the possibilities of his experience.

One recurrent problem in theology is that theologians seldom come clean about the extent to which they would accept this implication. So appeal is made to Scripture as though that necessarily added weight to the argument, whereas it could only do so if some special divine initiative were involved. Otherwise it must remain subject to the same canons of evaluation as any insight you or I might have. It was one of the merits of Barth that he not only saw this clearly, he realized that, if this anthropological method were allowed sway, our knowledge of God, coming as it would only through such universal insights, would be drastically curtailed.

So, for example, commenting on Schleiermacher in his survey of intellectual thought *From Rousseau to Ritschl*, he is concerned to point out that, whatever he may have thought to the contrary, his method has in effect led Schleiermacher to a denial of the doctrine of the Incarnation. This is because he defines Christ's consciousness of God as human self-consciousness perfected. But this is only to make a quantitative and not a qualitative difference between him and us and so 'according to the premises . . . he was bound to renounce the idea of the Deity of Christ.'[21] Barth does not offer other examples, but they are not hard to find. Indeed, one question raised by exclusive concentration on this method is whether it could ever yield very much knowledge at all about God and his purposes for man. To take a very basic Christian belief, God as our Father, is it really plausible to claim that this is an insight that could potentially be had by anyone on the basis of their experience? Does not the status of Christ's teaching rather derive from the fact that God first came close to him and so opened a way in which this might become true for all of us? Or again, take the question of life after death. Why should it be thought that God is so involved with humanity that he should want to take us all up into a higher life? Does not most of ordinary human experience suggest that God is at a distance from us? What gives conviction that there might be something beyond is thus not our own mundane experience, far less a universal human experience, but the witness of those to whom God seems to have come particularly close, particularly in the midst of their suffering, and given them the assurance of a love beckoning them to something beyond. The fact that the so-called death of God theology, typified by Altizer's 1960s classic, *The Gospel of Christian Atheism*,[22] could question whether we experience anything at all of the nature of God except his absence, should in any case give pause for serious reflection about the viability of this method.

Though I think Altizer goes too far, I personally believe in the
essential soundness of Barth's analysis of the limitations of the
method.[23] But, whether the reader is persuaded of the necessity of such
appeals to the authority of others' 'revelatory' experience or not, such
considerations lead naturally into the second positive feature of Barth's
theology to which I want to draw attention. This is his emphasis on the
shocking or surprising quality of revelation, that it is not at all
something that natural reflection would suggest. It is at this point that it
becomes important to recall the precise historical situation in which
Barth's theology was forged. Having been trained in the Liberal
theological tradition before the First World War, it was while he was a
parish minister in the small country village of Safenwil in the north-east
of Switzerland that he heard not only of the outbreak of the war but
also of the fact that ninety-three German intellectuals, including most
of his former professors, had issued a manifesto supporting the Kaiser's
declaration of war. The fact that theology in the tradition of
Schleiermacher should so closely identify itself with the prevailing
culture led him to question its credentials, as also how his own
preaching of the Gospel was to be distinguished from the mere word of
man. The result was *The Epistle to the Romans*, first published in 1919.
It is a clarion call to see God once again as the proper object of
theology and not man, and it was a theme which he continued to
emphasize in his massive and most important systematic work, *Church
Dogmatics*, which he continued working at almost up to his death in
1968.

In *The Epistle to the Romans* God is described as he 'who is
distinguished qualitatively from men and from everything human, and
must never be identified with anything which we name, or experience,
or conceive, or worship, as God'. So in revelation what happens is that
'above and beyond the apparently infinite series of possibilities and
visibilities in this world there breaks forth, like a flash of lightning . . .
the Truth of God which is now hidden.'[24] Little wonder, then, that he
rejects all natural theology and is led to the belief that it is only possible
to preach to the world, not argue with it. Indeed, not only does *Church
Dogmatics* sometimes read like a sermon, it is even the case that bound
with the Index are 'Aids for the Preacher' with appropriate references
to the text.

Such hostility is in marked continuity with the Reformed tradition to
which he belonged, and he shares at least one reason for this hostility in
common with Calvin, and for that matter Luther. This is the conviction
that the Fall has so defaced the image of God in man as to make
impossible any human move towards God. We are too blinded by sin to
achieve any true perceptions on our own. 'Man has completely lost the
capacity for God.'[25] The result is that he wishes to substitute an

analogia fidei ('analogy of faith') for the traditional *analogia entis* ('analogy of being' – the view that God and man share sufficient in common to justify the use of the same predicates, however greatly qualified). By this he means that instead of the meaning of religious terms gaining their meaning first from the secular context and then being transferred to the religious, the process should be seen as being reversed. Meaning first comes from the context of revelation. So, for example, he would hold that it is not the case that we first understand the meaning of 'father' from everyday discourse and then apply it by analogy to God. Rather, we have no clear idea of what the word properly means until that meaning is disclosed in the context of revelation.

But to all this there are two clear objections. First, it is hard to see how we could recognize 'father' as an appropriate term, unless we had first discovered its positive character elsewhere. In other words, language cannot function as a bolt out of the blue. Revelation could modify our understandings of the correct way in which a word is to be used; it could not simply create it. If this linguistic point is difficult to understand, essentially the same argument can be expressed non-linguistically. For it is impossible to see how man could respond to revelation unless there was something there first that enabled him to see such revelation positively as answering his questions. Otherwise it would simply appear as an irrelevance. So a total lack of previous contact is equally ruled out in this way. But, secondly, the Calvinist view of man's prior condition is not just derogatory of man, it is also demeaning of God. For it suggests that, rather than being seen as their ultimate author, God is indifferent to all those splendid outpourings of human creativity that do not explicitly bear his name.

That in his rejection of Liberal Theology he erred too much in the opposite direction, Barth seems to have come slowly to appreciate. At all events, in a brief autobiographical passage in *Church Dogmatics* he remarks in passing that 'in the attempt to free ourselves . . . from these early forms of one-sidedness . . . we took the surest possible way to make ourselves guilty of a new one-sidedness',[26] while in a later volume there is a fascinating passage where, contrary to what one might expect from his theology, there is a eulogy of Mozart 'because he knew something about creation in its total goodness' and that despite the fact that he 'does not seem to have been a particularly active Christian and was a Roman Catholic'.[27] But the clearest indication of a change of heart is in his 1956 lectures on *The Humanity of God*, where he admits to being 'only partially in the right' in his earlier theology.[28] But even so there is no acknowledgement of the essential rightness of natural theology, and that is a pity. Barth's strength lies in the denial that that is all there is. But equally, as we saw earlier, without some natural

theology it is impossible to see why revelation should be of interest. It
only becomes so when we see that there are certain questions posed by
human experience to which it could possibly be the answer.

If that is one criticism one might make of Barth, another stems from
a label that is frequently applied to his theology, Neo-orthodoxy or the
new orthodoxy. For although *Church Dogmatics* is full of marvellous
exegeses of Scripture, there is very little to suggest that his orthodoxy
took seriously the questions posed by historical criticism of the Bible.
That at least could not be said of the Liberal theologians like Harnack
and Troeltsch against whom he was reacting. But whether they
produced the right conclusions is quite another matter. Admittedly, in
so far as Barth sometimes retreats in sharply differentiating 'a maxim of
faith' and 'a maxim of historical knowledge'[29] and seems to imply that
the one can be had without the other, that must be pronounced entirely
wrong. The Christian, no more than anyone else, can escape from
questions of historicity. But it is one thing to admit this, and quite
another to say that it follows from this that a particular world-view or
the world-view most commonly adopted by historians must therefore
also be accepted. Here Barth's instincts were quite right.

The danger of giving normative status to the secular world-view is
well illustrated by the case of Harnack. Already a distinguished
historian in virtue of his seven-volumed *History of Dogma*, in 1900 he
brought out his celebrated book on the essence of Christianity, *What is
Christianity?* Though obviously much of what he says about criticism of
the Bible is valid, the method reduces itself to absurdity when all we are
in effect left with is Jesus promulgating the same sort of values as any
German liberal intellectual at the turn of the century.[30] Despite this
inherent danger of simply endorsing the secular culture, it is still widely
accepted that his younger contemporary, Ernst Troeltsch, offered a
successful means of drawing a distinction between improperly accepting
the world-view of one's own culture and endorsing the world-view that
is an essential prerequisite of doing historical research at all.

So, for example, the American scholar Van Harvey in *The Historian
and the Believer* uses Troeltsch's criteria to attack Barth for accepting
the historicity of the Resurrection: 'The issue is, by what right does
Barth in this particular case suspend those warrants he normally uses
and which he applies when, say, dealing with the story of Jonah or
Joshua?'[31] The argument of the 1898 essay in which Troeltsch most
clearly presents his case, *Über historische und dogmatische Methode in
der Theologie*,[32] can be briefly presented. It is that there are three main
criteria with which the historical method operates, and that all three
must inevitably rule out of court any theology which appeals to miracle
or assigns a specific causal role to the supernatural. The three in
question are criticism (by which he means that historical judgements

are always subject to revision and so never get beyond the status of assessments of probability), analogy (the need to assess such probability by comparison with our own experience and what we know to have happened elsewhere) and correlation (the assumption that events are intelligible only in so far as they can be shown to be part of an already existing causal pattern). As a rough characterization of the way in which historians operate, this is no doubt correct. It is also true that in consequence most would exclude the action of the supernatural as part of their explanation of what has happened. None the less it does not follow from this that such exclusion is integral to the method.

So, for example, in respect of the principle of correlation, precisely because God is regarded as personal and not arbitrary, his actions can be seen as relating to a wider causal context of personal interaction. Again with analogy, though we may have no experience of our own to give confidence in the possibility of miracle, that does not mean that belief in them becomes entirely arbitrary. One can set each alleged case against what we believe to be the general pattern of divine motives for action. Thus Barth might have justified himself by saying that what we know about the nature of God from the Bible as a whole makes it inherently unlikely that he would halt the sun for Joshua and his men to 'avenge themselves upon their enemies',[33] whereas there were particularly good reasons why he might raise Christ from the dead. So what a Christian historian who accepts the Resurrection as a miracle is doing is not opting out of the normal canons of historical method, but supplementing them with the conviction that there is an additional personal agent to be taken into account, i.e. God – supplementing because, apart from this proviso, the usual questions about reliability of sources, alternative explanations and so forth will still apply.

But, it may be said, I have misunderstood Troeltsch's main point. For how could belief in such a God be derived if not from the historical facts. But no historical fact could be the basis of such a belief. For following the rule of analogy with our present experience would prevent us from ever taking any alleged instance seriously. But this is to ignore the way in which shifts of perspective occur. It is not a matter of isolated instances, but of doubts occurring over a whole range of cases such that there then eventually occurs what Thomas Kuhn in his influential *The Structure of Scientific Revolutions* has called a paradigm shift.[34] The supreme irony is that Troeltsch's editors have placed immediately after the present essay under discussion another one published eleven years later, *Zur Frage des religiösen Apriori*, in which he finds himself forced to admit that 'for the pure psychologiser and positivist my theory of religion is just as grossly superstitious as papal encyclicals.'[35] The reason is that he too views the world through a perspective that is in conflict with much modern thought and which equally can find no straightforward historical justification. For he presupposes the real existence of an absolute value as the *a priori* of all knowledge.

There remains one of Troeltsch's criteria which we have not discussed, namely the first, what he calls criticism, with its emphasis on the probably and provisional character of historical judgements. Does not faith require certainty, and so are not faith and the historical method after all in irreconcilable conflict? The philosopher who most influenced Barth certainly thought so, and it is therefore to him that we must now turn.

Kierkegaard

Kierkegaard (1813–55) is often treated as the complete antithesis of rationality, as a defender of a fideistic view of religion, that faith alone matters and thus need furnish no objective grounds for belief. So, for example, Alistair MacIntyre charges him with advocating 'criterionless' choices.[36] Certainly it must be conceded that there is much in his writings to justify such accusations, and, in so far as such views are present, for the reasons given above they must be pronounced wrong. Faith cannot escape the question of justification. But I do not think that this is the only interpretation of what he has to say. For, once he is placed in his historical context it is possible to see him as making an entirely valid and important point about the nature of faith.

Two features of his time need to be remembered, the fact that the dominant philosophy was Hegelianism and conditions in the state, Lutheran church of his native Denmark. H. L. Martensen, who was Kierkegaard's university tutor and was later to become Danish Primate, was a devoted Hegelian. But, as we saw earlier, Hegel's response to Kant's relegation of God beyond the sphere of knowledge was to relocate him within the world as finding expression in the march of history. The result was that God and the world became in *some* ways synonymous, and because of this near-equivalence Christianity was conceived of as being essentially reasonable, at least when expressed in this philosophical form. But, if the intellectual climate tended to identify Christianity with reasonableness and the present state of the world, so equally did the Church of his day. It was essentially conformist, and, as the standard biography by Walter Lowrie informs us, Kierkegaard rebelled against this even to his dying breath, refusing the eucharist on his death-bed with the words: 'The parsons are royal functionaries, and royal functionaries are not related to Christianity.'[37] He saw the Gospels as offering a very different message, and this was undoubtedly one of the features which attracted Barth towards him. So of the several quotations from him in *The Epistle to the Romans*, the following is typical: 'May we be preserved from the blasphemy of men who "without being terrified and afraid in the presence of God . . . without the trembling which is the first requirement of adoration . . . hope to have direct knowledge" .'[38]

It was in his views on ethics that his rebellion was first worked out. Integral to Hegel's view of ethics was rejection of the Kantian emphasis on *Moralität* (personal decision) and its replacement with *Sittlichkeit* (conformity with social norms). Kierkegaard restored the Kantian stress on personal responsibility, but in a way which fundamentally challenged the conformist character of the Hegelian position. Thus in his first major work, *Either-Or*, he sees the fundamental moral contrast as lying between the 'aesthetic' and moral perspectives, with the former characterized as a search for immediate satisfaction and the latter by unconditional demands. It was an argument which he carried a stage further with the publication of *Fear and Trembling* later that same year (1843). In it he interprets Abraham's sacrifice of Isaac as involving a still higher demand in 'the teleological suspension of the ethical'.[39] But it is hard to follow him here and understand what it could mean to have a demand that transcends morality, if God is himself the ultimate author of all morality (though some commentators do attempt a reconciliation[40]).

But, whether Kierkegaard was right or not in this instance, it does illustrate well his main strategy, which is to challenge Hegelian certainties both about what we know and about the way in which we acquire such knowledge. In short, for Kierkegaard this form of the Romantic reaction to the Enlightenment, Hegel's easy confidence about God, just will not do. Kierkegaard retains a Kantian pessimism about the limits of our knowledge. But at the same time he equally firmly insists that we cannot halt there. For man has a passion for the infinite that keeps pressing him beyond. Kierkegaard fully admits that there may not be any objective correlate to such desires. But he is equally insistent that philosophy could not in any case provide us with knowledge of it. This is not only because of the admitted Kantian limitations but also because the very nature of philosophy is inappropriate to the search. In his most important work, *Concluding Unscientific Postscript* (1846), he provides a vivid analogy to illustrate the point. Philosophical method requires objective lightness, as with the use of a saw, whereas at the limits of our knowledge understanding will come only through subjective heaviness, i.e. through passion.[41]

In saying this he surely has a legitimate point. If we admit that there is some evidence to justify a particular moral or religious perspective, but keep holding back and demanding still stronger evidence, the net result may simply be the loss of any understanding at all, which none the less could have been ours, had we been willing to take the initial risk of belief. Putting it like that helps to put in a better light what is often regarded as Kierkegaard's most conspicuous irrationalist utterance in the *Postscript*: 'If the mode of this relationship is in the truth, the individual is in the truth even if he should happen to be thus related to what is not true.'[42] From the context it is clear that he is not saying that truth is unimportant, but that at the limits understanding only comes through commitment, and without commitment one cannot attain to the truth at all.

Perhaps a Biblical parallel will help. One might compare the numerous conditions that Jacob imposes upon belief in God with the unqualified character of the commitment in the psalm that concludes the book of Habakkuk.[43] One could of course read the latter as irrationalism pure and simple, but equally one can see that to adopt Jacob's attitude would effectively preclude one from ever properly acquiring a religious attitude to life. One's attitude would be always provisional and so always under the control of one's former perspective. This explains the attitude Kierkegaard adopts to history in the *Postscript*. He complains of its approximate and provisional character. In saying this he should not be taken as denying the relevance of historical considerations. But they can only take us so far and not beyond into the most important stage, through 'the leap of faith'. It is only through living the perspective with passion that it can properly be tested, just as it is also true when one falls in love or adopts a particular moral perspective such as pacifism or patriotism that the only way to fully appreciate what it means is to try it.

This straining at the limits also explains why, like Barth, he places such emphasis on the Incarnation and indeed insists that 'if one does away with the God-Man, one does away with Christianity.'[44] Man is straining at the infinite, but the attractiveness of Christianity lies precisely in the fact that it claims that the infinite has met man in this straining by becoming finite. It thus opens up the possibility of the limits of our knowledge being transcended. This is one reason why he likes the element of paradox in Christianity and can even claim that 'the thinker without a paradox is like a lover without feeling.'[45] For paradox can indicate a serious engagement with those limits, rather than simply a retreat before them.

The main lesson, then, we might derive from Kierkegaard is this: though Kant was right that there are strict limits to what we can know by formal reasoning, that does not mean that there is nothing beyond those limits, nor that, provided there are reasonable grounds for taking the 'risk of faith', faith itself might not provide some kind of subjective certainty, as we seek to live in the light of that belief. Nor should we think it a peculiarity of religion; it is equally true of moral beliefs.

Barth has undoubtedly been the most important conservative

Protestant theologian of the twentieth century. The person who holds the equivalent position in Catholic thought has also been heavily influenced by Kierkegaard, 'the witness of truth in our times'[46] as he calls him. But inevitably because of his Catholicism there is more stress on tradition in Hans Urs von Balthasar. It is therefore to the question of the role of tradition in theological method that I next turn.

The role of tradition

von Balthasar

There is no doubt that appeal to tradition is often synonymous with unthinking conservatism, with reaction taking the place of reason. But what makes von Balthasar one of this century's great theologians is precisely the fact that this cannot be said of him. For, though he does speak out in favour of many conservative but unpopular causes such as the celibacy of the clergy, all this has to be set in the context of a sustained intellectual defence of the view that the Church should adopt a very different perspective from the 'world'.

Unfortunately, until very recently the monoglot English reader would have had considerable difficulty in appreciating this intellectual depth. For, although a number of his more popular works have been available for some time, it is only recently that we have been given *The von Balthasar Reader*, selections that provide some indication of his range and approach. But much more importantly the task of translating his major work has now begun.[47] This von Balthasar had intended to be in three parts, each occupying several volumes, but so far only the first two parts are complete. His age (b. 1905) in any case now makes completion unlikely. He sees theology as concerned with the beautiful, the good and the true. The third part, *Theological Logic*, would have been concerned with the true. The second deals with the good, with the divine goodness as it has expressed itself in action, but there is still a strong aesthetic emphasis carried over from the first part, as its German title, *Theodramatik*, makes clear. But it is the first part that is the most important. For it is there that he attempts to reverse current theological trends and 'show how impoverished Christian thinking has been by the growing loss of this perspective which once so strongly informed theology.'[48] That perspective is perhaps more clearly indicated by the German title of the work as a whole, *Herrlichkeit*, with its wider aesthetic resonances, than the English translation, *The Glory of the Lord*, but the subtitle of Part I makes it clear what is going on, 'A Theological Aesthetics', and still more so the title of the first volume (of the seven in that part) 'Seeing the Form'. It is possible to identify two major theses underlying his position.

The first is his claim that understanding is possible only by viewing something as a whole, by examining its form, and that too much attention to the parts has in fact distorted theology. On the Protestant side things went wrong, he suggests, right from the start with Luther. For his insistence on the 'scandal' of the absolute contrast between this world of ours and the divine irruption into history means that 'no harmonising, no skill, no comprehension is permitted. Every form which man tries to impose on revelation in order to achieve an overview that makes comprehension possible – for this is presupposed in beauty – every such form must disintegrate in the face of the "contradiction".'[49] But he observes a similar disintegration within Roman Catholic theology, this time the impetus coming from Decartes' modelling of philosophy 'on the scientific ideal of the rising natural sciences'[50] and theology's resultant attempt to justify itself in relation to them, particularly through a concern for historical detail. Instead he argues that theology's proper task is to look at the form of reality as a whole, particularly at the way in which 'God's Incarnation perfects the whole ontology and aesthetics of created Being.'[51] It is in this context that he is prepared to say that 'even Scripture is not an isolated book, but rather is embedded in the context of everything created, established, and effected by Christ.'[52] In other words, in attempting to understand the nature of the Christian faith one must look at the system as a whole, at the history of the Church and God's involvement with the world, not just some allegedly key passages in Scripture. 'For we can be sure of one thing: we can never again recapture the living totality of form once it has been dissected and sawed into pieces.'[53]

From the quotations given so far it might seem that all we have is an intensely conservative desire to maintain the system as it always has been. But that would be wrong. He is highlighting a common problem. For it is often the case that we get so obsessed with details that we fail to see the wood for the trees, or may even refuse to make a commitment to faith because of anxiety about details such as the fallibility of Scripture or corruption in the history of the Church when these can find a perfectly clear rationale in terms of the system of belief as a whole. So, for instance, von Balthasar does attempt an original explanation of those scriptural passages which imply the imminence of the world's end, as also some explanation of why imperfection has always characterized the office of leadership in the Church, with 'Peter' always being in need of supplement by the love of 'John'.[54] Such examples demonstrate that he is not unwilling to take account of historical criticism, though as with Barth I do not think that he goes far enough. But, that said, his major point remains. A particular perspective on the world must be judged in terms of its coherence as a whole, i.e. on its form, not on particular items of content, taken in isolation and perhaps judged on the basis of wholly irrelevant criteria.

His other main thesis is perhaps the more contentious of the two. It is that a particular type of perceptual capacity is required in assessing the form.. In saying this he does not claim to be saying anything new, but rather to be following a long tradition in the Church of emphasizing the need for contemplation.[55] 'Works of art can die as a result of being looked at by too many dull eyes, and even the radiance of holiness can, in a way, become blunted when it encounters nothing but hollow indifference. But this remains but an external offence to beauty which may be rectified by purifying the heart and by exhuming what has been buried under the ruins.'[56] Certainly the parallel, if justified, would help to prove his point. For the perception of beauty is sometimes dependent on training; this is obviously so in the case of music. But does one really need purity of heart in order to do theology? Of von Balthasar himself there is no doubt that he is a holy man. His leaving of the Jesuits in order to found his Johannine Community of love is well known. But it is not hard to find instances of great theologians whose lives have none the less been anything but holy. One thinks of the unscrupulous Cyril of Alexandria from the patristic period or the libertine Paul Tillich from modern times.

My suspicion is that von Balthasar has in fact confused two very different claims, that one needs holiness to do theology as an intellectual discipline (which is untrue) and that one needs holiness to have religious insight – to produce, as it were, the building blocks of the system (which is true). The contrast I am trying to get at is between theology as a system concerned with questions of overall coherence and justification, and what it is attempting to cohere and systematize, religious experience of all kinds, including revelation. It is often claimed even by Liberal theologians that one needs empathy in order to study theology, but it is important to note why. It is not in order to assess good and bad arguments in the task of systematization and justification; that is exclusively a task of reason and intellect. Rather, it is in order to treat with sufficient seriousness the import of another's experience for which one may have no standard of comparison within one's own personal experience.

It is precisely here that sanctity becomes relevant. For it may well be that the saint, precisely because he is open to the divine will in a way we ordinary mortals are not, can attain new levels of perception that are entitled to a special status simply in virtue of the sort of person who has had them. Now, of course, this cannot mean automatic endorsement. It will depend, for example, how well the alleged perception fits in with what we already know of the divine will and purposes. But some such concession to von Balthasar cannot I think be avoided by anyone who assigns a unique position to Biblical revelation, though von Balthasar also wants to speak of 'new illuminations'[57] in the history of the Church.

Sympathy for this type of approach is by no means confined within the Roman Catholic tradition. Contributions from admittedly lesser figures in other confessions would include the Methodist Geoffrey Wainwright's *Doxology* and the Anglican Andrew Louth's *Discerning the Mystery*,[58] though interestingly neither mentions von Balthasar in his text. The former is an impressive attempt to produce a systematic theology on the basis of worship. While accepting that there should be congruity between belief and worship,[59] he is at pains to point out that liturgy may show us to be more deeply committed to some particular doctrine than some theologians would like us to believe. So, for example, Jesus was worshipped before he was formally called God.[60] Again the extent of kenotic incarnational language from St Cosmas to Charles Wesley is used to challenge the deistic and unitarian tendencies of some modern theologians: 'Once such language has been used religiously . . . it is hard for the worshipper to be satisfied with a God who would be less committed to the world in self-giving love.'[61] Unfortunately, he nowhere properly discussed whether worship might of itself give access to a knowledge not achievable by other means.

That had been the claim of von Balthasar, and it is renewed in Louth. The absence of any reference to von Balthasar is all the more surprising as his earlier book, *The Origins of the Christian Mystical Tradition*, not only contains several allusions to him but also discusses the very tradition that produced the form of aesthetics to which von Balthasar wishes to return.[62] But the explanation is not hard to find. It is that Louth believes that he has found a more effective philosophy on which to base his total rejection of attitudes stemming from the Enlightenment, namely that of Hans-Georg Gadamer. The net result is conservatism of a kind that even countenances a return to patristic uses of allegory.[63] Gadamer is part of a wider philosophical tradition known as hermeneutics, and so it will be appropriate to consider the relevance of Gadamer against that wider philosophical background.

Hermeneutics and Gadamer

Serious discussion of hermeneutics, of the philosophical problems underlying the interpretation of texts, is most commonly dated as beginning with Schleiermacher, perhaps largely because of the influence he had on the great German philosopher of history, Wilhelm Dilthey (1833–1911). Gadamer describes Schleiermacher's 'original contribution' as 'psychological interpretation': 'It is ultimately a divinatory process, a placing of oneself within the mind of the author, an apprehension of the inner origin of the composition of a work, a recreation of the creative act.'[64] To many, perhaps most, people today that will seem an obvious requirement in understanding a text. To see its originality one must place Schleiermacher in his historical context. It was an age still largely dominated by confessional interpretations of Scripture, without reference to their original setting. What Dilthey then did was to extend this claim to the whole field of literature and history, and thus reclaim for knowledge areas that Kant in his *Critique of Pure Reason* had excluded from the status of science. Thus, though he does acknowledge distinctive elements in the method of *Geistes- wissenschaften*, 'the human sciences', such as the need for an interpretative (*verstehenden*) psychology, his undoubted aim was to claim the same degree of objectivity for them as exists in the natural sciences. Such strong claims for them still exist today, for example in the Italian writer on hermeneutics Emilio Betti. However, the net result of such aspirations has been the tendency in the Arts to retreat into more tractable questions such as philology and textual criticism where objectivity is easier to obtain, rather than deal with the ultimately more important issue of aesthetics and appreciation. As an illustration, I well remember the hours of lectures on the great Greek dramas I endured as a classics student, where attention was exclusively focused on problems of textual criticism. No doubt others have encountered similar difficulties in the treatment of the Bible.

Long before Gadamer challenged such mimicking of the natural sciences and exaggerated claims to objectivity, the gauntlet had already been thrown down by the philosopher Martin Heidegger and the theologian most influenced by him, Rudolph Bultmann. The former's major work of 1926, *Sein und Zeit*, is best known for its Existentialism, which will be considered in chapter 3. But he also makes an important contribution to hermeneutics through his notion of the fore-structure of understanding. According to this, already before we even raise the question of meaning, meaning is present in the very fact of our being in the world. There is no neutral starting-point; rather, being placed where we are has already produced a vast fund of assumptions, with which we are likely to approach any text. In saying this he is not discounting the possibility of getting beyond the fore-structure to a point of better insight. But its decisive role is stressed by the suggestion that such insight always takes place within a 'hermeneutic circle',[65] merely making explicit what is in some sense already understood.

Bultmann took up Heidegger's notion with his own term of *Vorverständnis* (pre-understanding), and again emphasizes the im- possibility of approaching a text free of all presuppositions. Not only does he accept that a hermeneutic circle will assert itself in the fact that some form of belief will be necessary for complete comprehension of

Scripture, he insists that that belief can only be acquired if one already
in some sense comprehends its meaning. That, of course, is to put the
'circle' at its most paradoxical. Put more simply, the point is that pre-
understanding and text interact, and meaning only comes from the text
if there is already a basis in pre-understanding. Such a basis Bultmann
finds in man's existential condition, though it is important to add that
he claims for the text an ability to challenge that condition once the link
has been made.

A notable feature of the approaches of both Heidegger and
Bultmann is the way in which emphasis has moved away from
identifying the meaning of a text with the author's intention towards
locating it in the text's meaning for us. Bultmann does not carry this
process nearly so far as some modern French philosophers. But the
trend is also present in contemporary German thought, as can be seen
in their younger philosophy colleague at Marburg, Hans-Georg
Gadamer (b. 1900), and his major 1960 work, *Truth and Method*. He
writes: 'Not occasionally only, but always, the meaning of a text goes
beyond its author. That is why understanding is not merely a
reproductive, but always a productive attitude as well.'[66] The reason
why he is prepared to speak like this is again because of what is seen as
the interpreter's decisive role. 'We understand texts that have been
handed down to us on the basis of expectations of meaning which are
drawn from our own anterior relation to the subject.'[67]

To such anterior relations he gives a provocative name, prejudices
(*Vorurteil*). But the intention is not to deride, but to commend. For he
sees such anterior meanings as formed by the authority of tradition,
and it is his wish to reinstate both authority and tradition in a positive
way, against the assumptions of the Enlightenment. For he sees the
Enlightenment's pursuit of 'absolute reason' and objectivity as a
hopeless will-o'-the-wisp. 'In fact, history does not belong to us, but we
belong to it. Long before we understand ourselves through the process
of self-examination, we understand ourselves in a self-evident way in
the family, society and state in which we live.'[68]

It is Gadamer's treatment of authority rather than tradition which
has come in for the most criticism. In his defence he notes that even the
philosopher Descartes exempted morality from his reconstruction of
the truths of reason, and in this at least seemed content to rely on
others' wisdom. Indeed, Gadamer suggests that recognition of authority
rests on 'an act of reason itself which, aware of its own limitations,
accepts that others have better understanding'.[69] In an exchange of
articles another major contemporary German philosopher, Jürgen
Habermas, has debated this point with him. In essence his position is:
'Gadamer's argument pre-supposes that legitimising recognition and
the consensus on which authority is founded can arise and develop free

from force. The experience of distorted communication contradicts this pre-supposition.'[70] The notion of distorted communication is one Habermas has pursued throughout his writings. What he has in mind is the way in which ideology, whether conscious or unconscious, can distort communication through functioning as a 'power-legitimating world-view'.[71] He therefore continues to support the Enlightenment search, expressing it in terms of an 'ideal speech situation' in which truth would be revealed by universal consensus, formed as a result of free communication and decision. But while he was surely to challenge Gadamer's too ready acceptance of authority as something good and involving an exercise of reason, his own hermeneutic proposal seems equally implausible. Not only is it unlikely that we would ever agree on what constitutes truly free communication (we don't experience the same things as oppressive), in his attack on authority Habermas ignores the positive role that tradition can undoubtedly sometimes play.

Thus, for instance, Gadamer points out the way in which tradition helps bridge the gap between the text and our present situation. 'It is not a yawning abyss, but is filled with the continuity of custom and tradition, in the light of which all that is handed down presents itself to us.'[72] The result is that the sort of questions that we put to the text are to some degree determined by that tradition. But not wholly. For tradition is also something that we help to create by participating in its evolution. This we can do partly by the questions we ask but also partly by the questions the text puts to us. The process he describes as 'effective-history' (*Wirkungsgeschichte*), and the result a 'fusion of horizons' (*Horizontverschmelzung*).

An intriguing feature of this emphasis on the creative role of tradition is the extent to which he sees Aristotle as a precursor, particularly in *Reason in the Age of Science*.[73] For one finds a similar positive assessment of tradition based on Aristotle in one much acclaimed book about morality from within the Anglo-Saxon philosophical tradition, namely in Alasdair MacIntyre's *After Virtue*.[74] Gadamer's examples are derived mainly from law, theology and classics, though unfortunately they are never very specific. This is a pity, as I think that it would have strengthened his case. For had he considered the Bible in any detail, it would surely have been obvious that today, no less than in the past, it is not approached 'neat' or 'raw'. Thus, so far as the ordinary reader is concerned, one need only reflect what the uninitiated might make of it if they were to start at Genesis and work their way through the text. They would find themselves just as repelled as the average Christian is by the Koran or the scriptures of some other religion, if he has been given no prior guidance as to what is significant and what subordinate to that significance. But equally the same is true of the professional scholar. For, as already observed in discussing Troeltsch, there is no such thing as a totally impartial perspective.

The role of tradition is shaping our interpretations thus cannot be ignored. Nor should we see this as a curse, any more than that the formation of our morals by our society should be seen as such. Not only is all the richness of others' wisdom ours, if we believe in Providence, then that wisdom will also be seen as having ultimately a divine origin. But none of this is to justify an unyielding conservatism. As Gadamer says, each time we read a text 'our own prejudice is properly brought into play through its being put at risk.'[75] It is perhaps no accident that in his introduction to *Reason in the Age of Science* Frederick Lawrence quotes England's greatest theologian, John Henry Newman, whose writings helped to produce the revolution of the Second Vatican Council. Even in 1845 he was writing: 'here below to live is to change, and to be perfect is to have changed often.'[76]

So far we have been looking at general principles of method. Before turning to specific issues, what now remains to be done is to consider what use the systematic theologian should make of the work of the Biblical scholar, especially given the fact that their conclusions are also by no means infrequently influenced by theological or philosophical considerations.

Reading the text

Bultmann

It is possible to ask various questions of a text, and in this the Bible is no exception. Thus, though they may overlap, generally it is one thing to ask about historical accuracy, another to ask about meaning and the way in which a text successfully conveys this, and yet another to ask about its truth or intellectual significance. In doing the first the Biblical critic conceives of himself as an historian and in doing the second as a literary critic, while it is the third, of course, that is properly the concern of the systematic theologian. But clearly all three are interrelated and so the systematic theologian cannot avoid taking seriously the conclusions of the Biblical critic, just as he must also be on his guard against the sort of Biblical scholar who presents answers to the first two types of questions as though they were also necessarily the only answer available to the third question. One of the great merits of Bultmann was that he fully appreciated this distinction. But before we assess the tenability or otherwise of the conclusions he drew from it, it will be as well to set him in a wider framework of the various approaches currently available to the Biblical critic.

There is no doubt that until relatively recently it was the historical rather than the literary question that preoccupied Biblical scholars. Thus modern Biblical criticism effectively began in the eighteenth century with Source Criticism, the attempt to recover the underlying sources, in particular for the Pentateuch and the Gospels. It is interesting to note that it was only at this initial point that the Biblical critic seems to have given a decisive impetus to another discipline. For we know that Michaelis and Eichhorn had a marked influence on Wolf's pioneering and celebrated *Prolegomena* to Homer (1795).[77] But since then the influence seems to have been overwhelmingly the other way, with Biblical critics drawing fresh inspiration for new methods of approach from secular literary critics or from philosophy. Even so this is not to suggest that these early attempts at Source Criticism were particularly successful. So, for instance, the Griesbach Hypothesis (1783), that Luke and Mark used Matthew, was eventually abandoned in favour of the Two Source Hypothesis of H.J. Holtzmann (1863), that Matthew and Luke relied on Mark and another source, called Q (from the German for source, *Quelle*).

Form criticism is really a further development of Source Criticism, and first made its appearance in studies of the Old Testament. The Graf-Wellhausen Hypothesis had suggested four sources for the Pentateuch of varying date (J.E.D. and P.). Hermann Gunkel (1862–1932) argued that further dissection was possible by looking at the various genres (*Gattungen*) to which the material belonged, e.g. legends, hymns, thanksgivings, etc., and that the use of a genre could reveal something of the life-situation (*Sitz-im-Leben*) of those using it. Martin Dibelius and Rudolph Bultmann (1884–1976) were responsible for applying the approach to the New Testament, though they tended to use the word *Formgeschichte* rather than *Gattungsgeschichte*. Bultmann wrote his *History of the Synoptic Tradition* (1921),[78] a classic for this type of approach, while holding a teaching post at Breslau. Its main feature is the emphasis placed on the way in which Jesus' teaching has so often been adapted to a new *Sitz-im-Leben* in the subsequent life of the Church. An example might be the way in which Jesus' original teaching on marriage was modified to allow for the exception of adultery or again to take account of the fact that in Roman, unlike Jewish law, a woman could divorce her husband.[79]

The relevance of Redaction Criticism to historical questions is shown in an early anticipation like Wrede's *The Messianic Secret* (1901), in which he argued that this was an invention of Mark to explain the failure of the disciples to recognize who Jesus was. But the term *Redaktionsgeschichte* was not in fact coined until 1954 by Willi Marxsen, and it is only really from about that time that it begins to achieve major prominence in, for example, Marxsen's own work on Mark, Conzelmann's on Luke and the slightly earlier work of

Bornkamm on Matthew. Its principal feature is the move away from dissection of the text and towards looking at the redactor's aims as expressed in the shaping of his material as a whole. Inevitably it also meant a move away from the recovery of history to an appreciation of literary structure and overall theological purpose, since these, rather than any straightforward attempt to write history in the modern sense, were clearly what motivated the various differences between the Evangelists. This new stress in its turn prepared the ground for two further developments, the more obviously literary approach inspired by Structuralism (examined below) and what is known as Canonical Criticism, where the theological aim of not just one book is examined but the shaping of the canon as a whole. This latter approach is particularly associated with the distinguished American Old Testament scholar Brevard Childs as, for instance, in his *Introduction to the Old Testament as Scripture* (1979).

With this last type of criticism a complete fudging of our first two questions with the third, the systematic theologian's question, has occurred. For Childs see his role as not only to indicate what considerations historically led to the present shape of the Protestant canon but also to defend the legitimacy of that shape. It would have been much better if he had clearly acknowledged that they are two distinct questions, something Bultmann would undoubtedly have done. As he is the only man this century who could have claimed to be as distinguished in Biblical criticism as in doctrinal theology, it will be profitable to assess the value of all these different types of approach for the systematic theologian against the background of his own largely negative attitude to the relationship.

One surprising feature about Bultmann that is not often realized is that despite the fact that he is probably the most conspicuous example of Liberal Theology in the twentieth century, his theology was as much forged in reaction to nineteenth-century Liberal Theology as Barth's had been. The explanation for this is that his historical investigation of the New Testament convinced him that faith could not be reliably based on any attempt to recover the historical Jesus, and that therefore an alternative foundation must be sought. But because he believed himself to have found just such an alternative foundation, in *Faith and Understanding* he is content to assert: 'I calmly let the fire burn, for I see that what is consumed is only the fanciful portraits of Life-of-Jesus theology, and that means nothing other than "Christ after the flesh".'[80]

What he proposes instead is a faith that has a minimal dependence on history. All we really need to know is that Jesus lived and died, the *dass* of his existence. Apart from that everything of importance is encapsulated in the preached word, not in the details of history. 'Faith is directed to the Word, and to the authorised proclamation of the

Word.'[81] So even the Resurrection is interpreted purely as an expression of the meaning of the Cross: 'Faith in the resurrection is really the same thing as faith in the saving efficacy of the cross.'[82] The rationale he finds for this employs a distinction that goes back at least to 1892 and Martin Kähler's book *The So-called Historical Jesus and the Historic Biblical Christ*, in which two different German words for history are used, *Historie* and *Geschichte*. Roughly speaking, *Historie* is simply what happened, whereas *Geschichte* is the continuing significance of the past in the present. Bultmann holds that it is only the latter that matters for faith and that to discover this a massive translation exercise in necessary, what he calls *Entmythologisierung* (demythologization), translating the mythological language of the first century into the existentialist language of the twentieth. Since the notion of myth is discussed in chapter 2 and Existentialism in chapter 3, nothing more about this programme need be said here, except to note the extent to which the Jesus of history is relegated to *Historie*. For notoriously in his *Primitive Christianity* Bultmann discusses Jesus in the section dealing with Judaism and not in that dealing with Christianity.

Even those who admire the existentialist approach to theology often find themselves worried by the extremes to which Bultmann is prepared to go. So, for example, John MacQuarrie in his book on Bultmann, *An Existentialist Theology*, comments 'Yet it seems to me that there is a residual truth in the myth that cannot be translated into any existential form because it refers to something beyond existence. The truth is that this act of forgiveness cost something to God . . . It was the Son of God who died.'[83] Bultmann's refusal to accept such an irreducible element in fact seems to be based on two reasons, neither of which are legitimate. First, he felt himself bound as an historian to exclude any possibility of miracle. As he puts it in *Jesus Christ and Mythology*, 'the modern study of history . . . does not take account of any intervention of God.'[84] At one level this is of course true, but, as I have already observed when discussing Troeltsch, allowing the possibility is not necessarily pernicious to the exercise of the historical method. But perhaps the deeper reason motivating him was a desire to escape the ambiguities and uncertainties of history, and give faith an unshakeable foundation. If so, it was quite misconceived. For, as noted several times already in the course of this chapter, faith cannot escape the element of risk. But, so far is this from being a defect that it is precisely this that constitutes its challenge and marks it as belonging to so much else that is worthwhile, like personal relationships, morality and aesthetics.

Thus, so far from regarding the types of Criticism outlined above as perhaps interesting but irrelevant to his task, the systematic theologian must actively engage with its arguments and, where necessary, come to terms with its conclusions. Those worried by the way in which such techniques undermine the possibility of any literalistic understanding of the inspiration of Scripture might perhaps turn to the later and more eirenic of James Barr's two books on the subject, *Escaping from Fundamentalism*.[85] But in any case there is an alternative model for understanding the process ready to hand. We can conceive of God engaging, as it were, in a dialogue with the community of faith, and trying to advance their understanding of himself and his purposes, but always in a way that respects their freedom.[86] Inevitably, if this is so, the Bible will be a mixture of sublimity and nonsense (and much in between!). Inevitably too, this makes harder the task of assessing the relevance of scriptural passages to specific doctrines. But that is not to say that the task is an impossible one, nor that there are no criteria available. Rather than discuss them here, it will be easiest to let them emerge in practice, as specific doctrines are tackled in subsequent chapters.

Lévi-Strauss to Derrida

But before concluding this chapter, it will be profitable to look at one recent trend in Biblical criticism that originates in recent French philosophy. Structuralism reached the height of its influence in France in the 1960s largely in reaction to the subjectivism of Existentialism, but ironically it has now been superseded by an even fiercer subjectivism. In chapter 5 another version of this reaction will be encountered when we examine Deleuze's response to Lacan's structuralist psychology. But here I shall take the best-known, the Structuralism of Lévi-Strauss and the early Barthes, and Derrida's subjectivist response, which has come to be known as Deconstructionism. Of the two it is still Structuralism which exercises by far the greater influence on theology, particularly in the work of Biblical critics, though Deconstructionism is beginning to make its influence felt.

The earliest roots of Structuralism are in fact to be found not in philosophy but in linguistics, particularly the work of Ferdinand de Saussure (d. 1913), though his major work *Cours de linguistique générale* was only published posthumously by his former students in 1922. The basic idea is that adequate sense can only be made of a language by looking at its structure or system as a whole. The leading exponent of Saussurean linguistics in Britain, John Lyons, has a favourite simple example to illustrate the point.[87] He asks us to consider the difficulties involved in translating a basic English sentence like 'The cat sat on the mat' into French. Decisions about the gender of the cat, the tense of the verb and type of mat have all to be made before translation is possible because French, unlike English, is not content to leave any of this ambiguous. In other words, the point is that one has not understood how English and French operate as languages until one has mastered their relational or structural assumptions as a whole, rather than just word for word translation.

All this is non-subjectivist in the sense that clearly there are right and wrong answers to whether structures have been correctly identified. It is not just a matter of personal preference. But the application of these techniques to anthropology by Claude Lévi-Strauss (b. 1908) was to give the claim to objectivity a deeper meaning. For he intended his theories to apply not just to a particular language or culture but to be of universal application, and herein lay a threat to Christianity since the contention could be made that the 'myths' of the Bible are simply one variant of a common pattern.

Lévi-Strauss did obtain an *agrégation de philosophie*[88] but, as he tells us in his intellectual biography *Tristes tropiques*, he turned to anthropology because of disappointment with existentialism which he saw as too 'indulgent towards the illusions of subjectivity'.[89] While previous anthropologists had either (like Malinowski) treated the thought of primitive peoples are being entirely directed by basic needs or (like Levy-Bruhl) regarded it as a function of emotion, Lévi-Strauss tried to show in books like *The Savage Mind* (1962) and its four-volumed successor *Mythologiques* that their thinking was just as much motivated by a desire to understand the world about them as ours is. The deceptive element was its mythological character, but once this is deciphered, it becomes readily intelligible and is found to exhibit common underlying (though often unconscious) patterns. An excellent but brief example of this is given by his pursuit of a connection between harelips and twins in *Myth and Meaning*.[90] By comparing myths from all over north and south America he provides an explanation of why harelips are frequently regarded among primitive peoples with suspicion. It is because they are regarded as a form of incipient twinhood, twinhood containing within itself the inherent likelihood of division into good and bad.

Lévi-Strauss very much saw his aim as being through the study of the 'unconscious infrastructure' to produce a 'system' of 'general laws'.[91] So much is this so that he can even declare that 'the ultimate goal of the human sciences is not to constitute, but to dissolve man',[92] meaning thereby that it is the aim of anthropology to discover these largely unconscious, universal social determinants that shape man's beliefs, including his mythology. However, as we have seen, the word 'structuralism' is often used in a weaker sense, and so one must always be on one's guard against possible misunderstanding. For example, the philosopher and literary critic Roland Barthes during his structuralist phase seems to have frequently meant no more by the term than to stress the objectivity of his analysis of a particular narrative.

Structuralism in both senses has had its effect on theology. Barthes provides a readily intelligible illustration of its application to the Bible in his treatment[93] of the story of Jacob wrestling with the angel in Genesis 32. His suggestion is that it functions like a typical folk-tale in which the hero is sent on a quest against an opponent, but that its strength lies in the way in which, unlike the normal pattern, this opponent also turns out to be the originator of the quest, that is, God. The alert reader may already have been reminded of the assumptions underlying Form and Redaction Criticism, and indeed McKnight has not been slow to suggest that, had Form Criticism 'been less historically orientated', it could have developed into a structuralist approach.[94] But for the actual use made by professional Biblical scholars one should look at something like McKnight's own application of the techniques to Luke 5, Daniel Patte's introductory *What is Structural Analysis?* or *Semeia*, the American periodical inspired by this approach.[95]

That the application of structuralist techniques to the Bible has many merits cannot be denied, just as it has helped in the understanding of other works of literature. My reservations about its usefulness would be twofold.

First, it is often unnecessarily technical, partly because some of its practitioners wish to give it the pretensions of a science. Indeed, even what is supposed to be an elementary treatment like Patte's produces a highly complex analysis of the Parable of the Good Samaritan and of Galatians 1.[96] But there are structuralist-inspired treatments that avoid this defect. A good example, though from a Cambridge English scholar, would be Frank Kermode's treatment of St Mark's Gospel in *The Genesis of Secrecy* (1979). Yet even he at one point gets carried away by a presumed common pattern of such narrative, into characterizing Judas as an invention to fulfil the alleged necessity for a Betrayer.[97]

Secondly, in the way it is most commonly practised, it helps literary understanding more than it advances religious perception. Thus, if anything of religious worth can be extracted from the Jacob story, it will surely not be via what Barthes says, but much more likely to come from the sort of insight which Origen was already proposing in the third century, that it might serve as an image of spiritual combat (with success in the battle against evil bringing God's presence nearer) or of the value of perseverance in prayer, as in Christ's parable of the widow and the judge in Luke 18. A conspicuous example of where exclusive concern with such an analysis has been positively harmful in obscuring the possibility of perceiving truth in any deeper, non-literary sense, is to be found in the writings of Lévi-Strauss's most distinguished English disciple, Edmund Leach. Perhaps it is really his atheism that is to blame, but certainly his insistence in *Structuralist Interpretations of*

Biblical Myth (1983) that the entire Bible, Old and New Testament, should be treated as myth and not history distorts more than it helps. This perhaps emerges even more clearly in the treatment he has elsewhere accorded the life of Jesus, where it is seen entirely in terms of a myth that works by means of difference and reversal, in contrast with John the Baptist and the Old Testament. But is it really helpful to make the historically absurd suggestion that '*human* destruction of the first born son of *God*' was intended as a deliberate reversal of 'the *divine* destruction of all the first born sons of the *Egyptian oppressors*' (his italics)?[98]

Deconstructionism is pre-eminently associated with the name of Jacques Derrida (b. 1930), though one can see even Barthes moving in this direction from 1970 onwards with his study of Balzac's *Sarrasine* in his cryptically titled work *S/Z*. The principal idea of Deconstructionism, as the name implies, is hostility towards what is seen as an essentially man-made construction of structures. The deconstructionist considers that they have no ultimate justification in reality, and in order to underline this point he attempts to undermine (deconstruct) all suggestions of structure.

A major motive for Derrida's belief is his conviction of the infinite richness of language and its open-ended character. One way he expresses this is his notion of *différance*. Derrida's unusual spelling with an 'a' is intended to stress derivation from the verb *différer*, which can mean 'to defer' as well as 'to be different from'. Not only can every word or linguistic sign mean a number of different things, no complete account can ever be given. Such is the richness of language and the range of its possible significance, he argues, that a complete explanation remains infinitely deferred. Another element is his view that no clear line can be drawn between the literal and the metaphorical. Thus in *Writing and Difference*, written in 1967 but not translated until 1978, he describes metaphor as 'the emergence of language itself' and speaks of it as having 'infinite equivocality'.[99] It is this linguistic aspect that has so far had the most influence on the English-speaking world, through what has become known as the Yale school of deconstruction and which is particularly associated with the name of the literary critic Paul de Man.

Derrida, himself a non-practising Jew, studied under the greatest Jewish philosopher of our time, Emmanuel Levinas. It is perhaps therefore not surprising that he has given an anti-religious interpretation of the import of his views on language. This can best be illustrated by an essay in *Of Grammatology*, 'The End of the Book and the Beginning of Writing'. There he argues that the rise of a deconstructionist perspective reflects a decline in a religious attitude to meaning. Thus he informs us that 'the age of the sign is essentially theological' and that 'the difference between signified and signifier belongs in a profound and implicit way to the totality of the great epoch covered by the history of metaphysics, and in a more explicit and more systematically articulated way to the narrower epoch of Christian creationism'.[100] Derrida likes the gnomic phrase, as when he says later on the same page that 'the intelligible face of the sign remains turned towards the word and the face of God.' But fortunately the meaning is not in doubt. It is that certainly until the Reformation and possibily until the rise of Rationalism the world and its constituents were viewed as a Book of Nature that was also God's Book. The result was a conception of language as 'a sign signifying a signifier, itself signifying an eternal verity, eternally thought and spoken'.[101] In other words, because language referred ultimately to forms pre-existing in the mind of the Creator there was no serious danger of failure of reference or of language being open-ended in its possible implications. Then came the seventeenth century with God no longer viewed as the sole creator of meaning, but every individual who gives utterance to thought. From there it was but a short step to 'the end of the book and the beginning of writing'. For with the myriad of creators language was no longer subject to the same kind of controls, and so the signifier acquired a considerable degree of independence over against its author. Now 'the concept of writing exceeds and comprehends that of language.'[102] One way of viewing Structuralism is to see it as attempting to halt this process. For in so far as it attempted to postulate structures of meaning independent of particular individuals, it can be seen as offering a new, more secure locus of meaning. Hence one reason for Derrida's hostility to Structuralism in all its forms, though he is open-minded enough to admit that the theological age of the sign 'perhaps will never end'.[103]

However, it is important to be aware that behind these views on language also lie a second, metaphysical thesis, namely anti-foundationalism, that is to say his opposition to the notion, best exhibited in Descartes, that the foundations of our knowledge are such that certain beliefs can be shown to be more basic than others. His argument is that all attempts to demonstrate this fail because what is alleged to be less basic will be found to have been covertly assumed all the time among the alleged foundational beliefs. So, for instance, he has argued that, despite the explicit aim of challenging the metaphysics of Husserl, 'Levinas's metaphysics in a sense presupposes . . . . the transcendental phenomenology that it seeks to put into question.'[104] To give one more example, this time from English philosophy, more recently he has challenged J. L. Austin's attempt to produce a theory of meaning based on conventions which he called 'performatives' (such as promising), in terms of which descriptive statements would simply function as a sub-class. Derrida notes that Austin had complained that his predecessors had relegated forms of speech other than statement to insignificance, but finds exactly the same attitude in Austin himself to what Austin calls 'non-serious' uses of performatives. His conclusion is that, just as Austin had deconstructed his predecessors, so the same can be done to Austin.[105]

The use made so far of Deconstructionism by theologians does not in general bode well. The most common response has been simply to accept Derrida's position wholesale and adopt an extreme form of subjectivism. The Bible is interpreted entirely non-literally (i.e. atheistically), though the richness of its language is seen as having considerable merit in allowing a more subversive rebellion than most, against all forms of foundationalism and authority. This is very much the message of the contributors to a collection edited by the American Thomas Altizer, *Deconstructionism and Theology* (1982). So for example Carl Raschke writes: 'The demise of man is only the toppling of the last icon of the great circle . . . Deconstructionism does not announce the death of God through writing in order to install a new fetishism, a kind of anthropomancy, the mumbo-jumbo of pronouncing the awesome name of "humanity".'[106] So the assertion of the primacy of a 'writing' that subverts any possible objective foundations of our knowledge should not be read as especially singling God out for attack, but as much an attack on any form of authority, even if it is merely a unified conception of ourselves. Again, another American, Mark Taylor, in his deliberately playfully entitled *Erring: a postmodern a/theology* (1984), though he begins by quoting Derrida to the effect that deconstruction 'blocks every relation to theology',[107] ends by talking of 'this gay affirmation of a world without truth' in which 'the unending erring of scripture' is 'a vast pun, a free play, with unlimited substitutions' that can offer 'the joyous affirmation of the play of the world and of the innocence of becoming'.[108] So what he sees the Bible as offering us is a subjectivist, atheistic 'carnival' type of religion.[109]

It would indeed be a great pity if the reactions of theologians were to remain just on this level. Even Derrida has recently expressed himself unhappy with the total relativism which has been deduced from his theories.[110] This may even be because he has never quite escaped the clutches of foundationalism. For it has certainly been argued that his talk of the infinite deferral of meaning only makes sense in the context of a foundational claim that language *needs* an ultimate ground to have a determinate meaning.[111] But, more probably, rather than an unacknowledged longing for a return to foundationalism, what we have is simply the common French trait of rhetorical exaggeration, and it would be a shame if that exaggeration blinded us to the undoubted merits in his position.

Let me mention just two. First, while it would be absurd to suggest that no belief is ever more basic than any other, Derrida is surely right to draw our attention to the frequency with which our beliefs are in fact interdependent and mutually reinforcing. In other words, the position is commonly much more complex than either foundationalism or a parity stance would have us believe. Two brief articles by Kerr and Eagleton[112] do indicate that the implications of this for systematic theology are sometimes heeded. But the point is equally applicable to the work of Biblical scholars. For nothing is more common than to find Biblical scholars claiming a foundational core to, say, the teaching of Jesus or Paul, with everything in the former's vision subsumed under the concept of the Kingdom of God or everything in the latter's thought deemed to be under the controlling idea of justification by faith. Now, of course this might be true, but one's suspicion is that in each case there are a number of leading ideas which interact and are mutually interdependent. Does, for example, Jesus' notion of the fatherhood of God necessarily have to be explained in terms of the approaching Kingdom or Paul's concern for his nation in terms of justification? The thought of New Testament writers, like the epistemological foundations of religious belief, are more complex than we commonly like to admit.

Secondly, Derrida's stress on the richness of language, particularly the irreducible richness of metaphor, needs to be taken seriously. For example, probably Jülicher was right that Jesus originally only intended one point to be made by a parable, but even so, if that point is expressed metaphorically, it may well have a richness that defies a single point analysis. But I shall delay considering metaphor in detail until chapter 5 when Paul Ricoeur's position on the matter will be examined. Suffice it to say for the moment that Derrida gives us a timely warning that it is a mistake to tie down Biblical images too precisely. Their meaning is a complex function of their literal meaning, the history of their use as images, the cultural context to which they are addressed and the immediate linguistic context of their use. How all these elements balance out against each other is no easy matter to determine, and the reader of the Bible needs to be on his guard against thinking so. A good illustration of this is the significance of masculine imagery in the Bible. The challenge to this from Feminist Theology is the first specific doctrinal question to which we turn our attention in the next chapter.

2

Doctrine of God

Though there have recently been some theologians who have challenged whether Christian theology does have God as an objective being as the core of its subject matter, their views are so marginal both to the history and intelligibility of the subject that they can safely be ignored. Cupitt's *Taking Leave of God* (1980) is responsible for reviving the idea in England that the function of God might simply be a mythological way of expressing purely human ethical concerns, but its genesis is to be found thirteen years before in the American Thomas Altizer's *The Gospel of Christian Atheism* (1967). This is interesting to observe as American theology has often been the theology of extremes, of both extreme radicalism and extreme conservatism. Thus it is no accident that fundamentalism traces its roots to the nineteenth-century Princeton theologian B. B. Warfield. Fundamentalism gives scant attention to its critics, but the same can equally be said of much Liberal Theology in the United States. So, for example, in a recent American introduction to theology[1] most of the contributors simply assume certain positions as necessary since the Enlightenment and in their desire to avoid the dogmatism of fundamentalism seem almost to delight in doubt and uncertainty in a way that is still very much the exception rather than the rule in England.

Two major preoccupations of American Liberal Theology, feminism and God as process, will be the concern of the first half of this present chapter. But before we proceed to this task it will be useful to raise the question why there are such strong national differences in the way in which systematic theology is pursued. There is an old adage of the three Cs: 'Theology is created in Germany, corrected in England, and corrupted in the United States.' Given the corrective role assigned to England, it was probably written by an Englishman! Even so it does I believe contain a measure of truth. The creativity of Germany I would

put down to the fact that even today there is a healthy interaction
between theology and other disciplines at university level in a way that
would be unthinkable in England. This is not just a matter of the close
relation between individual thinkers such as existed between Heidegger
and Bultmann, but also of the way in which many another continental
philosopher such as Levinas or Gadamer can take a serious interest in
theology. Another relevant difference from England is the fact that two
different Christian traditions, Lutheranism and Roman Catholicism,
exist in a position of rough equality, and so feel the need to make sense
of, and justify, their origins. By contrast England has until relatively
recently been much more integrated both in society and church. This,
coupled with a strong sense of history, has inevitably produced a
moderating influence that has deflected German ideas into channels
more suited to the preservation of that unity. Cupitt is but one small
indicator that this consensus is in the process of collapse, and that
England is moving more in the American direction. For what most
characterizes America is the absence of rigid social constraints in what
is a highly pluralist society. The plethora of Christian sects gives ample
witness to this fact. Nor is the university campus immune. For, given
the separation of religion and state, American theologians, especially
those in 'Religion' departments, frequently feel the need to demonstrate
the objectivity of their subject by producing conclusions that are at
variance with religious tradition. But, as I argued in my discussion of
Troeltsch in the previous chapter, the Liberal pursuit of neutrality is an
unattainable ideal, since to say anything at all on religion is already to
adopt a perspective the objectivity of which can be questioned. Yet one
should not end on a negative note about American theology. For that
very pluralism results sometimes in an openness to new ideas that is
genuinely creative and without clear parallel in the more staid
atmosphere of English theology. Feminist Theology indicates well both
the richer creativity and the inherent danger of degeneration into
absurd extremes that goes with it.

The divine attributes

Feminist Theology

This is an interesting phenomenon to consider when discussing the
divine attributes because, while it illustrates well the tendency of much
American theology towards extremes, it also raises important issues
which can all too easily be missed by one's amusement at the absurdity
of some of the suggestions being made. The issues can most usefully be
pursued by considering two recent books on the subject, both
published in 1983, one offering a systematic theology from this

perspective, R. R. Ruether's *Sexism and God-Talk*, and the other an analysis of the Biblical picture, E. S. Fiorenza's *In Memory of Her*. I shall make two negative critical comments before attempting to draw out what I see as its more worthwhile features.

The first serious ground for concern is its failure to give due attention to the metaphorical character of religious discourse. Ruether's book opens with a myth in terms of which the harsh Father learns a better way from the ultimate source of his being, 'the Queen of Heaven'. Though she insists that her intention is to transcend sexual language, as with her proposed term 'God/ess', it is significant that she believes that this can only be a distant aim. In the meantime, the symbolism must be corrected by the substitution of alternative female images such as the 'Divine Wisdom' and 'empowering Matrix' with which the book ends. All this is done with the object of questioning the 'assumption that the highest symbol of divine sovereignty still remains exclusively male'.[2] But in response one wants to ask whether she has an adequate grasp of the nature of religious language. For one has surely failed to understand what a metaphor is, if one carries over every aspect of meaning from the original context. So, just as in calling a girl a rose one would not expect to have one's fingers pricked, so equally in calling God Father one does not expect any sexual element to be present. Indeed, millions of men, far less women, must have automatically corrected the image when they saw the loving concern it indicates better demonstrated by the mother in their homes. It is father as he ought to be, not as he is.

But equally there is a naïvety about language in the alternative being proposed. For, though Ruether rejects the so-called Goddess or Wicca Movement, found in writers like Christ and Starhawk,[3] she does so for the wrong reason. She objects that they have an 'historically inaccurate'[4] view of the pagan religion they wish to espouse as an alternative to male-dominated Christianity. This may well be true, but much more important is the fact that it reintroduces highly anthropomorphic conceptions of God. So far is Ruether from accepting this that in the vain pursuit of neutrality she even gives capitals to the term 'Goddesses', 'rejecting the traditional Western usage that left them lowercase to signal that these were false deities'.[5] For on her view, despite her professed Christianity, 'theological reflections drawn from Judeo-Christian . . . traditions do not have a privileged relation to God.'[6]

One of her two favoured symbols, the Matrix, bears obvious analogies with Process Theology,[7] whereas the other, 'Divine Wisdom', which is also Fiorenza's favoured term, is more firmly rooted in the Biblical tradition. Fiorenza is the more scholarly of the two, but even so like Ruether she is insufficiently sensitive to the nature of metaphorical language. She tells us that 'Divine Sophia is Israel's God in the

language and Gestalt of the goddess.'[8] But to use feminine imagery is
not necessarily to make a sexual commitment, whereas historically to
speak of a 'goddess' would be. More importantly, this leads on to my
second major criticism of Feminist Theology, that is, its failure to take
the historicity of religion seriously enough. For, interestingly, both
Ruether and Fiorenza assume that Jesus was on the 'right side'.

That Fiorenza does much to correct our perception of the role of
women in the Gospels I shall shortly go on to concede. But that either
Jesus or the early Church believed in anything like the egalitarianism
desired by the modern women's liberation movement is very hard to
credit. Doubts can be raised on historical, moral and cultural grounds.
It is on the last of these that I would wish to place most stress, but the
other two also deserve mention. Historically, the problem is that she
builds an enormous amount on very little evidence. So, for example,
the words of the Syro-Phoenician woman are taken as 'a sign of the
historical leadership women had';[9] Mary Magdalene is called 'the
apostle of the apostles'[10] in virtue of her role at the empty tomb; again,
she moves without clear rationale from the acknowledged role of some
women like Junia to the claim that 'without question they were equal
and sometimes even superior to Paul in their work for the gospel.'[11]
Secondly, morally there is something almost obscene about the way in
which privileged women academics treat the feminist issue as on a par
with God's 'preferential option for the poor'.[12] The attempt is made to
strengthen the link by the observation that most of those suffering
acute hardship are women, but even so like should not be compared
with unlike. If there is oppression in a middle-class American home, it
is on an altogether different scale from the anguish of the starving slum-
dweller. But, finally and most importantly, culturally it makes no sense
at all to ascribe to Jesus anything very much like the preoccupations of
the modern feminist movement. Certainly he was remarkably free in
his attitude to women; certainly too his comments on divorce could
have been as directed against mistreatment of women as against easy
divorce.[13] But this is quite different from envisaging Jesus as the
inaugurator of a new social order in which the primary responsibility
for the home would cease to reside with the mother. Fiorenza herself
acknowledges how deeply inbred Jewish attitudes were,[14] but fails to
draw the obvious implication from this. This is that Jesus must have at
most aimed at equal consideration for all people, not at the undermining
of what was universally assumed to be a natural feature of the human
condition until modern times.

To say this is neither to challenge Jesus' moral perfection nor to deny
the need for change today. Jesus could not help but be bound by what
were then perceived to be universal empirical facts relevant to
morality, just as now we accept that his insight was also circumscribed

by 'facts' of science and history. But, again, just as we admit that this 'knowledge' needs correction in the light of, for example, our changed understanding of the authorship of the books of the Old Testament,[15] so similarly his moral perceptions may need adjustment in the light of our new understanding of the facts about male and female nature. On my view this involves not only the need to acknowledge women's right to positions of leadership in the Church but also the recognition that parenthood is an equal responsibility. However, the really important thing to emphasize is that acceptance of this depends on empirical questions about the nature of the two sexes, not on an appeal to Jesus' authority, the roots of whose teaching lay elsewhere, in the claim that every individual ought equally to be the object of our love as they are of God's, irrespective of whatever status, subjective or objective, they may have. In other words, even objective inferiority, for example in intelligence, should be no bar to equality of consideration.

However, while I do not accept the extreme form of the feminist thesis about Jesus, there is no doubt that scholars like Fiorenza have demonstrated the need for us to acknowledge the extent to which the Scriptures are male orientated. Thus, I am convinced that Mary Magdalene was the first witness to the Resurrection despite Paul's omission, especially as it effectively has the support of all four Gospels.[16] To give one more example, it is hard to resist Fiorenza's conclusion that it is simply male bias that makes Junia into a man or demotes the significance of Phoebe,[17] thus considerably underestimating the extent of women's contribution to the early expansion of the Church. Likewise, insufficient attention has been paid to the amount of female imagery for God already present within the Scriptures, ranging from the presentation of him as a pregnant woman by Deutero-Isaiah[18] to Jesus' and Paul's use of the image of Wisdom.[19] Yet it is only fair to add that cultural prejudice can be seen at least once to be operating in the reverse direction, with Fiorenza failing to take adequate account of the role of the mother of Jesus, presumably for no other reason than that she is not regarded as a suitable feminist symbol. At all events, not only does Fiorenza implausibly attempt to reduce her significance in the passages she does discuss, she totally ignores the fact that she is the only woman mentioned by name as being present at the first missionary meeting of the incipient Church.[20]

Back to Plato and beyond

In the previous section we have been examining the extent to which Feminist Theology's proposals for a revision of our images for God are justified. In the course of that examination we noted how reasons (in the form of an appeal to our natural knowledge) might lead to the

correction or further development of Biblical insights, and also how
Biblical criticism might restore to their proper place images that had
been neglected in conventional analyses. In this section what I now
want to do is look at attributes rather than images, and in particular
discuss the way in which on this issue as well theology is faced with the
two types of question mentioned in the previous sentence: to be more
specific, both with the question whether rational considerations
(deriving ultimately from Plato) have not moved our conception of
God in the wrong direction, and also secondly whether the Bible may
not perhaps contain a rather different conception of the divine
attributes from the Platonic one commonly given. Here I propose to
look at two specific attributes, God's timelessness and his impassibility.
Such reflections will provide a natural transition to a discussion of
Process Theology, where traditional accounts of the divine attributes
are even more seriously under attack.

The view that God is outside of time and does not suffer are both
subsumed under a more fundamental claim about God, that he does
not change, since time is a measure of change and suffering commonly
taken as a negative indicator of change for the worse. It is important
therefore first to be clear about why this notion of divine immutability
has embedded itself so deeply in the traditions of Christian systematic
theology. For better or worse, the decisive factor in the development of
the view was the influence of Platonism, the dominant philosophy at
the time of the formation of the Creeds in the patristic period. A
leading feature of Plato's thought (427–347 BC) and of its subsequent
development in Middle (*c*.80 BC–AD 220) and Neo-Platonism (stemming from Plotinus who died in 270) is a suspicion of change. Thus one
of Plato's main arguments for his Theory of Forms is that knowledge of
the sensible or empirical world is impossible because it is in a constant
state of flux;[21] so the proper objects of knowledge must instead be
perfect exemplars or forms of each empirical thing, which necessarily
because perfect are not part of sensible reality. Indeed, so deep does
the suspicion run that (helped by the use of the same word in Greek for
both existence and truth[22]) even the very existence of sensible things is
called into question.[23]

Plato comes nearest to the Christian conception of a personal God
with his notion of the demiurge or creator God in his *Timaeus*, but even
there the demiurge is clearly subordinate to the Forms in imitation of
which he creates the world. In fact, in his most famous dialogue, the
Republic, the position of God is clearly usurped by the Form of the
Good, the Form that gives intelligibility to all other Forms in virtue of
their striving teleologically to represent the fulfilment of their own
kind. (Each Form is 'good at', successful at, being the thing in question,
unlike sensible particulars which are a mere pale imitation and only have

reality in so far as they are able to copy the Form.) That being so, it is intriguing to observe that the Good is described as 'not itself identical with reality, but beyond reality, and superior to it in dignity and power'. The process by which that which limits and defines everything else comes to be seen as itself beyond all limits has begun. At all events, the process has gone much further by the time of Plotinus, in whose philosophy the One has taken over the role of the Good, though the initial idea probably comes from Plato's late and difficult dialogue, the *Parmenides*. Already present there is the notion of intelligibility and shape being given to something only through its determination as a unity by the One.[24] However, it is only with Plotinus' *Enneads* that we find the One being treated as divine in virtue of its status as being the highest form of reality that limits and determines everything else.[25]

Both Plato and Plotinus assume that the Good and the One are not subject to any temporal restraints. But it is someone very much later in this tradition, the medieval philosopher Anselm (d. 1109), who perhaps gives clearest expression to the worry about time that arises once one pursues this understanding of the divine as what gives limit and definition to everything else. In his *Monologion* he describes it as 'shameless ignorance' to think of God as 'delimited' by either space or time. For, just as 'a thing has a place only if a place contains the thing's size by delimiting it', so 'a thing has a time only if a time somehow limits the thing's duration by measuring it and measures the thing's duration by limiting it.'[26]

But in response to this whole tradition which sees God as what gives limits rather than himself being subject to any, one needs to ask whether too high a price has been paid. The fact that Plato and Plotinus conceive of the ultimate source of reality as impersonal should in itself be a sufficient warning. For to describe God as personal is already to impose a large number of constraints upon what he must be like. This is not in itself enough to exclude the notion of God as a timeless being, since it is just possible to conceive of a personal being who is outside time. But what cannot be conceived is a timeless being who can also relate to personal beings within time like ourselves. At most he could leave 'traces' that would constitute his response, but there could be no sense of personal interaction, still less of God being directly experienced.[27] When one adds to this all the conceptual difficulties recently identified by analytic philosophers,[28] one can I think no longer refrain from the conclusion that the kind of mystical tradition which Platonism brought to Christianity is misconceived. For nothing could be a greater perversion of the God of the Christian revelation than this unknowable God without limits and without attributes.

In the Platonic tradition coupled with this view of the ultimate source of reality as that which determines everything else while remaining itself undefined went the notion that it must also be simple and not complex. One obvious reason for this is that if it were complex then there would be certain things which were constituted part of its being rather than themselves being determined by it.[29] But another reason as old as Plato[30] is that the complex or composite is seen as inherently liable to dissolution. Only the completely simple has a sufficient internal guarantee of always remaining the same, since there is nothing from within that can produce an imbalance that would lead to dissolution into component parts. Whatever the reason, this demand for divine simplicity has continued to exercise a major influence until modern times. But, as Wittgenstein has pointed out,[31] anything at all can be seen as simple or complex depending on the perspective one adopts.

With such a strong demand for internal simplicity, it is hardly surprising that any complexity introduced from without was dismissed with barely a moment's thought. The divine could not suffer both because this would imply that it is determined rather than determining and because it would introduce an unstable element of complexity into an essentially simple entity. But on the latter point not only, as we have noticed, is complexity a matter of perspective but also in any case there is no reason to accept a connection between durability and simplicity. An ant is a relatively simple entity, but its life is soon over; the universe is enormously complex, but it is still in existence. As for the first point about divine aseity, this is clearly a more substantial issue since one could argue that God cannot be God unless he has such complete independence. Process Theology denies this by insisting that God necessarily suffers in virtue of being what he is. What is wrong with this claim I shall discuss in the next section. But, even so, there is still room for the more modest proposal that God *chooses* to expose himself to suffering.

This is the position of Jürgen Moltmann in *The Crucified God* (1973). Commenting on the claim that God is not changeable, he remarks: 'But that statement is not absolute; it is only a simile. God is not changeable as creatures are changeable.'[32] In saying that he has the Bible entirely on his side. In passages like 'I am the Lord, I change not',[33] what the writers have in mind is the steadfastness of God to his purposes, not any metaphysical notion of immutability. It is also from revelation that Moltmann identifies the main pressure to speak of a divine passibility. Of the two natures doctrine he declares that 'it cannot seek to maintain only a dialectical relationship between the divine being and human being, leaving each of these unaffected; in its own way the divine being must encompass the human being and vice versa.'[34] The result is the crucified God of the title. God 'voluntarily opens himself to the possibility of being affected by another',[35] not just in the Cross but wherever human suffering is to be found. So of one incident at Auschwitz he comments: 'To speak here of a God who could not suffer would make God a demon.'[36] Moltmann I think is right, but one must beware of too easy an anthropomorphism. For any suffering God endures will still be subject to the enormous transformation an omniscient consciousness brings. So much of human misery is due to uncertainty about the outcome or duration of the pain, from both of which God would be exempt.[37]

Creation

Torrance and Process Theology

So far in this chapter we have been examining the way in which greater awareness of the cultural conditioning of our concepts may force on us a revision in our understanding of the divine attributes. However, one source of this pressure which many theologians regard as acute has hitherto been ignored. This is our transformed scientific understanding of the world. That the Bible cannot be used as a source of scientific information, as for instance Archbishop Ussher did in the seventeenth century with his dating of the creation to 4004 BC, should go without saying. The divine dialogue with man, in order to be comprehensible to the men of the time clearly had to assume the science of the time, including a three-decker universe with water below and above the earth.[38] But if there can be no influence of theology on science,[39] this still leaves unresolved the question of whether it is legitimate to expect some effect the other way.

It is important to distinguish two different ways in which such influence might be felt. For it is one thing to admit that science poses questions for theology; quite another to claim that it it can direct theology to the sort of answers it ought to give. Thus it is clear that facts like the nature of the origin of the universe, its age and extent, the role played by evolution, etc., all raise questions for theology about the nature of God's relation to the world. But that does not mean that science can tell us the answers. For it is a totally different type of question that is being asked. At most, science can modify the theological perspective.

But it might modify it in two very different kinds of ways. It might do so either with respect to specific issues or through science being seen as offering general analogies to theology in its method or concepts. What is meant by the latter will become clear in due course when we examine the writings of T. F. Torrance and Process Theology. But first let me give two illustrations of the danger of tying theology too closely to specific scientific theories.

Most scientists have now moved towards acceptance of the so-called Big Bang account of the origin of the universe. On this view we live in an expanding universe that is the result of an explosion about fifteen thousand million years ago that happened to 'the cosmic singularity', the matter of the universe that was then compressed to the size of little more than the point of a needle. Such an account may sound inherently more creative than the alternative theory of Bondi, Gold and Hoyle that was once almost as popular, the so-called steady-state theory. But one should beware of confusing scientific and theological issues. For what is central to the Christian doctrine of creation is not the temporal origin of the world but its utter dependence on God, and that is something that holds equally for all points of time. So, even if the steady-state theory were to return to popularity, this would do nothing to undermine the truth of the Christian claim. It would simply mean that this eternal world of ours was God's 'first thought', as it were. For, irrespective of whether we conceive of him as in or outside time, such an infinite mind would clearly need no time to reflect before he thought the world into existence.

Equally, theologians need to be careful in the use they make of the so-called anthropic principle, the view of the astrophysicist Brandon Carter and others that 'the universe must be such as to admit conscious beings in it at some stage.'[40] The principle can be formulated at various levels. A strong version would claim that necessarily the world had to be the way it is for there to be conscious observers capable of observing it, whereas a weaker version would merely point to the remarkably fine tuning that was essential for it to be possible for anything analogous to human life to emerge. Certainly, the path that led to man was a narrow one. So, for example, had the ratio of nucleons to photons, electrons and neutrinos been only slightly different in the early stages, then there could have been no nuclei heavier than hydrogen and so no carbon or the possibility of life that that brings. Again, had the universe been either slightly less or slightly more homogeneous, life could not have occurred: slightly less would have meant the universe collapsing into black holes; slightly more, the impossibility of galaxies developing. One way of challenging the surprising character of facts like these would be to raise the possibility of parallel universes, that is, of this universe being only one of many, the others, of which we are unaware, having failed to develop life as we know it. But this seems a rather desperate attempt to reduce the improbabilities. However, science is changing so fast that theologians would be unwise to rely too much on such facts as evidence for design; especially dangerous would be the temptation to make man once again the centre of the universe. What the anthropic principle shows is that, if this universe has a purpose, then clearly the emergence of life is a central element in that purpose.

But there are still a large number of scientific facts where the path did not need to be so finely tuned, and in any case we can conceive of alternative explanations of the fine tuning that exists eventually being given. So I think theologians still cannot escape the question of what significance does attach to the vast tracts of the universe where man seems not at all relevant. Should we not say that God often delights in creation simply for its own sake, and that this need not have any reference or relevance to man? Recall the image of creation as play in Proverbs.[41]

But if both these illustrations, i.e. Big Bang and the anthropic principle, call into question any simple attempt to mould the Christian doctrine of creation on the most recent scientific theories, there remains the problem of how theology should respond to the prestige of science. The two major theologies which I now want to discuss in this section, Torrance and Process, seek to respond in general terms rather than with respect to the narrower issues raised above. But, that said, each offers a very different sort of response. Both detect an underlying similarity of form, but whereas Torrance finds this in a similarity of method, for Process Theology this lies in the similarity of basic categories of thought. Whether such attempts to link theology and science through general principles rather than specific issues are any more successful is the question to which we must now direct our attention.

T. F. Torrance's 1969 work, *Theological Science*, has almost the status of a minor classic. Winner of the Templeton Prize 'for progress in religion' and a former Moderator of the General Assembly of the Church of Scotland, this Edinburgh professor is one of the very few British theologians whose name is widely known abroad. The major influence on his thought has been Karl Barth, and this emerges clearly in *Theological Science*. His major claim is that theology, like science, is controlled by its object, and so does not have its source simply in the aspirations of the inquirer, as some radical theology would have us believe.[42] He notes that the chemist philosopher Polanyi detects the rationality of nature to lie in the way in which it 'so commands our respect for it that we are ready to let it speak for itself' and sees an obvious parallel to this in the fact that 'theological thinking is more like listening than any other knowledge, a listening for and to a rational Word from beyond anything we can tell to ourselves and distinct from our rational elaborations of it.'[43] The result is his claim that 'it is this very devotion of theology to its proper object that is the scientific passion of theology.'[44] Given the stress on the indispensable role of the observer in modern quantum physics, the reader can therefore hardly be surprised when Torrance goes on to deduce from his parallel between theology and science the important subsidiary point, that the role of the observer is also indispensable[45] if we are to gain a proper understanding of theology's own object ('God in Christ').[46] 'True objectivity is to be found only within personal communion or dialogical relation with God.'[47]

There is much of value in what Torrance says, particularly his insistence that theology too must be controlled by its object and not by purely human projections. Right too is his claim that this will require us to modify many of the ways in which we think of God. For example, 'theology is forced to reconstruct the notions of power and goodness as aplied to God from what God has done.'[48] But combined with such insight is a regrettable tendency for him to overplay his hand. As a highly specific example one might mention the strange passage in which he attempts to justify the interpretation of the parable of the sower and the seed in Mark 4 as dominical by drawing a parallel with Frege on arithmetic.[49] More generally, he seems to overstress the parallel, as in the following: 'theological thinking is essential . . . *a posteriori*, thinking that follows and is obedient to the given and communicated Word . . . and empirical, thinking out of real experience of God determined by God.'[50] But all this is highly misleading, since theology is *a posteriori* and empirical in a very different sense from science. Thus, to mention just one obvious difference, for the Christian the crucial factor in determining doctrine is not his own experience but reflection on the experience of the early Church. So, unlike with science, the key empirical content is mediated and indirect, as for example in respect of our knowledge of the Resurrection.

However, this is not to say that we are left with just those two general points of comparison that Torrance chooses to stress. He also mentions the communal character of the enterprise on which both science and theology are engaged,[51] a point which is also taken up by someone who is both a scientist and theologian, namely Arthur Peacocke in *Science and the Christian Experiment*. Apart from noting the way in which both accept the limited authority of a community, he also sees other parallels – in the role of imagination (e.g. Kekulé's dream of a snake grasping its tail in its mouth suggesting to him the ring form of benzine) or again in the way in which the appeal to experience helped to shape credal 'laws'.[52]

What these comparisons of Torrance and Peacocke undoubtedly show is that theological and scientific methods are not as remote from one another as might initially be supposed. But if more is intended, for example that theology cash in on the prestige of science, nothing could be more wrong-headed. For, as I have already argued in chapter 1 when discussing Gadamer, what is most urgently required in all Arts subjects, including theology, is release from the baneful influence of the conviction that knowledge is only possible through something approaching the scientific method. Rather, different methods are appropriate in different contexts.

One possible point of comparison which Peacocke mentions[53] is the way in which theology by returning to Biblical categories might produce the more dynamic imagery that is characteristic of science. This is certainly a fundamental aim of Process Theology which seeks to replace the static notion of substance that has dominated theology for so long with a dynamic notion of God as process. The actual term 'process theology' seems only to have gained currency in the fifties, though its antecedents are much older than that. The Cambridge mathematician and philosopher A. N. Whitehead (1861–1947) is the seminal influence. During his fellowship at Trinity he collaborated with Bertrand Russell on *Principia Mathematica*, but by the time he produced *Process and Reality* he had already accepted a professorship of philosophy at Harvard. There Charles Hartshorne was one of his assistants. In 1928 Hartshorne moved to the philosophy department at the University of Chicago, where he remained until 1955. It was largely thanks to him that Whitehead's often difficult ideas were popularized in theology, and by the sixties a whole stream of books was appearing on the subject, of which John Cobb's *A Christian Natural Theology* and Schubert Ogden's *The Reality of God* are typical.

The basic idea of what Whitehead calls his 'philosophy of organism'[54] is that science reveals to us that all reality is in movement and that being so we are not entitled to make God an exception. Thus, despite Newton's discovery, *contra* Aristotle, that motion was no less natural than rest, Whitehead upbraids him for not carrying his insight far enough. Newton in his *Scholium*[55] had accepted notions of absolute space and time, whereas Plato in his *Timaeus*, he claims, saw the essential point of universal growth. 'The full sweep of the modern doctrine of evolution would have confused the Newton of the *Scholium*, but would have enlightened the Plato of the *Timaeus*.'[56] Other contrasts to which Whitehead points in Plato's favour are the way in which his preference for mathematical analysis would have made him better disposed to the modern dissolution of quanta into vibrations, as would his acceptance of primordial matter make more readily acceptable its evolution.[57] Any reader recalling my earlier section on Plato in which his hostility to change was stressed cannot but now he puzzled how sense is to be made of these remarks of Whitehead. But the explanation is relatively simple. Plato accepted an immanent divine principle that teleologically directs all things towards their 'telos' or end, and this is the source of Whitehead's praise for Plato. But it is important also to remember that for Plato this was the lowest level of reality, and that what is most truly divine remains totally beyond change. How the subsequent Platonic tradition reconciled these two claims we will observe when we look briefly at the philosophy of Plotinus later in this chapter.

Suffice it to note at this stage that Plato could never have accepted the way in which Whitehead develops this notion in relation to God. His suggestion is that we think of God as having what he calls a 'primordial' and 'consequent' nature. 'Analogously to all actual entities, the nature of God is dipolar . . . The consequent nature of God is conscious; and it is the realisation of the actual world in the unity of his nature . . . The primordial nature is conceptual, the consequent nature is the weaving of God's physical feelings upon the primordial concepts.'[58] Not perhaps surprisingly this language has led some commentators[59] to doubt whether the primordial nature is anything more than an abstract concept. Whether correct as an interpretation of Whitehead or not, it is certainly a defect that his followers have sought to rectify. Ogden does this in part by making the analogy of the world as God's body more explicit. 'God is by analogy a living and ever growing God . . . and is related to the universe of other beings somewhat as the human self is related to its body. And yet, just as surely implied, is that God is even in these respects the truly eminent or perfect reality, whose unsurpassability is a matter of principle, not simply of fact.'[60] The primordial nature is thus clearly conceived of as taking initiatives, as well as in turn being affected by the world.

As for what led Process theologians to these conclusions apart from the alleged greater compatibility of its fundamental category with a scientific outlook, two major types of argument can I think be detected. What seems to have weighed most with Whitehead was what he called his 'reformed subjectivist principle', 'the denial of . . . any meaning not abstracted from the experiential meaning'.[61] In other words, the claim is that no sense can be attached to an account of God that is not based on that alone of which we have knowledge, namely our own experience. He informs us that 'consciousness presupposes experience, and not experience consciousness,'[62] and applies this as much to God as to all physical reality. Hartshorne in similar vein argues that God cannot be described as personal unless like us he is capable of change in response to his environment, as also that he cannot properly be said to love unless his experience is like ours in being pained by others' sufferings and enriched by their achievements.[63] If the first argument is conceptual, the second is primarily pragmatic. It is that if Christianity is to make an adequate response to secularism and restore something of the involved God of the Bible, then he must be located where men's real concerns are, i.e. in the world. This is an argument particularly popular with Ogden. Of traditional theism he remarks that 'the difficulty with the old theism's dymythologizing is that it does not really interpret the scriptural myths, but rather eliminates them.'[64] His point is that classical analyses like that of Aquinas make the meaning of God's acts lie in what happens to men and not what happens to God.

That the first, conceptual argument has some force cannot be denied. Indeed, it continues to persuade some contemporary philosophers of religion that God must therefore have a body.[65] But this seems to me an over-reaction. In the first place, although as a matter of fact neural firings in the brain may always accompany all human mental acts, we have no difficulty in conceiving them taking place without any such physical base. It must thus be a purely contingent fact, not part of the meaning of the terms. But secondly we have already noted the way in which even when something like suffering is ascribed to God the character of the experience is fundamentally transformed because applied to an omniscient consciousness. The other, pragmatic argument is more difficult to assess. The most obvious criticism to make is that of course wishing God to be relevant does not mean that he is or can be made so. Indeed, there are some grounds for objecting that all Ogden offers us is an alternative mythology. Thus it is significant that in his chapter on divine action in history he proposes as an analogy the relation between our minds and brain cells.[66] But strictly speaking it is inappropriate to talk here of the mind's action: the activity of the brain cells is indispensable to what we do, but our intentions (which is what defines something as an action) are directed to the world, not to these unknown brain cells. Not only that, the mind is not conscious of any interaction with the cells, and so there is no real parallel with personal action. This cannot help but make one wonder whether Ogden is not really using God just as a mythological prop on which to base his optimism about the world, rather than actually saying anything about a conscious director of the process. It is a suspicion which is considerably strengthened when one reads sentences like the following: 'I hold that the primary use or function of "God" is to refer to the objective ground in reality itself of our ineradicable confidence in the final worth of our existence.'[67] To be fair to him he does here talk of 'the objective ground', but the question remains how secondary this is to 'our ineradicable confidence . . .'.

Hegel

That it was to Plato, despite his limited relevance, that Whitehead appealed has already been noticed. What makes this appeal all the more strange is the fact that his life was almost exactly contemporaneous with the brief flourishing in England of a philosopher's ideas that were far more naturally congenial to his own viewpoint. For British interest in Hegel can be dated from Stirling's *The Secret of Hegel*, published not long after Whitehead's birth (1865), with important works by Green,

Bosanquet and Bradley appearing in the decades thereafter. Not only that; Cambridge's leading Hegelian and Whitehead's junior, McTaggart, overlapped with him for nineteen years of his fellowship at Trinity. Yet *Process and Reality* fails even to mention Hegel, except once in a long list of philosophers. Perhaps he felt (rightly) that by the time he came to write the book the influence of Hegel was on the decline, and so it would be unwise to tar his own ideas with that brush. Perhaps he simply failed to understand the significance of Hegel. But, whatever the reason, there can be no doubt about his relevance. For like Process Theology he offers a view of God as immanent in the world and dependent on it.

Admittedly this interpretation of Hegel is hotly contested and some of his commentators deny him any Christian commitment. But it seems to me that he could in fact with some legitimacy be described as the last great Christian philosopher, though this is not of course to declare him orthodox. One example of such an alternative interpretation is Walter Kaufmann's *Hegel: a reinterpretation*.[68] His argument is that Hegel needs to be understood not against the background of the *Lectures on* the Philosophy of Religion which he gave towards the end of his life, while a professor at Berlin, but in the light of his *Theologische Jugendschriften*, his early writings on theology. From these he locates the reason for Hegel's revolt against Kant in his admiration for the Greeks and which has therefore nothing to do with Christianity. Likewise, he sees the introduction of Hegel's central category for the divine, *Geist* (literally 'Spirit') as inspired by the Romantic reaction to the Enlightenment. Thus he uses the poet Schiller to argue both that Hegel intended by the term 'a creative force',[69] and that the quotation from him at the end of Hegel's major work *The Phenomenology of the Spirit* is intended to convey, that 'there is no supreme being beyond' and that ' "history comprehended" must replace theology.'[70] So his conclusion is the same as that of J. N. Findlay that Hegel's position was really one of atheistic humanism.[71]

But there is just too much counter-evidence for Kaufmann to be right that all that Hegel's views underwent was a change of emphasis, with Christianity now commended as 'an important, if somewhat benighted, anticipation of modern philosophy'.[72] Indeed at one point his argument degenerates into silly prejudice when he remarks of one, more positive early writing that 'Hegel filed this latest attempt into a desk drawer, where it belonged',[73] forgetting that this was the initial fate of them all! At the same time one must avoid the other extreme, such as Emil Fackenheim's *The Religious Dimension in Hegel's Thought*, in which despite Fackenheim's Jewish faith, Hegel is turned into an orthodox Christian. In his key chapter on 'The Hegelian Middle' he argues both against 'the right-wing interpretation' of Hegel as a Platonist, as a 'transcendent metaphysician',[74] and also against 'the left-wing interpretation', 'the immanentist interpretation' in which 'the world of human experience exhausts Reality.'[75] One might have thought that such a mediating view of Hegel would have produced an account in which *Geist* is seen as wholly immanent but yet not reduced to simply the sum of human experience, and indeed at one point he seems to concede the necessity for Hegel of divine embodiment.[76] But equally there are other passages in Fackenheim which draw Hegel closer to Christian orthodoxy, as when he speaks of 'a total and gratuitous divine Love for the human; a total identification with the man, by a Divinity which does not need it'.[77] But against that has to be set emphatic declarations of Hegel like the following: 'Ohne Welt ist Gott nicht Gott' (God is not God without the world).[78]

The existence of such rival interpretations demonstrates I think not just lack of clarity in Hegel's exposition but also the richness of his ideas, with opposed viewpoints each wishing to claim him as their trailblazer. My own suggested interpretation would run something along the following lines. Hegel does seem initially to have accepted the Kantian expulsion of God beyond the realms of knowledge and to have reacted by accepting the Greeks' very humanistic celebration of man. But his return to Christianity was I think sincere, and motivated by the thought that only through an immanent but all-encompassing notion of *Geist* was it possible to make sense of reality as a whole. It had to be immanent because like Whitehead he held that all mental activity must necessarily be embodied. Where his most original contribution lies, however, is in his explanation of the form such embodiment takes.

His argument is that personality is only forged in opposition to another, and so it is only by *Geist* going out of itself into man that the divine self-consciousness can be formed. Thus the famous passage on 'Lordship and Bondage' in the *Phenomenology* opens with the emphatic declaration that 'self-consciousness exists in and for itself when and by the fact that it so exists for another; that is, it exists only through being acknowledged.'[79] Human beings are seen as able to move from 'an sich', a merely implicit personality, to 'für sich' (sometimes called 'an und für sich'), a full self-consciousness only through what he calls 'a life-and-death struggle': 'They must engage in this struggle, for they must raise their being for themselves ("für sich") to truth.'[80] But it is a struggle in which at least in the human case the real victor is not always the apparent victor. For Hegel claims that in the master–slave relationship, it is the slave who first obtains free selfhood, since the master remains dependent on his need to dominate the slave. This is then applied to God in the section on 'The Revealed Religion'. In explaining the origin of the world he writes: 'This individual Self as at first thus immediately posited, is not yet Spirit for itself; it does not exist as Spirit . . . Before it can in fact be Self and Spirit it must first become an "other" to its own self.'[81] This he holds explains not only the presence of human consciousness in the world but also what he sees as the necessity of the Fall since the movement to 'für sich' cannot take place without conflict. Thus, though Hegel certainly believes that the march of history will culminate in *Geist*'s complete self-realization, this should not be equated with a naïve optimism. The presence of evil is fully acknowledged, as indeed his own personal tragedies might have led one to expect.[82]

It is against this background that Hegel's acceptance of the Christian doctrines of Incarnation and Trinity must be set. In a sense in positing the world as the other, *Geist* has been incarnate in all men from the beginning. But it has been an imperfect realization, and that is why Hegel attaches so much importance to the doctrine of one particular individual as uniquely incarnate. Unlike Judaism which makes God completely transcendent and Greek religion which never gets beyond partial immanent realizations, Christianity alone offers a complete realization of God as man and man as God, a fulfilment which then paves the way for a community inspired by the Spirit, one which will make such identity possible for all men, and thus hasten the full realization of *Geist für sich*. Put like that, it of course becomes clear that, as Charles Taylor notes in his definitive work *Hegel*, 'he did not . . . believe in the Incarnation in the ordinary sense, since ultimately Jesus is not God in any sense in which all other men are not.'[83] The Incarnation is the next topic to which we shall turn, but in the meantime it will be profitable first to critically examine the two main theses that underpin the above account, his view of language and his account of personality.

Hegel finds it easy enough to claim that he is accepting orthodox Christianity because of the distinction he draws between *Vorstellungen* (images) and *Begriffe* (concepts). Only philosophy deals with the latter, whereas religion is essentially a matter of the former, and of course if Incarnation is a *Vorstellung* rather than a *Begriff* then there can be no difficulty with his claim that he has fully accepted it: images must not be taken too literally. But the irony is that discussion within revisionary theologies like Process and Hegel tends to be conducted in terms that are treated as conceptual but in fact are more appropriately regarded as imagist, namely the terms immanent and transcendent. To explain. Those sympathetic to Hegel or Process often claim that the conception of God as immanent enables us to conceive of him as more involved with the world and so as more real to us. But what they forget is that the root meanings of 'immanent' and 'transcendent' are based on spatial imagery, and hence that their meaning is not primarily conceptual at all. Thus, if pressed to yield what literal force they do have, not only is their meaning far from clear but also, more worrying for the whole strategy, it becomes obvious that an immanent picture of God can produce just as little experiential and conceptual involvement as a transcendent one.

That the Latin roots of the two words mean 'going beyond' and 'remaining within', presumably no one would deny. But problems arise as soon as one attempts to penetrate this spatial imagery and detect some clear conceptual content. One might, for example, suggest that the intended contrast is between God as apart from the world and God as involved in it. But this won't do. God as transcendent can still be involved with the world in various different ways, e.g. through continuing to support it in existence, through revelation or through miracles. Equally inadequate is the suggestion that the contrast is between God as independent of the world and God as dependent on it. Here one might quote the traditional Christian doctrine of the Holy Spirit which sees the Spirit as immanent, but certainly not as dependent. All this makes one suspect that theology has become hopelessly bewitched by what is after all only a metaphor, a metaphor that has its *raison d'être* in human experience where the spatial image, unlike in the divine case, after all makes some kind of sense. For it comes naturally to us to identify our experience of God as internal or external, with at one extreme the Spirit's inner prompting and at the other the experience of the numinous, of awe at the distancing majesty that compels us to bend the knee in worship. But from the fact that he is experienced like this nothing follows about his actual location, since by definition he is present everywhere, omnipresent.

Still more critical for this type of approach is the fact that, even if clear sense could be attached to the contrast, there is no guarantee that conceiving of God as immanent will make him more involved and real to us. It is the old problem of holding something too close to one's eyes, with the result that one cannot see it. Ogden's analogy of the relation between the mind and the brain ought to have given us due warning. The brain is so close that we are not normally conscious of any interaction at all, and for almost all practical purposes we can ignore its existence. Thus while excessive emphasis on the divine transcendence through the *via negativa* (saying what God is not) has sometimes pushed God off the edge of the precipice into non-existence, as in the past unintentionally in some writings strongly influenced by the Neo-Platonic tradition and nowadays intentionally in the more recent writings of Don Cupitt,[84] so excessive emphasis on the divine immanence has the same inherent possibility. Indeed, it is surely no accident that Hegel's two most distinguished immediate followers, Marx and Feuerbach, both turned in an atheist direction. Not only that, Feuerbach in his *Essence of Christianity* (1841) makes the connection quite explicit. Having just quoted a remark of Augustine's on divine immanence, that 'God is nearer, more related to us . . . than sensible, corporeal things', he then goes on to deduce that 'consciousness of God is self-consciousness, knowledge of God self-knowledge.'[85] God has become so immanent as to be identical with us.

So the key issue turns out not to be immanence versus transcendence but Hegel's claims about the logic of personality. This has two aspects, that personality requires physical expression and that it can only be produced in interaction with other persons. My objections to his first thesis I have already mentioned when discussing Process Theology. A similar complaint can be made about his second claim, that it is an illegitimate extrapolation from the human case. For there is an obvious explanation of why the necessity holds in our case, and why equally it cannot apply in God's. Our problem is that as children we start with no independent consciousness at all, with us even having to learn of the existence of other, independent minds.

But to say that much is not to dismiss Hegel's point entirely. For, just as I have argued that the contrast between immanence and transcendence has been exaggerated, so here I would wish to argue, though less strongly, that the contrast between divine need and divine independence has been overplayed. Theologians as different as Barth and Tillich have complained that Hegel's scheme destroys the freedom of God,[86] and as it stands this is of course true. But what they have failed to notice is the possibility of a mediating position, that while neither physical expression nor interaction may be necessary for God, it could be natural. This might seem like a subterfuge, but in fact the distinction between the appropriate and the necessary is an old one in theology.[87] Here what I have in mind can perhaps best be introduced by drawing a parallel with some human cases. For example, it is not necessary for love to be present between two people that it attains physical expression, though it is natural that it should do so. Again, for health to exist it is not necessary that regular exercise be taken, but arguably this is its most natural expression and reinforcement. Similarly then with God. He does not need persons, and he does not need the world. But arguably it is natural for any personality, including God, to express himself creatively and among other things that will mean expressing himself responsively to other persons. That is to say, God would be no less a person if none of this happened, but what would be missing would be the natural tendency of personalities to flow beyond themselves into creativity, both in respect of things and personal relationships.

To that degree, then, I think that Hegel was right. We do need to see creation as more than just an optional extra for God. Though unlike us he didn't need another medium in which to express himself, his thoughts being entirely adequate, the world represents the spontaneous and natural desire all persons have to create something of themselves outside of themselves. The world can thus in a sense be seen as the divine expression, comparable to the mother's expression of herself in her care for her children or the artist's expression of himself in his picture or bronze.

Thus paradoxically, though Hegel's greatest influence on twentieth-century theology has been through his immanentist conception of God (whether one takes Tillich's conception of God as 'the Ground of our Being' or John Robinson's best-seller popularization in *Honest to God*[88]), my suggestion is that all this really represents is theology mesmerized by images. The real importance of Hegel lies elsewhere, in the way in which he forces us to reconsider our conception of the divine personality.

For Hegel, not only is the world the divine expression, it reaches its pre-eminent expression in the Incarnation, and so it will be appropriate to turn to that issue next. Of the two theologians to whom we shall devote most attention ironically it is the one uninfluenced by Hegel (Maurice Wiles) who exhibits most affinity with his doctrinal position, while the other, Wolfhart Pannenberg, though profoundly influenced by Hegel in many ways, none the less transcends that influence to produce something approaching an orthodox account of the Incarnation.

Christology

Pannenberg and Wiles

Despite the paucity of references to Hegel in his major innovating work *Jesus: God and man*, it is clear that Pannenberg (b. 1928) has been profoundly influenced by him. Thus, in one of the two short passages in which his ideas are discussed Hegel's account of the Trinity is praised for 'this profound thought that the essence of the person is to exist in self-dedication to another person',[89] and it is significant that in the other it is this very notion of 'becoming in the other'[90] that is used to help explain what he understands by the Incarnation. He goes beyond Hegel in two key respects. First, though he agrees that the consummation of the divine life is tied to the end of history, he disagrees that there is any logical means available to us whereby we can plot its course from now until that *eschaton*. Secondly, and more importantly for our present concerns, he uses Augustine's analysis of the divine eternity as 'never-ending present'[91] to argue that what from our perspective may seem a becoming, has from God's always been part of his divine life, and so at least from an eternal perspective Jesus has always been God.

His argument is far from simple, and I believe ultimately flawed. Its significance lies in his willingness to takes seriously the conclusions of critical Biblical scholarship and despite this to take with equal seriousness the Biblical witness that rather more was involved than the life of an ordinary man. That is to say, modern theologians tend to be either critical and unorthodox or orthodox and uncritical. Pannenberg's achievement is that he tries to be both, and has had no serious rival in attempting this since the German edition of his book came out over twenty years ago in 1964. On the critical level he fully accepts the overwhelming view among Biblical scholars that there was no divine consciousness present in Christ, but equally refuses to concede that this is the end of the argument. Instead, he stresses the Resurrection and the significance it would have against the backdrop of the apocalyptic expectations of that time. He summarizes his own argument as follows: 'Only at the end of all events can God be revealed in his divinity . . . Only because in Jesus' resurrection the end of all things, which for us has not yet happened, has already occurred can it be said of Jesus that the ultimate is already present in him, and so also that God himself, his glory, has made its appearance in Jesus in a way that cannot be surpassed . . . If these apocalyptic ideas are translated into Hellenistic terminology and conceptuality, their meaning is: in Jesus, God himself has appeared on earth.'[92] In other words, it is because Jesus is held to anticipate completely in his person the end of all things in which the Hegelian return of the other into God will at last be fully realized, that he is considered to be God in that anticipatory disclosure event. I have criticized the form of this argument elsewhere.[93] Suffice it to say that I do none the less think that he has correctly located where the historical burden must lie in any adequate defence of a strong incarnational view. Only some such remarkable event as this could have legitimated the transformation between the limited consciousness of Jesus of which we learn from the Synoptic Gospels and the increasingly august role assigned to him that culminates in St John's Gospel's explicit acknowledgement of his divinity.

But it is not just a different form of historical justification from the past that Pannenberg offers. As already noted, he also departs from the past in offering a new model for understanding what took place. Thus, not only is the first serious attempt of orthodoxy to come to terms with modern critical scholarship rejected, namely the kenotic model of God literally becoming man, so too is the traditional Chalcedonian model of Christ being the God-man, i.e. simultaneously God and man rather than successively as with the kenotic model. Against the kenotic model he objects that it pays 'the price of God's identity',[94] his point presumably being that God emptying himself of his divinity is tantamount to his ceasing to be identical with God. The section in which he discusses the Chalcedonian model is significantly entitled 'The Impasse of the Doctrine of the Two Natures'.[95] While emphasizing that 'vere deus, vere homo is an indispensable statement of Christian theology', he sees the basic problem of the model to lie in the fact that 'one cannot speak of divine being and human being as though they were on the same plane.'[96] That is why he sees all attempts to relate Jesus' human consciousness to the Son and not to the Father as a mistake.[97] Not only is it untrue historically (that is not how Jesus saw himself) such 'absence of individual concreteness in Jesus' human nature as such . . . would make the completeness of his humanity problematic.'[98] Instead therefore he proposes that we take the two very different perspectives of the human and divine seriously. Then we shall see that it is only from God's timeless 'eternal present' that we can pronounce Jesus as God. This is true whether we take his favourite theme of the Resurrection perspective,[99] or a more Hegelian argument like the following: ' "Person" is a relational concept, and because the relation of Jesus to the Father in his dedication to him is identical with the relation to the Father intended by the designation "the Son", Jesus in his human dedication to the Father is identical with the eternal person of the Son of God.'[100]

Two comments need to be made about this strategy of Pannenberg's. The first concerns the inadequacy of his own proposals, and the second observes the greater cogency of the options he has rejected. On the first point the trouble is that, whichever way one takes his proposal, one runs into problems. Thus from the divine eternal perspective it could mean either (a) that the human Jesus, foreknown from eternity, has always been 'part' of the second Person of the Trinity (in which case the problem of the two natures is simply transferred to the eternal realm), or (b) that at the Resurrection Jesus was taken up into the eternal realm to be the Second divine Person (which means that what we then have is a variant of the kenotic model with the added complication of a consciousness that from our perspective expands at the Resurrection but from God's eternal present has somehow always timelessly been there), or (c) that from the eternal perspective there only ever has been a human consciousness but in virtue of its perfect anticipatory disclosure of the End it is always one with God (with the resultant difficulty that, all Pannenberg's protestations notwithstanding, Jesus is not in any literal sense God).[101] Thus it seems to me that we must pronounce Pannenberg's attempt to produce an alternative model a failure It engenders just as many difficulties as its predecessors, if not more.

But in any case Pannenberg's objections to the Chalcedonian and kenotic models are not nearly as decisive as he supposes. I have elsewhere[102] defended at length the coherence of both models. So there is no need to repeat that defence here. Suffice it to note that the likely source of the difficulty for Pannenberg as for so many theologians is resistance to postulating change in the Godhead. But, as we saw when we looked at Plato, such resistance has no secure basis. That conceded, the kenotic model can be seen to have no more logical difficulties than those raised by reincarnation, and the Chalcedonian 'impasse' resolves itself with the unity of the two natures guaranteed by the degree of interaction between them, with not only the divine nature inspiring the human but, uniquely in this case, the human experience directly being taken up into and affecting the divine nature.

One last word on the kenotic model. It is often summarily dismissed as though there was something particularly unbecoming in conceiving of God in this way. But that God should associate with a being of such vastly inferior intellect as man is astonishing enough, and once the model is put in that context, I can see no additional special obstacle from the divine dignity in God becoming man in this way. Indeed, one suspects that, though at an academic level it was only first canvassed as a model in the nineteenth century in response to Biblical criticism, it may well have been the predominant way of conceiving the Incarnation at the popular level throughout the centuries, though no doubt with an element of docetism thrown in. Certainly Loofs finds traces of its popular expression throughout the history of the Church, even in the patristic period,[103] and as evidence of its continuing esteem today at that level let me record the following headline over a feature in a popular Spanish magazine: 'La tierra en la que DIOS nació' '(The land in which God was born).[104] Theologians therefore seem to me unnecessarily contemptuous of popular piety in giving the theory such scant attention in comparison with the Chalcedonian model.

In comparison with the earlier dominating influence of Bultmann, more recent German Protestant thought through its leading representatives, Pannenberg and Moltmann, has tended towards more conservative doctrinal positions. English theology, on the other hand, has moved in precisely the opposite direction. Here a typical example would be the Regius Professor of Divinity at Oxford, Maurice Wiles, who was also one of the contributors to *The Myth of God Incarnate* (1977). Certainly, with Wiles not only is there no influence from Hegel, there are at least two major contrasts. First, he detects no meaning or direction in history. The notion of Providence at most has justification in the fact that 'there are occasions which arouse in us, either at the time or in retrospect, a sense of divine purpose.'[105] Wiles' view can perhaps best be characterized by saying that for him God has left 'traces' of himself in the universe, features that especially give access to what he is like, but these are open to all men equally at all times. Religious insight is simply the ability of some to better grasp what those features are. In theory at least you or I could have made the same discovery, but, others having made the discovery, we may be prepared to rest content in reliance on what they have done. The fact that God is thus providentially directing neither Church nor world perhaps helps explain the second major contrast with Hegel, his emphasis on divine transcendence rather than immanence. Indeed, significantly transcendence is the very first attribute which he assigns to God in his *Remaking of Christian Doctrine*: 'First, then, everything that suggests the validity of belief in God at all points to belief in his transcendence.'[106] The contrast with Hegel is ironically still further heightened by the fact that Wiles's first appeal by way of justification is to 'Schleiermacher's feeling of absolute dependence', the very feeling that Hegel ridiculed when he remarked that then 'a dog would be the best Christian, since it possesses this feeling of "salvation" when it hungers for a bone!'[107]

But, despite these contrasts, there is one obvious point of contact where Wiles is nearer to Hegel than Pannenberg, and that is in his view of the Incarnation. For, though both insist on the uniqueness of Christ, equally for both the language of Incarnation is not conceptual but imagistic or metaphorical, or as Wiles chooses to put it, the language of myth. This has at least the merit of honesty. For British theology, as represented for example by Donald Baillie's *God was in Christ* (1956) or John Robinson's *The Human Face of God* (1973), had in effect been adopting this position for some time and, in using the same language of incarnation, had laid claim to a continuity with the tradition to which they were not entitled. Wiles' candour is a breath of fresh air in a discipline in which issues are constantly being obfuscated by the apparent endorsement of traditional language, when the theologians concerned are in fact advocating something quite different.

Wiles traces the introduction of the term 'myth' into English theological discussion, and notes positive appraisal as 'a doctrine expressed in narrative form . . . where the object is to enforce faith not in the parable but in the moral'[108] as early as Baden Powell, one of the contributors to the Liberal manifesto of 1860, *Essays and Reviews*. Wiles adopts a very similar view himself, though he prefers to use the term 'ontological'[109] rather than 'moral' for the element that remains true despite the falsity of the literal interpretation. In the case of the incarnational narrative of God becoming man the true 'ontological' element is 'first that his own life in its relation to God embodied that openness to God, that unity of human and divine to which the doctrine points . . . And secondly . . . that in his attitude towards other men his life was a parable of the loving outreach of God to the world.'[110] However, he is willing to concede that his position is not without its difficulties, and interestingly, though he thinks the problem superable, his discussion ends with the comment that the 'possibly most searching difficulty of all is the question whether a myth can continue to function as a potent myth, once it is acknowledged that it is not literally true'.[111] That clearly is the nub of the matter. It is also an issue that exercised

Roland Barthes, one of the great French thinkers of the post-war period.

Barthes and myth

A wide variety of interests characterized a career that culminated in his election as professor of semiology in the prestigious College de France three years prior to his death in a traffic accident in 1980. His earlier career was dominated by an interest in structuralist literary criticism of the kind discussed in chapter 1, though even then his interests extended widely enough to include a sociological study of fashion (his *Système de la mode* of 1967). But by his 1973 work *Le plaisir du texte* Structuralism had already been transcended into a sort of Derrida-type hedonistic enjoyment of words for their own sake without regard to their role in any particular underlying structure. His inaugural lecture still further limited exaggerated pretensions for Structuralism by emphatically declaring that 'semiology is not a grid; it does not permit a direct apprehension of the real through the imposition of a general transparency which would render it intelligible. It seeks instead to elicit the real.'[112] In other words, semiology (the study of signs in general) can only help to clarify and enlighten: it 'has no substitutory role with regard to any other discipline'. Such comments make it all the more significant that his last work, *Camera Lucida*, studies the power of the camera without resort to any of his earlier technical vocabulary, apart from his notion of a 'punctum', the discordant element that punctures one's consciousness and gives power to the photograph.[113]

Formal works of semiology, literary criticism, biography, studies of fashion and photography may not seem to have much in common or to have much to do with philosophy. But there is an underlying link, and that is in Barthes' fascination with the analysis of culture. It is in this context that his early work *Mythologies* belongs. Despite its brevity, it is one of the most penetrating studies of the relation between myth and society ever written, not least because it looks at the myths of contemporary culture. For Barthes it is indispensable to the power of the myth that people believe it, and so it will be particularly interesting to compare his view with the very different view of another literary critic and indeed one of the most esteemed literary critics of the English-speaking world, namely Northrop Frye. It will be my claim that Barthes has an insight that Frye lacks.

Barthes detects myth in an extraordinary range of contemporary contexts – in soap-powders, in steak and chips, in the brain of Einstein, in the Blue Guide and in striptease, to name but a few. One of the most intriguing is his analysis of 'The World of Wrestling' in which he considers 'that power of transmutation which is common to the

Spectacle and to Religious Worship'.[114] Essential to his argument is the contrast between boxing and wrestling. In the former there is a real contest, with the result uncertain, whereas in wrestling the spectator suspends disbelief, and sees everything in terms of a straightforward conflict between Good and Evil. Thus, not only does the *salaud* (the 'baddy') play dirty, he is expected to look fat and ugly as well. When the 'goody' falls he can even be compared to Jesus on the Cross,[115] but all know that justice must be done in the end. Thus, essential to Barthes' analysis of wrestling as a form of myth is that for the duration of the contest the story is believed, that it really does give access to reality as it is: 'In the ring, and even in the depths of their voluntary ignomity, wrestlers remain gods because they are, for a few moments, the key which opens Nature.'[116]

After giving numerous examples the book ends with an extended but difficult abstract discussion of the nature of myth. Of the many points he makes there – not all plausible – three in particular seem to me to merit special attention. The first is his insistence that 'everything can be a myth.'[117] Not only does he refuse to confine the term to stories, he does not even confine its appropriateness to language. He does not tell us his reason in the former case, but it is not hard to guess. For whether something is presented as a story or as a single image is not necessarily in itself very significant. So, for example, it is possible to present the wrestling match as the story of a contest or with equal appropriateness frame it in a single image, that of 'the beautiful and the good' standing in triumph over the ugly bully. His interest in semiology explains why he refuses to confine the term to language. Language is only one form of communication and the same message could equally well be conveyed by actions or pictorial images, such as photography or cinema.

Secondly, the power of the myth is to be found in the way in which the imaginative sign, whether it be story or image, outruns what can easily be said at the literal level. Through its power of encapsulation it acquires a life of its own, and becomes more likely to invoke a ready response than when its content is spelt out in a more matter of fact way. Barthes makes this point in a very memorable way, by drawing a comparison with an alibi. 'Nothing prevents myth from being a perpetual alibi: it is enough that its signifier has two sides for it always to have an "elsewhere" at its disposal. The meaning is always there to present the form; the form is always there to outdistance the meaning.'[118] However, the image is not altogether fortunate. For 'alibi' suggests that the literal meaning does not matter at all (meaning lies 'elsewhere'), whereas, as his metaphor of 'outdistancing' and the following pages make clear, what he wants to suggest is that myth gains its power through transcending the literal, not through supplanting it.

Thus, the force of 'alibi' is that myth is a slippery customer, as it were, who has always got another locus of meaning up his sleeve, whose meaning, it claims, is never exhausted by the literal truth of the story or image. This point emerges with particular clarity in his recurring example of a *Paris-Match* photograph of a young Negro in a French uniform with uplifted eyes saluting the tricolour.[119] That this is actually taking place is not denied. The mythical character of the photograph rather lies in the way in which it transcends this literal meaning into a general claim about the nature of the French Empire.

This example of his may also be used to illustrate the third main feature of his analysis to which I wish to draw attention. Barthes sees the work of the 'mythologist' (someone like him who studies myths) as a task of decipherment, of understanding how the 'distortion' takes place, and in this context of the Negro salute he remarks: 'if I decipher the Negro's salute as an alibi of coloniality, I shatter the myth even more surely by the obviousness of its motivation.'[120] But at the same time he contrasts this with what acceptance of the myth would mean: 'If I focus on the mythical signifier as on an inextricable whole made of meaning and form . . . I respond to the constituting mechanism of myth, to its own dynamics . . . The saluting Negro is no longer an example or a symbol, still less an alibi: he is the very presence of French imperiality.'[121] In other words, it is integral to Barthes' analysis of the power of myth that the whole, literal and transcendent meaning be believed. This too explains why Barthes crusades so much against their belief. For he sees belief in them as what gives ideological strength to bourgeois society, as when for example 'a typist earning twenty pounds a month recognises herself in the big wedding of the bourgeoisie.'[122] But his left-wing politics does lead him seriously astray when he is found claiming that there are no left-wing myths, on the grounds that revolutionary politics is concerned to transform reality, not preserve images.[123] For surely the attraction of Marxism is exhibited in the way in which people can continue to believe in its myth of a truly egalitarian society, despite all the evidence to the contrary from existing communist societies.

Now contrast all this with what the leading English-speaking literary critic, Northrop Frye, has to say on the subject of myth in the Bible in his recent book *The Great Code*. His argument is that three stages in the development of language can be distinguished, the metaphorical, the metonymic and the literal,[124] and that in the light of this we should see poetry as 'genuinely primitive, and not as an artificial way of decorating and distorting "prose" '.[125] Not only does he thus attempt to validate poetry as a legitimate alternative mode of discourse, he also argues that, despite the dominance of our own society by the literal, myth deserves to continue to find a place within it because of what it attempts to achieve. Thus he identifies two aspects to myth, 'its story-structure' and 'its social function as concerned knowledge, what it is important for society to know'.[126] In such a context he argues it is unimportant whether the myths are histories or fictions, and in any case it is undecidable.[127]

There is a great deal of valuable analysis of Biblical language, particularly I think in the two chapters he devotes to typology. But it is hard to see his account of myth as anything other than wrong-headed. This is not because he makes the usual narrow identification of myth with story, nor because of his identification of its social function. Rather, the problem is the way in which, like Wiles, he thinks we can choose our myths. Added to this is their failure to appreciate the way in which the power of the myth is tied to believing it true at all levels. Thus on the first point, it is almost farcical to read of the ease with which he thinks we can abandon a central Biblical image like 'the body of Christ';[128] still more so to discover his proposal for an 'open community of vision',[129] in which our society's myths are to be chosen from many sources, including the Bible. What this ignores is what Barthes has so rightly stressed, that it is myths that choose us, not we them. It is because they encapsulate so well what we struggle to express that we fall prey, rightly or wrongly as the case may be, to their power. This failure to reflect on what gives myth its power equally explains his indifference to questions of history. In fact, remarks such as 'it is the bits of credible history that are expendable'[130] expose his real attitude, and it is not without significance that the final message he derives from the decoded myths[131] is little more than some vague sense of hope.

But, if Barthes is to be preferred to Frye and Wiles, how is his analysis to be applied to the Bible? Let us take the two standard cases of the Fall and the Incarnation. In the first case I would suggest that the reason why the Fall continues to exercise a power and fascination over the Christian mind, despite the non-historicity of the opening chapters of Genesis, is not because we now treat the story as a myth but because a single image has taken over and the story been entirely discarded. Thus there are numerous details of the story which we would wish to challenge, that all evil in the world is the fault of human decision, that morality is a matter of an externally imposed divine ethic, that God did not wish man to have certain basic forms of knowledge, that sexuality and sin are necessarily connected and so on. Indeed, the longer one reflects on the story, the clearer does it become that the continuing power of the myth has nothing whatsoever to do with the story. Rather, I suggest, it is a matter of a pictorial image, of the contrast between living with the divine Goodness and doing what one knows to be wrong. Thus, far more than the Bible story it is pictures like Thomas

Coles' Boston painting 'The Expulsion from the Garden of Eden', in which Adam is portrayed defiantly leaving Paradise for a wolf-ridden terrain, that most powerfully achieve a mythological effect on me. That is to say, it successfully encapsulates a meaning and a commitment for me that resists easy unpacking, not just despite the fact but precisely because through the painting one is only minimally reminded of the Biblical story. For with the tree of forbidden fruit, the serpent and so forth removed, the literal truth of the image strikes home immediately. It is any man and every man in that darkness, with the expulsion from the light of the divine Goodness caused by one's own decision. On that foundation the deeper level of the myth is then based, with its insistent invitation to reflect further on one's own sinfulness.

With the Incarnation there is certainly much more justification for saying that it is the Biblical story that is the basis, but even here I am not entirely convinced. For, so far as its mythological power is concerned, does this not focus on two aspects only, with the rest of his life-story largely ignored? Is it not God defenceless in the stable and suffering on the Cross around which all the emotive and evocative power is concentrated? But, whether this is so or not, again note that it is indispensable to that power that the literal content of the image be true, that just as in the case of the Fall the image must be of any man so in this case it can only be of God. To suppose otherwise would be to misunderstand completely thousands of Christian sermons throughout the ages such as Luther's talk of 'Mary suckling God with her breasts' and so forth. It is simply because the image is so shocking when taken as the literal truth it is that it compels further reflection on what it must imply about the nature of the divine love.

I conclude therefore that, so far from offering a mythological account of the Incarnation, Wiles' interpretation actually undermines what is probably the most powerful myth the world has ever known. With that judgement on Wiles I am sure Barthes would have had no hesitation in agreeing. But it still leaves me with a major problem. For, as noted earlier, Barthes refuses to concede the truth of any myths, whereas I have been concerned to argue above that both the Fall and Incarnation function like his notion of myth but are also true. Despite numerous attempts to do so, it is probably too late to save the word for a more neutral interpretation. Perhaps the best term currently available is 'symbol', which I discuss in chapter 5. Certainly the more recent use of story[132] is no less unsatisfactory. Not only does it narrowly confine us to the verbal, as Frye notes,[133] it normally tends to be contrasted with history and so carries the same disparaging connotations about factual truth as myth itself.

The Trinity

Moltmann and Augustine

One possible way of interpreting Jürgen Moltmann's recent book *The Trinity and the Kingdom of God* is as an attempt to rehabilitate the doctrine to the status of a Barthes-type 'myth', a status which it has never really had within the Western theological tradition. That is to say, in contrast with that tradition shaped by Augustine in which the Trinity, unlike the Incarnation, has been little more than a formal idea, Moltmann is seeking through use of a different model associated with Eastern Christendom to make the doctrine a focus of commitment in the same way as we find with Barthes' 'myths'. Thus clearly for him 'three persons in one God' is not to be seen as something requiring formal definition, but as a concept in which meaning outruns the form, a rich concentration that not only points beyond itself to tell us a great deal about the nature of the divine life but that also, in its turn, can be seen as a legitimate reflection of our deepest personal and political aspirations. Given my suggestion in the previous section that images are often more effective in fulfilling this role than stories or words, it is interesting to observe that in his Preface Moltmann stresses the influence upon him of Andrei Rublev's icon of the Trinity in which the distinct and personal character of its three members is of course heavily stressed.[134]

Moltmann in fact launches a major attack on the whole Western approach. Its effect, he argues, has been to make Christians 'monotheists' rather than trinitarians.[135] Kant's comment that 'it is impossible to extract from this difference any different rules for practical living' he regards as both justified and typical.[136] Nor have twentieth-century trends in theology been any more helpful. Barth's view is described as 'eternal repetition' or 'holy tautology', while Rahner's is equally summarily dismissed on the grounds of its 'astonishing similarity to Barth' with 'almost the same presuppositions'.[137]

The source of his objection is the Western stress on the divine unity that makes the nature of the differentiation between the 'persons' problematic. Indeed, the core of the problem is detected by Moltmann in the reluctance of the Western tradition to take the term seriously, a reluctance which, as we shall see, was particularly prominent in Augustine. But it is a retreat which Moltmann sees as based on a false understanding of the nature of personhood. Thus he reprimands Rahner for reacting against what is in fact a very inadequate view of personhood: 'What he describes is actually extreme individualism: everyone is a self-possessing, self-disposing centre of action which sets itself apart from other persons.'[138] He notes too its effect in 'the modern bourgeois world's cultivation of the individual' with each person seen as a unit and others as a restraint on one's freedom: 'The other person is the only thing that limits the development of one's own personality and the realisation of one's own self.'[139] Moltmann then contrasts this view with his own, in which he sees personhood as necessarily relational and involving others. Antecedents, however, are admitted in the Cappadocians in the patristic period and in Richard of St Victor in the medieval, though significantly the culmination is seen as being reached in Hegel: 'Hegel then picked up this idea and deepened it. It is the nature of the person to give himself entirely to a counterpart, and to find himself in the other most of all. The person only comes to himself by expressing and expending himself in others.'[140]

A previous section on Hegel has already discussed the extent to which such claims about the nature of personality are true. So there is no need to repeat the discussion here except to note one puzzle about Moltmann's position. Like Hegel he claims that this means that the world is necessary, but, unlike Hegel, he believes that the persons of the Trinity have a life of their own apart from the world. So in theory at least this should mean that Hegel's point has already been met through the existence of the other persons of the Trinity. Though he is hard to interpret here, the reason why Moltmann regards this as insufficient[141] seems to be because of his belief that love is not completely fulfilled unless there is some need in the beloved and this obviously does not apply to the other persons of the Trinity. If that is his argument, it is surely wrong. Some of our deepest experiences of love consist simply in the enjoyment of the other with no need implied at all, as for example in the pleasure of a friend's company at a meal or on a walk.

But neither my earlier criticisms of Hegel nor these present objections to Moltmann should blind us to the important insight in his position. For, while there may be no necessity for the divine personality to be like our own in needing others for its expression, this does not preclude the possibility that as a matter of fact this is its character. As such it would then provide a powerful underpinning not only of our own dependence on social relations but of our hope that we can at times transcend them, however imperfectly, into a higher unity.

That it was this insight that the fourth-century Cappadocian fathers, particularly Gregory of Nyssa, were struggling towards, I have argued elsewhere.[142] Nor is there any shortage of analogies from our own experience that help to give credence to the idea that this is what the Godhead might be like. Every time we find our individuality transcended into a common perceived unity, whether it be in friendship or marriage or college or nation, we are given some inkling of what the divine unity might be like. Of course, this is so often fleeting and even in our deepest commitments fundamental disagreements occur. Admittedly also, sometimes such feelings of a common identity can be demonic, as in great fascist rallies of the past; sometimes too one can feel sucked in against one's better judgement – powerfully evoked for me in the film *Cabaret* by the boy singing a Nazi song and one by one his audience rising to join him. But none of this can alter the fact that such moments also mark man at his best, in sympathetic or emphatic identification with another. Moltmann cannot therefore but be right in urging the power of this social analogy for the Trinity compared with 'the mystic solitariness of God'[143] that Rahner and most modern theology continue to advocate.

But why do they do so? Four years after the last of the Cappadocians died St Augustine began work on *De Trinitate*, one of his three great masterpieces along with the *Confessions* and *The City of God*. Completed over twenty years later in 420, it has continued to exercise an enormous influence on Western theology right up to the present day. To be fair to Augustine, the main problem was the sheer genius of the man. In the patristic period he had no serious rival apart from Origen (d. 254) and, though Origen had offered an account of the Trinity in which the persons are sharply distinguished, Origen was under strong suspicion for heresy even in Augustine's own lifetime and finally formally condemned at the Second Council of Constantinople in AD 553.

Two aspects of Augustine's presentation seem particularly worthy of note, his alternative proposal of a psychological rather than a social analogy, and the way in which his stress on distinctions based on relations effectively reduces the doctrine to a meaningless form of words.

Initially his comparison of the Trinity to a single person or mind might seem a valuable course to pursue. For it leaves one in no doubt about the divine unity, especially when to this is added his attack on the adequacy of the term 'person' to identify successfully the three elements in the Godhead.[144] Of the psychological analogies Augustine offers, the clearest is to be found in Book X, with his comparison of the three members of the Trinity to the three human faculties of memory, understanding and will. That it has a number of advantages certainly must be conceded. Apart from safeguarding the divine unity by choosing something like mind that seems almost necessarily to be one, the analogy reinforces this sense of unity both by its choice of three faculties, each of which is indispensable to the successful operation of the mind, and by the fact that they are constantly interacting. Augustine believed that it has an additional advantage, with Father, Son and Holy Spirit corresponding to these three faculties, but I do not find this plausible. In any case, there are three decisive objections to his proposed analogy. First, if the New Testament reveals an Incarnation at all, it reveals two persons interacting, and this clearly favours the social analogy. Secondly, in the analogy the divine unity is bought at the expense of any real distinctness between the three elements. As Augustine himself remarks, 'all are mutually comprehended by each' (e.g. 'I remember the whole of my understanding and the whole of my will').[145] But, if this is so, it is hard to see why the matter is not better put by saying that there is really only one thing, the mind, but it can be seen from three different perspectives, and a perspective is not an ontological difference. Finally, to be told that our minds are like God in this way carries no practical import. We are at a loss to see what difference it could make to the way we act, or even to the type of mental life we lead. Yet it would surely be reasonable to expect some difference, if we really had at our disposal some great truth about the nature of the divine life.

But the nadir in Augustine's discussion had in fact been reached several books earlier, in Book V. There he impressively displays his powers of logic, but at the cost of assigning any meaningful content to the doctrine. The details of the argument need not concern us here.[146] Suffice it to say that he finds it impossible to distinguish the 'persons' except by their relations. But the relationships of sonship, procession, etc. have only clear sense in their original revelatory context. After all, what difference could there be in an eternal context between sonship and procession?[147] That being so, all we have left with, once the Filioque is taken into account, is the purely formal contrast that one person alone (i.e. the Father) relates and is not related, one person alone (the Son) both relates and is related (since in virtue of the Filioque like the Father he sends the Spirit, but is himself begotten of the Father), and one alone (the Spirit) is related but does not actively relate. This is surely logic at its most barren and uninformative!

But what led Augustine to this impasse? To answer that question, we need to examine the philosophical tradition that had most influence upon him.

Plotinus and Neo-Platonism

It is largely thanks to Plotinus' reshaping of Plato's ideas in the third century that Platonism acquired its dominant influence on Christian theology that was to last until the Aristotelian revival in the thirteenth century brought about largely by Aquinas. Admittedly, prior to this time theologians like the second-century Apologists had already made use of the eclectic Middle Platonism that combined features of Platonism and Stoicism,[148] but one very much gains the impression of second-rank theologians borrowing from philosophers who are themselves second-rank. That being so, nothing very much seems to hang on the borrowings. Justin Martyr (d.165) would probably have sought to express Christianity in the dominant philosophy of his day, whether leading philosophical contemporaries like Albinus had been Platonist or not. But with Origen, Plotinus' contemporary, and still more so with Augustine, it is clear that much more is at stake. Both, rather than simply adopting a Platonic perspective, seem to have been genuinely convinced by the force of Platonist arguments. That being so, someone with the intellectual stature of Plotinus could not but help to further accentuate the challenge to them to integrate their Christian faith and Platonism, especially as he continued the Middle Platonist trend in moving the emphasis away from Plato's own concern with ethics and epistemology towards a concentration on the religious question.

In the case of Origen the challenge was most likely mediated through their common philosophy tutor, Ammonius Saccas, but some direct influence is not impossible, as Plotinus, the younger man, was a philosophy student at Alexandria for ten years (approximately 232–42), during which time Origen was at his most productive. Certainly, in respect of the language they use to talk about God, Wolfson is prepared to declare that 'the similarity between Origen and Plotinus is striking, and it certainly cannot be explained as a mere coincidence.'[149] But there is not just similarity of language. Origen has Father, Son and Holy Spirit as three gradated levels of divinity in much the same way as Plotinus speaks of the One, Nous (i.e. Mind) and the World Soul. Nor is the similarity merely a formal one. The same reasons are given in explanation both of why there must be an Original of a certain kind at a higher level and of why none the less lesser levels of deity will be produced. Thus on the former point a previous section has already identified the kinds of factors that led to a stress in the Platonic tradition on an ultimate divine simplicity, though it is worth adding that Armstrong sees the unbounded character of this simplicity only clearly emerging with Plotinus.[150] However that may be, we find exactly the same stress in Origen's major work *De Principiis* in which he describes the Father as a 'simplex intellectualis natura' and also later in the same section as a 'Monad'.[151] Likewise it is the same kind of reasons that are seen as implying gradations in the divine being. Plotinus tells us: 'Whenever anything reaches its own perfection, we see that it cannot endure to remain in itself, but generates and produces some other thing . . . How then should the most perfect being and the first good remain shut up in itself, as though it were jealous or impotent – itself the potency of all things? . . . Something must therefore be begotten of it.'[152] Lovejoy in a famous book was to dub this idea *The Great Chain of Being*. In similar vein Origen on more than one occasion does not hesitate to gloss the Book of Wisdom's reference to an 'effluence of the divine glory' as an 'emanation' or 'outflow'.[153]

Given these two principles it now becomes clear why after the Council of Nicaea (325) someone like Augustine was presented with what was probably an insoluble dilemma. In several passages Augustine is lavish in acknowledging his debt to Plotinus' influence.[154] But Nicaea's declaration of the equality of the persons of the Trinity meant that that influence had to be resisted. For, while in Neo-Platonism the divine principles could exist easily in harmony, tension was inevitable once the graded character of the second principle was denied but the simplicity of the originating Monad maintained. Something just had to give. Armstrong seems implicitly to acknowledge this when, while noting that Augustine 'felt it his duty to make philosophical sense of the Trinity in terms of Neoplatonism',[155] he none the less makes the extraordinary comment that 'the doctrine of the Trinity seems to be quite compatible with the Neoplatonic doctrine of the One as long as one does no philosophising, either avowed or disguised as theological speculation or dogmatic formulation, about the Trinity.'[156] In other words, Augustine has succeeded, provided we do not take any of his analogies too seriously! That that was also Augustine's assessment of the situation seems to be confirmed by the final book of *De Trinitate*, in which he takes back most, if not all, of the force of those analogies by contrasting our own complexity with 'the simplicity of that Highest nature',[157] which is 'absolutely indivisible and truly unchangeable'.[158] Indeed, it cannot be without significance that his very last act before the concluding prayer is to return to the Filioque as the only way of distinguishing generation and procession in that 'ineffably unchangeable and indivisible Trinity'.[159] This is a formal success, bought at reduction of the doctrine to a mere empty shell of words.

Unfortunately, the influence of Neo-Platonism did not cease with Augustine. Permeated by its influence are the works of Dionysius the Areopagite (also known as Pseudo-Denys) who was probably writing at the end of the fifth century or the beginning of the sixth. Thus, though he claims to be advocating orthodox trinitarianism, it is significant that in *The Divine Names* he urges that 'we must, in the power of the Divine Unity, turn from the Many to the One and declare the Unity of the whole single Godhead, which is the one Cause of all things; before all distinctions of One and Many, Part and Whole, Definiteness and Indefiniteness, Finitude and Infinitude . . . beyond all titles, expressing under the form of Being That Which is beyond being.'[160] Partly because throughout the Middle Ages he was identified with the person who heard Paul's speech on the Areopagus and believed,[161] and partly because of Aquinas' respect for tradition, he and Augustine continued to ensure a continuing impact of Neo-Platonism even on St Thomas' 'Aristotelian' revolution.

The extent of the influence of such apophatic or negative theology on

Aquinas is still a matter of dispute. But what for me is incontestable is that, so far from offering a profound approach to the nature of God, it contains within itself the means of destroying any intelligible account not only of the Trinity but of God at all. One recent commentator on Aquinas, David Burrell, may be used to illustrate the point. In his book *Aquinas: God and Action* he interprets Aquinas very much along these lines. Of Aquinas' use of relations to explain the Trinity, he concedes that 'it brings little illumination', but insists that it 'has none the less served its purpose' because it defends 'the unity which divinity must exhibit'.[162] It is a unity, however, that he has already expounded in terms of the more basic category of simpleness, a simpleness which for Aquinas he warns us 'does not name a characteristic of God, but a formal feature . . . It is a shorthand term for saying that God lacks composition of any kind. And that bit of metaphysical jargon is itself a shorthand way of remarking that no articulated form of expression can succeed in stating anything about God.'[163] Aquinas we are told was only concerned to say what God is not,[164] and so 'it would be . . . obtuse to ask whether Aquinas' concept of God is a true one. For such a question presupposes that he was engaged in developing a concept of God.'[165]

Nowadays this is a common interpretation of Aquinas, in Germany and France as much as in the English-speaking world.[166] It is in marked contrast to the more positive emphasis of previous generations of Thomist scholars, even the immediately preceding generation of men like Garrigou-Lagrange, Gilson and Maritain. That the Neo-Platonist strand in Aquinas' thought is now taken so seriously is surely welcome. But I cannot help wondering whether it has not been overdone. Why should the few passages which strongly support this interpretation be allowed to control so totally our understanding of the *Summa* as a whole, when so much else reads much more positively? May not Aquinas simply have been inconsistent? But, whether the correct interpretation of Aquinas or not, it is quite inadequate as an account of our concept of God. For a purely negative approach makes anything and everything equally inappropriate to predicate of him, and so equally appropriate. But the notion will only make sense if incompatibles and contradictories are excluded, which is already to concede that certain terms are more appropriate than others and thus an acknowledgement that in fact we already do know something positive about God.

Burrell remarks that 'Aquinas displays his religious discipline most clearly by the ease with which he is able to endure so unknown a God.'[167] But, if the above is correct, that cannot possibly be the religious motivation behind Neo-Platonism since unless God has some definition he cannot give definition to the religious quest or to worship.

What then was the explanation for its religious appeal? Rist in his book on Plotinus provides the key when he observes that for Plotinus corresponding to the divine simplicity there is a similar need for simplicity in us: 'The One is pre-eminently simple and to attain likeness to it we too must be pre-eminently simple. Hence Plotinus' cry through all the stages of the "mystic way" is the more insistent here: "Strip away everything." '[168] The relevance of this may not be immediately obvious, but a central theme of Plotinus lies behind it, a theme that was even to find its echo in the structure of Aquinas' *Summa Theologiae*, which, despite its formal division in three parts, is 'ultimately divided into two vast visions of God: the exitus of all things from God, and the reditus of all things, particularly man, to God as to his ultimate goal'.[169] This Plotinian vision of all things flowing out of God and thus only finding their happiness by flowing back to him is I think the feature which exerted most religious fascination. In a world like Augustine's and Pseudo-Denys', in which the Roman Empire was collapsing about them, it offered a path to salvation that bypassed the world. It offered the possibility of ascent to God through 'stripping' off the inessentials of the world, a world whose perceived transience Peter Brown in his biography of Augustine sees as one of the great bonds between him and Neo-Platonism.[170] Thus the real source of Neo-Platonism's attractiveness lay not in an emphasis on the unknowability, transcendence, or mysteriousness of God, but in the hope it held out of escaping a troubled world by a retreat inwards that was also seen as an ascent upwards to the original source of one's being. Indeed, on this matter there is no more significant sentence in the *Enneads* than the following: 'This is the life of gods and of the godlike and blessed among men, liberation from the alien that besets us here, a life taking no pleasure in the things of earth, a flight of the alone to the Alone.'[171]

To justify this flight Plotinus frequently[172] employs an image that had originally been little more than a passing remark in Plato. Plato writes that 'we should make all speed to take flight from this world to the other; and that means becoming like the divine so far as we can.'[173] Indeed, much of Plotinus' philosophy can be seen as an extended meditation on that sentence, giving it a depth that Plato never intended. But can such a claim to divine likeness be justified in Christian theology, and, if so, what does this say about man's relationship to the world? It is to such questions as these that we must next turn.

3

Doctrine of Human Nature

The divine image

Irenaeus and Calvin

The doctrine of salvation, the subject of the next chapter, is clearly what makes of more than abstract interest the subject of the previous chapter. But salvation suggests deliverance from something, and so a prior question inevitably raises itself, namely what there is in human nature that requires such deliverance. That is the topic of the central sections of this chapter, but the content of the chapter as a whole is wider because one cannot artificially isolate the features that need redemption and then simply ignore other aspects of human nature. For to do so would be to fail to take account of the fact that man's nature is a unity and that interactions are taking place between the various aspects of his personality all the time. But to express matters like that is already to take sides on one major doctrinal divide, the extent to which man's nature needs redemption. For in acknowledging features in man from which he does not need deliverance it suggests that I would side with the typically Catholic stance of Irenaeus (d. *c.*200) rather than with the characteristically Protestant position of Calvin (1509–64).

The usual theological way of expressing the issue is in terms of the divine image in man. For Irenaeus it remains, whereas for Calvin it has been effaced. But simply to put it like that tells us very little. What we need to do is to go behind the language to underlying motives. Perhaps the best way of comprehending the difference is to see it as generated by a different starting-point, depending on whether one takes the doctrine of God as Creator or the doctrine of salvation as the more basic, controlling element for one's view of human nature. If one starts from the former, the question that raises itself is what it is that God has put of himself into his creation, such that man and God now share something significant in common. But if from the latter, the issue instead becomes how proper weight can be attached to the divine deliverance unless it is seen as applying to the whole of human nature. It is a difference of perspective that one finds reflected as much within the Bible itself as in later theology. Arguably, this is the best way of interpreting the contrast between the Old Testament and the New. For, while the former treats the divine image as an actual possession of man, for the latter it is only something to which he can aspire.

One is so used to hearing in sermons and so forth that the image was lost at the Fall that it comes as something of a surprise to discover that this is not actually what Genesis says. The author of the famous verse ('And God said, Let us make man in our image, after our likeness'[1]), the so-called Priestly Source (P), makes no such claim. For later in his narrative he has God declaring to Noah: 'Whoso sheddeth man's blood, by man shall his blood be shed: for in the image of God made he man.'[2] This surely implies that the image is still present. Otherwise it is impossible to see why a reason has been given, since without the image there would be nothing of value worth preserving. But in any case a careful reading of the earlier passage confirms this interpretation. Barth[3] uses the following verse with its reference to 'male and female created he them' to argue that a trinitarian reference is intended, but that is ridiculously over-subtle. The meaning is plain. The image is one of power – 'and let them have dominion over . . . all the earth.' Man is like God because he has been given some of God's creative power to rule and direct the earth. Nor is this the only place in the Old Testament where such an understanding occurs. One might compare Psalm 8: 'What is man that thou art mindful of him? . . . Thou hast made him to have dominion over the works of thy hands.' Later the Book of Wisdom was to offer a rather different account, with the divine image reflected in man's immortality. But the stress is once again on actual possession: 'God made man imperishable, he made him in the image of his own nature.'[4]

Now contrast this with the New Testament. While both Old Testament notions sprang from reflections on the way the world is,[5] for St Paul the question of the image is all about what man might become. His most famous allusion is christological, when he calls Jesus 'the image of the invisible God',[6] and it is this soteriological reference which controls all he has to say on the possibility of the divine image existing in ordinary men and women. So, for example, we are told that we are 'predestined to be conformed to the image of his Son' and that 'just as we have borne the image of the man of dust, we shall also bear the image of the man in heaven.'[7] Thus clearly for Paul there is no actual image present. It is a potential possession that can only be actualized through Christ. This is also normally how he handles his more mystical theme of the image reflecting the divine glory.[8] But there is one passage in which he appears to treat it as an actual possession. The intriguing thing about it (he is discussing why women unlike men should have their heads covered in church[9]) is that the reason given is to symbolize man's power or authority over woman,[10] which of course brings us back to what I suggested was the original point of Genesis.

Despite this lack of consistency in Paul, there can be no doubt that it was the Old Testament's notion of the image as an actual possession which exerted the greater influence on pre-Reformation theology, though thanks to a misunderstanding of Hebrew parallelism it is tempered by something of the Pauline vision. Writing at the end of the second century, Irenaeus, the Greek bishop of Lyons, drew a distinction between 'image' and 'likeness' that has no justification whatsoever in terms of P's original intentions. In his most important work, *Adversus Haereses*, he suggests that the likeness was lost at the Fall, but the image retained.[11] However, he identifies that original image with neither creative power nor immortality but with rationality and freedom, as in the following passage where it is used as a justification for punishment: 'But man, being endowed with reason, and in this respect like to God, having been made free in his will, and with power over himself, is himself the cause of himself, that sometimes he becomes wheat, and sometimes chaff. Wherefore also he shall be justly condemned.'[12] Though Irenaeus does not say so, one might argue in view of his reference to 'power over oneself' that his interpretation of the image is a legitimate identification of what underpins the notion of creative power. For what gives man dominion over himself and the rest of creation is precisely the freedom he has to reason and make plans. However that may be, his version of the image was certainly very widely adopted in subsequent thought. For instance, Augustine declares of the soul that 'it is made after the image of God in respect to this, that it is able to use reason and intellect in order to understand and behold God.'[13]

At the same time Irenaeus uses the notion of 'likeness' to suggest potential, the transformation that can be effected through Christ.[14] This too is an idea that is taken up by later thought. Indeed, Aquinas in the *Summa* uses the Pauline notion of 'glory' in which to express it. He tells us that the divine image is only perfected 'according as man knows and loves God perfectly, and this is the image according to the likeness of glory'.[15] But it is in Orthodoxy that its most extensive use is to be found, a phenomenon that continues to the present day. This generally takes the form of a claim to divinization. Such language is already present in the patristic period, and indeed even occurs once in the Bible. But it is clear that both to the author of 2 Peter and to someone like Athanasius little more is meant by becoming divine than receiving the gift of immortality,[16] whereas a very different picture is presented in *The Triads* of what is perhaps Orthodoxy's greatest theologian, St Gregory Palamas (d. 1359). There, partly under the influence of Neo-Platonism, he conceives of perfection as such complete transparency to the work of the Spirit that it becomes appropriate to say of such individuals that 'they have become entirely God, and know God in God.'[17] That this Neo-Platonic influence on Orthodoxy continues to the present day is well illustrated by the modern Orthodox theologian Vladimir Lossky (d. 1958). When seeking to contrast with his opposite the 'deified man' who 'shows in himself by grace what God is by nature', he chooses 'the extremity of falling-away which Plotinus calls "the place of dissimilarity" '.[18] The return to the One is thus never very far absent, no matter how much Biblical notions of indwelling and incorporation also play their part.

Divinization as a sharing in the divine 'likeness' is an issue to which I shall return in the second half of chapter 5. But in the meantime some interim judgments must be offered in respect of these various accounts of the 'image' as present possession. In fact, whether we take Wisdom's immortality, Genesis's creative power or Irenaeus' and subsequent tradition's reasoning, they all, I think, share a basic defect. This can be illustrated both from the divine perspective and from the human. The problem from the former is that the link postulated between God and man seems insufficient to explain why God might have any strong interest in the lot of man. If man has immortality, it is still dependent on the Creator's whim, while human creative power and rationality seem very insignificant when compared to those of an infinite and omnipotent mind. This, of course, is not to deny that some link is provided. What it is to do is to challenge whether Irenaeus has gone far enough in searching for some more fundamental category than that to which Genesis appeals. In other words, one needs more than just man's ability to reason in order to explain the depth of the divine commitment to his human creation, to which Christianity lays claim. But, equally, there is a problem from the human perspective. If it is really appropriate to talk of a divine image in every man, then it would also seem reasonable to maintain that its presence acts as a reminder of the divine, at least to the more percipient of human beings. Otherwise it must be a peculiarly weak image. Yet, clearly, even to the most devout features of this kind, when encountered in their fellow human beings, do not immediately conjure up any thought of God. So something has gone wrong somewhere in such attempts to provide a suitable transition between the doctrines of God and human nature.

This is an appropriate point at which to turn to the Reformed tradition since it regards the entire project as misconceived. One need not look far to discover the reason for this attitude. It is because of the

Reformation's different theological method, with its rejection of natural theology and insistence that the only proper starting-point is not some general doctrine of God but only God as revealed in one's doctrine of salvation. Within such a framework any claim that the divine image is still present must inevitably be seen as a threat to the indispensability of that starting-point. So both Luther and Calvin find it necessary to deny the continued presence of the divine image in order to preserve the ubiquity of Christ's saving work. There must be no human contribution to salvation. For that would imply that human nature had some proper existence in its own right without reference to what God has done in Christ. So with that objective in view in their commentaries on Genesis both are equally emphatic in rejecting the possibility, Calvin for example unequivocally declaring that 'the image of God has been destroyed in us by the Fall.'

Yet even Calvin finds it hard to dispense with the notion altogether. So at one point in his *Institutes of the Christian Religion* we find him declaring: 'The Lord commands us to do good to all without exception, though the greater part, if estimated by their own merit, are unworthy of it. But scripture gives us an excellent reason when it tells us that we are not to look to what men themselves deserve but to attend to the image of God which is present in all men and to which we owe all honour and love.'[19] Perhaps he is simply speaking loosely in passages like this, when in fact he means the potential image. But more probably actual possession is intended, though in a way which preserves the universal salvific framework. This could be done by maintaining that the image is present in sinful man but only in the sense that its building blocks are still there, and that these remain totally ineffectual apart from the atoning work of Christ.

This is also perhaps the best way of explaining the difference between Barth's earlier and later positions in his *Church Dogmatics*. In the first volume we find him arguing against Brunner in favour of Calvin's most emphatic declaration. 'The Humanity and personality of sinful man can certainly not constitute a conformity with God or a point of contact with the word of God. In this sense, as a possibility for God belonging to man *qua* creature, the image of God is not only, as is said, destroyed with the exception of a few traces, but annihilated.'[20] But by the time he came to write the third volume a dramatic change seems to have occurred, though less dramatic than is commonly supposed. Certainly the language is very different. He is now prepared to write that man 'is God's image inasmuch as he is man'.[21] It is largely under the influence of the Jewish philosopher Martin Buber (d. 1964) that the change has been effected. Thus he adopts Buber's I–Thou terminology to express his new claim that the image continues to be present, with its presence displayed in two specific ways. First, man exists as a 'thou' addressed by the divine 'Thou'.[22] Secondly, there is present a similar 'I–Thou' relationship between man and woman that also cannot be destroyed by sin.[23]

However, there are a number of difficulties even in Barth's revised position. What these two aspects of man's actual life are supposed to reflect is a similar relation within the trinitarian character of God. This would make sense, if Barth was using a social analogy for the Trinity. But, as noted in the last chapter, he belongs to the Augustinian tradition, and Moltmann finds his account so formal and impersonal that he uses such phrases as 'eternal repetition' and 'holy tautology' to describe it. This cannot but call into question whether any significant common element has in fact been identified. Added to this is the problem that, given Barth's strictures on natural theology, not surprisingly when one reads between the lines one discovers that the first of the two features is only potential after all. For only in revelation does man actually experience God as a Thou addressing him.[24] With the second feature, the relationship between man and woman, it is at least an actual existent to which appeal is being made. But, given his views on the Trinity, one cannot help suspecting that its real motivation lay elsewhere – theologically, in the way in which one covenant relationship (between man and wife) can be used to reinforce the appropriateness of the other (man and God), and morally, in the rather dubious way in which he uses this 'image' to argue against religious orders and 'the malady called homosexuality'.[25]

In short, then, the claim that Barth made a really major shift in his theological position on the subject cannot be substained. It is not all that different from Calvin in some of his moods. Man in his covenant relation with woman exhibits the structural or relational possibility of a similarity encounter with God. But there is no necessary connection, still less any real parallel between the human and the divine case. Perhaps little else could be expected, given Barth's emphasis on the absolute comprehensiveness and indispensability of salvation through revelation.

Thus far, then our search for an appropriate focus for talk of the divine image in man has reached an impasse. What I would now like to suggest is that the Jewish philosopher Emmanuel Levinas offers the best way forward – a way forward which Barth might have anticipated through reading Buber, as Buber foreshadows some elements in Levinas' thought. But in order to understand Levinas properly one must set him in the context of the major philosophical movement of which he is part, namely Phenomenology. This has the added advantage that it will enable us to understand better a movement which is at the root of so much later continental philosophy.

Phenomenology and Levinas

Phenomenology as a philosophical movement is less widely known than Existentialism. But twentieth-century Existentialism is in fact largely a child of Phenomenology, and indeed almost all this century's trends in continental philosophy can be seen as deriving from it. The father of the movement was Edmund Husserl (1859–1938). With his first major book, *Philosophie der Arithmetik* (1893), which attempted to offer a psychological foundation for mathematics, he burnt his hands badly. His main critic was Gottlob Frege, who with Wittgenstein was to give such an impetus to linguistic analysis as the underlying rationale of Anglo-Saxon philosophy. But, while Husserl admitted his error about mathematics, he did not retreat from his general strategy of seeking for the truth through the analysis of consciousness rather than language. So, while the English-speaking world took as its basic datum language, something that necessarily assumes our corporate existence, and to this day remains preoccupied with the analysis of our concepts through the analysis of language (and sometimes with the creation of a more adequate, artificial language for comparison), Husserl gave to continental philosophy a very different turn. It was a turn towards the individual subject and the consciousness with which he faces the world.

Of Husserl's works the most easily accessible (both of which are described as introductions) are *Cartesian Meditations*, based on lectures given at the Sorbonne in 1929, and *Ideas*, a much longer work first published in 1913.[26] The allusion in the title of the former to Descartes effectively underlines both his central concern and the manner in which he attempts to realize it. For like Descartes he is concerned with the foundations of our knowledge and uses a similar method by which to discover those foundations. Borrowing a word from ancient Scepticism he describes his proposed procedure as an 'epoché' (holding back), though various German words are also used such as *ausschalten* (turn off) and *einklammern* (bracket). The source of his favourite term should not deceive the reader into thinking that his ultimate aim was a sceptical one. Rather, it is a temporary suspension of belief so that critical stock-taking can take place. The objective is to discover by this questioning what really are the basic structures of human consciousness.

What he believed he discovered was the existence of a simple 'transcendental Ego' that is not reducible to a bundle of perceptions but which relates intentionally to the objects of its experience. Through intuition (*Anschauung*) it is able to grasp the essence of things (*Wesensschau*), essences which likewise are not reducible to empirical generalizations. Two features in this brief summary are particularly worth stressing. First, the way in which, despite his appeal to experience, he insists on going beyond the standard empirical approach.

Thus, though for him intuition does not mean simply acceptance of the given but involves reflection and consideration of examples, the final say clearly lies with the mind, which is given a unique place, not subject to an empirical reduction to its particular experiences. Secondly, there is the connected point that the relation between the mind and its objects is seen as an 'intentional' one. That is to say, meaning is given to its objects by the mind and not vice versa. This inevitably raises the question of whether sense can be given to the notion of objects existing apart from consciousness if they are held to have no meaning apart from it. Though he appears to have resisted being called an 'idealist' until as late as 1929,[27] he did finally concede that on his view reality has no meaning apart from that which is conferred on it by mind.

Put like that, the connection with Existentialism should be obvious. Man creates meaning by imposing on the objects of his consciousness the structures and patterns he finds on reflection inherent within it. This much would be accepted by both Phenomenology and Existentialism, but with this difference. In Phenomenology the stress tends to be on intellectual concepts; in Existentialism on the emotions. Existentialism will be discussed in a separate section later in this chapter. Suffice it to note here that its two most famous twentieth-century exponents were both indebted to Husserl. Heidegger while at Freiburg acted as Husserl's seminar assistant. He was asked by Husserl to help write an article on Phenomenology for the *Encyclopaedia Britannica*, and was even nominated by him in 1928 as successor to his chair. Likewise with Sartre. Though he never called himself a phenomenologist, he studied Husserl during his year in Berlin (1933–4), and his first philosophical work, *L'imagination*, is heavily indebted to him.

But it is not just Existentialism that has important connections with Phenomenology. Similar comments can be made about that other major modern continental movement, Structuralism. Towards the end of his life Husserl became interested in the notion of *Lebenswelt* (life-world). This was inspired by the thought that questions of structures of consciousness could not be dissociated from consideration of the particular social life-world in which they are anchored. He appears to have first raised the question in a lecture at the University of Prague in 1935. These thoughts were subsequently expanded into his last major work, the posthumously published *The Crisis of European Sciences and Transcendental Phenomenology*.[28] Prior to publication the French phenomenologist Merleau-Ponty did much to popularize the notion in France. But, even while Structuralism was still an anthropological rather than a philosophical movement, Husserl saw the connection between their ideas and his. So in a letter of March 1935[29] he describes the anthropologist Lévy-Bruhl's analysis of the social structures of primitive mentality as an anticipation of his own ideas.

By now the more theological reader may have become impatient and be wondering what all this has to do with the question of the divine image or even more generally with producing an adequate theological account of human nature. Before I attempt to demonstrate the relevance of the Phenomenology of Emmanuel Levinas to the specific issue, it will be helpful to indicate first the wider context, the way in which Phenomenology is relevant to questions of human nature in general.

The answer is that it raises the issue of what really is integral to the nature of man and, so far as Husserl's later thought is concerned, how far this is affected by different social structures. For in effect what Husserl's phenomenological reduction attempts to determine is the relative priority and dispensability of the various intentional acts of meaning by which we constitute our world of experience. Husserl's own religious position seems to have been somewhat complex (a non-practising but not indifferent Protestant Jew!) but that he did expect his method eventually to yield some theological insights is widely accepted.[30] In a moment we shall observe how Levinas relates Phenomenology to his Jewish faith, and in chapter 5 how Paul Ricoeur does this for Christianity. Yet another example is Max Scheler (d. 1928) whose writings have exercised a large influence on the present pope. Marital difficulties prevented any deep involvement in the Roman Catholic church of his birth but he retained a lively interest in the moral and religious implications of Phenomenology, even when he finally moved to an atheistic position.

A major preoccupation of the writings of Scheler, like those of Levinas, is the attempt to answer the most common objection raised against the phenomenological reduction, that with the transcendental Ego alone guaranteed and all else, including the existence of other persons, cast in doubt, the net result is solipsism. Husserl himself admits that 'between the meaning of consciousness and reality yawns a veritable abyss.'[31] Little wonder then that many a later commentator has been led to remark that 'whatever Husserl may say in his defence it is his transcendental epoché that cuts us off from the reality of other people.'[32] Scheler's solution in *The Nature of Sympathy* is to argue that the primary phenomenological datum is the undifferentiated consciousness of infancy and that therefore 'it is by virtue of precisely the same act of discernment within an as yet undifferentiated whole that we come to a clear realisation both of what is ours and what belongs to others.'[33] The existence of others is thus necessarily given in a baby's first recognition of its own distinct existence.

Levinas (b. 1906) adopts a rather different solution. This is pursued in both his major works, *Totalité et infini* (1961) and *Autrement qu'être ou au delà de l'essence* (1973).[34] He argues that, whether one takes inanimate objects or persons, it is impossible to analyse their meaning simply as intentional constructions of the transcendental Ego. Rather one has to take account of the 'resistance' offered by the object of consciousness. So, in the case of material objects there is the fact that they can assert their difference from us by presenting themselves as a challenge to us to take possession of them or enjoy them. But it is on the resistance of the other person that Levinas lays most stress. For Husserl he points out we have at most 'the forever-indirect knowledge' of the inferred existence of others: 'I constitute the other on the basis of the perceived behaviour of a body analogous to the one I inhabit.' But such an analysis he argues does not correspond to our experience. Instead, using his recurring image of the face (*visage*), he puts it thus: 'Thought alert to the face of the other is the thought of an irreducible difference, a difference which is not a thematization and which disturbs the equilibrium of the impassible soul of knowing.'[35]

Significantly Derrida entitles his deconstructionist study of Levinas, 'Violence and Metaphysics'.[36] For essential to Levinas' argument is the perception of Husserl's phenomenology as a 'philosophy of violence'. Levinas comments that 'if the other could be possessed, seized, and known, it would not be the other. To possess, to know, to grasp are all synonyms of power.'[37] Whether this is a fair description of Husserl's inferred 'other' need not concern us here. What is important to note is the extent to which Levinas wishes to substitute in its place respect for the mystery of the other. Added to this is the claim that this mystery is most clearly known in weakness and not in power or violence. It is here that his image of the face finds its most obvious *raison d'être*. For we most clearly encounter 'the ethical resistance' of the other when the face of 'the stranger, widow and orphan', the face of the despised and deprived, look at us accusingly, demanding by their expressions that we take account of them in their weakness.

This may all sound rather sentimental, but Levinas has, I think, an important point. Nor should it be confused with what Martin Buber argued earlier in his classic *I and Thou*. Derrida in a very perceptive footnote recognizes three points of difference.[38] Of these the most fundamental seems to me to be Buber's emphasis on the reciprocal character of the relation. For example, he says that 'a person makes his appearance by entering into relation with other persons',[39] and goes on from this to declare that 'the word I is the true shibboleth of mankind.'[40] In fact, it is clear from the direction of Buber's argument that what really interests him is the surpassing of individuality in a mutual relationship, and in this connection it is interesting to observe that the relation between Jesus and his Father is taken as the model.[41]

By contrast, what interests Levinas is the exact opposite, the other as something essentially different, the face that challenges us to respect it as having a right to a distinct life and identity. But equally, in so far as we do enter into relation, Levinas would maintain that it is not in the overcoming of difference but in the exposure of our own weakness to the other that what is most important about personhood is revealed. Thus significantly he uses the phenomenological term 'reduction' to refer to the process of identifying what he regards as the most basic element in any turn towards the other, the fact that a desire to communicate presupposes a willingness to expose oneself to hurt. Thus even the master in conversation with the slave must acknowledge the ability of the slave to give mental, if not verbal expression to very different thoughts from what he would wish.

But how does all this relate to the question of the image of God in man? For Levinas this notion of the face is central. God's creative act is the allowing of a similar resistance, a divine act of self-restriction. Man is allowed independence of God, and it is that capacity for resistance that exhibits what man and God share in common. There is a resistance, particularly in weakness, to possession and categorization that requires recognition of the existence of an independent value. So in *Totalité et infini* he writes that 'an infinite which does not contract like a circle but withdraws from ontological space in order to make room for a separate being exists in a divine manner.'[42] In 'Beyond Intentionality' he puts it more poetically and more rhetorically: 'Is the way in which the stranger thrusts himself upon me not the very manner in which a God who loved the stranger and who put me into question by summoning me would "enter on the scene".'[43] Putting it in more prosaic English, what Levinas' oft repeated insistence on the resemblance between man and God amounts to is the claim that man and God share the same moral quality of 'resistance', an independence over and against ourselves that paradoxically is at its most evident in 'weakness'.

There seem to me to be at least three reasons why Levinas' suggestion is superior to anything hitherto proposed within the Christian tradition. The first is that it offers a more plausible explanation of why it is that God should have a special interest in man. The difficulty with earlier accounts is that human power, rationality, or freedom are so insignificant in comparison that it is hard to see how they could give a reason for God to take an interest in such a vastly inferior being. Levinas provides the answer, by identifying the underlying rationale behind the earlier suggestions. It is because of the personal and moral independence God has given man, an independence that like his is evident even in 'weakness' since it is impossible for it to be destroyed without first destroying the person. Putting it another way, what identifies us with God is the radical freedom he has given us to say 'No' to him or anyone else, even when we are totally powerless.

Secondly, it explains why no human being can ever lose his moral value. Notions like power, rationality, interpersonal relationship (as with Barth's proposal) and so forth all admit of degree. This makes it hard to see why one should resist varying estimates of the moral worth of particular individuals. Christian ethics has traditionally resisted that path, but little credit for this goes to the doctrine of the divine image. The most common line is to appeal to the divine love for all men, that 'while we were yet sinners, Christ died for us.'[44] But, while such verses argue against any comparison of merit between individuals, they leave the most important issue unresolved. For there cannot be a total lack of value. Otherwise there would be no reason why animals for example should not be equally included among those for whom Christ died. That is why the need to point to a feature unique to man and applicable to all men alike cannot be circumvented. Levinas again provides an answer. In the face of every 'other' we encounter a resistance to our own wills that is indicative of an independent, irreducible moral value. Experiencing the other as other is enough. It is clearly so basic to all our experience of humanity as not to raise the question of degrees of worth.

Finally, by accepting Levinas' explanation of the image it enables us to avoid the long-standing confrontation between Catholic and Reformed positions. On the one hand the Catholic insistence on the essential goodness of creation can be maintained by insisting that the image continues to be present even in sinful man. On the other hand this can be done in a way that does not challenge the Reformed insistence on the indispensability of Christ to every aspect of human salvation. This is possible because Levinas locates the image in an aspect of man where what is in question is the moral value of man, not any contribution to his salvation. That is to say, while for example rationality has sometimes been defined in such a way as to make possible a major independent human contribution to salvation and for this reason was decisively rejected at the Reformation as a possible account of man as he now is, Levinas' proposal presents no such obstacles. The resistance of the other is what gives man a shared value with God, but it is not a value that of itself can contribute in any way to the advancement of man. For that something further is required, whether it be rationality or divine grace or both.

Sin

Tillich and Niebuhr

If the previous section on the divine image was concerned to raise the question of what it is that gives God a special interest in man, with the topic of sin the focus shifts to why man needs that interest. For sin is the traditional answer. Nor is it hard to see why. For, though even in Scripture it sometimes means no more than that conventional morality has been scandalized,[45] the two most common Greek words for the notion both imply the idea of failing to hit a goal or mark, a want or deficiency that needs to be rectified.[46] Indeed in St Paul's famous phrase, 'all have sinned and come short of the glory of God',[47] 'come short' almost functions as an exegesis of the meaning of 'sinned'.

But why do we fall short? To what extent are we responsible for that falling short? Why does God allow it to happen? It is in answer to questions such as these that the traditional Christian doctrine of original sin was formulated. According to its classic expression in Augustine, we have all genetically inherited a tendency to sin as a result of the exercise of free choice by our universal first parent. However, thanks to his theory of seminal identity (based on a misunderstanding of the Greek of Romans 5)[48] he is able to insist that we too bear responsibility for that original decision of Adam. The stress is thus on human guilt, a stress which culminates in Calvin's doctrine of total depravity.[49]

With the abandonment of belief in the historicity of the Fall this is no longer a credible option. But that has not put an end to the questions, nor the need for a doctrine of original sin. What in effect has happened in modern theology is that the meaning of 'original' has moved from an historical first human act to identification of universal features of the human condition (prior to any acts) which incline us towards sin. In other words, rather than a temporal sense of 'original' we now have a structural or constitutional understanding. Two main types of such prior or 'original' features have been canvassed, the sociological and the psychological. Tillich and Niebuhr both represent one variant of the latter approach. But it will be as well to indicate first the variety of other proposals available before focusing more narrowly on their ideas.

The irony is that, even given belief in an historical Fall, the ultimate barrenness of the Augustinian approach need not have been the result. For, as N. P. Williams points out in his definitive study *The Ideas of the Fall and of Original Sin*, at least three other ways of explaining the presence of sin had been canvassed prior to the time of Christ. Even the Pentateuchal source 'J' offers two explanations. In Genesis 6 there is his story of a union between gods and men which later Judaism interpreted in terms of the lust of fallen angels, while Williams suggests that the original point of Genesis 3 was not Augustine's but a sort of Prometheus myth. 'Their sin lay in the illicit acquisition of scientific knowledge . . . he thinks that civilisation is a mistake, and that the increase of knowledge brings sorrow in its train.'[50] But, if neither of these two is likely to win any credence today, the third deserves more respect. This is the idea of *yeçer ha-ra* ('evil imagination'), derived from rabbinical speculation on Genesis 6, 5 and 8, 21. What particularly commends itself in these speculations is the way in which it represents an early attempt to identify an underlying feature of human nature inclining us to sin, of the sort now being considered by modern theology. Intriguingly too, then as now consideration was given to the question of whether in consequence God might be held ultimately responsible for sin. So, for example, while the later Greek text of Ecclesiasticus 15, 14 unequivocally asserts free will with 'man made in the beginning and then left free to make his own decisions',[51] the original Hebrew text views the *yeçer* as a direct creation of God, though yielding to its promptings remains a matter of free human choice.

But the Bible at most throws out hints, rather than definitive lines for further investigation. Of the two types of modern approach distinguished above, it is the sociological which is the more common. It finds its most conspicuous illustration in Liberation Theology, but it has penetrated even English theological writing. An example of this would be the collection of essays edited by the sociologist Martin and the theologian Whiteley, entitled *Sociology, Theology and Conflict.* Whiteley in his contribution suggests that 'we may with advantage use the term original sin when what an individual does, though he cannot disclaim responsibility for it, is due in an appreciable measure to "community forces".' As examples he gives the pressures of the advertising industry, the clash of standards in a child between those of the home and the local gang, and even a window cleaner having to pay "protection money" to a gangster in order to be able to work in a particular area. In the case of David Jenkins, the present Bishop of Durham, the extent of such 'original sin' is carried to the point where it is denied that criminals are responsible for their acts.[52] But there is no need to go that far in acknowledging the existence of sociologically conditioning factors predisposing the individual to sin. What we seem to have is varying degrees of diminished responsibility, though with responsibility perhaps never disappearing from view altogether.

Original sin in this sense then will be whatever sets us at a distance from God or alienates us from him, though we cannot be held fully responsible for that alienation. That there are such social forces beyond out complete control surely cannot be denied. Better examples than those offered by Whiteley might be the possession of slaves in a society in which no one has raised the moral issue, or perhaps eating meat today, if it is in fact morally wrong, given how seldom one is challenged to think about the issue. In other words, all wrong perceptions, even though they are socially induced and the individual has only minimal responsibility for them, will still have to be overcome before he can have a perfect relationship with God, with him able to see the imperfections of men as God sees them. Such complete insight will of course only come with the next life, but that does not alter the fact that such social constraints for the moment put us in a situation of sinfulness, of alienating distance from God, even though we cannot be held responsible for those constraints.

In identifying structural determinants to sin with psychological rather than sociological factors it is interesting to observe the Dominican Victor White in *God and the Unconscious* recalling the theme of the *yeçer ha-ra*. While rejecting the psychologist Jung's suggestion of the need for 'assimilation of the shadow' in man,[53] he does find it helpful to see reintegration as requiring 'the recognition and acceptance of the "Shadow" '.[54] That Shadow he subsequently suggest has its nearest ancient analogue in the notion of the 'evil imagination'. Intriguingly he also finds the notion embedded in St Paul: 'So also St. Paul, in Romans 7, will almost personify what he calls "the sin that dwells within me" . . . It is the adversary which is contrary to the "mind", the conscious ego, which delights in the law of God. It is the accuser which shows us up for what we really are despite our claims to righteousness. It is, in the jejune language of analytical psychology, an automonous complex, a shadow, which acts in and through us in spite of ourselves: "If I do what I do not want, it is no longer I that do it, but sin that dwells within me." '[55]

That since Freud we have been compelled to recognize hitherto unacknowledged dimensions of human existence surely needs no argument. Terms like repression, sublimation and the unconscious are all part of our common vocabulary. No doubt too St Paul's account of sin could be analysed in terms of desires repressed in the unconscious reasserting themselves. But there are least two difficulties in the way of assigning such psychological determinants a comparative status to ontologically prior sociological structures.

The first is whether they are really like them ontologically prior, or not in fact the product of complex interaction between conscious and unconscious. For are we not often indirectly responsible for what has been repressed and is now operative at the level of the unconscious? It is because we once failed to face up honestly to certain issues that they now confront us anew but in a very different form, with us apparently compelled to act for reasons we do not comprehend. A simple example of this would be the way in which we can take out our anger on some innocent party, when the guilty is beyond our power to affect, and yet believe that the reason why we act is because of justified indignation against the former. This seems quite different from the sociological case in which the predisposing factors are entirely antecedent to any decisions of ours.

But in response it may be observed that psychologists would claim that certain basic dispositions are innate, and so these would be antecedent in the requisite sense. This leads us on to the second main difficulty with this type of approach. For we are then faced with the acute problem of why God should have so constituted human nature. Personally I find it hard to see what evidence could compel one to assent to theories like Freud's Oedipus Complex, but perhaps the problems in accepting it are not as hard as one might initially have supposed. After all, even Freud acknowledged that civilization would be impossible without some sublimation of the two basic instincts which he identified, the libido and the death instinct. Moreover, some of his followers have not been slow to point out that, though the pattern of development may not sound particularly pleasant, the net result is a richer personality. So R. S. Lee in *Freud and Christianity* has no difficulty in accepting the way in which conscience (the 'Super-Ego') is alleged to develop in Freud's theory. What is important is that the development proceed in such a way that there is 'a just balance between Ego, Id and Super-Ego so that the Ego is free to handle the world, yet full of energy for its tasks because in good relations with the Id, and at the same time under enough control from the Super-Ego not to choose the first primitive satisfactions which offer, but to build up its energies for greater, more integrated, and more permanent satis-factions'.[56] When one adds to this Lee's defence of sublimation and his careful distinguishing of it from displacement,[57] and his limited endorsement of the fact that 'Christianity sets out to capture the unconscious',[58] it becomes clear that one can accept a great deal of Freud without this necessarily leading to the undermining of traditional Christian claims. But the irony is that the more one proceeds down this path, the less easily do Freudian conceptions fit under the category of original sin. For the psychological structures and process of develop-ment now turn out to be strictly neutral, with society, parents and the individual himself charged with the responsibility of whether they turn out for good or ill.

But, if psychological accounts of original sin would thus seem to dissolve into a mixture of social and personal responsibility, this is not finally to put to an end the relevance of psychological considerations. For existentialist theologians have suggested a rather different way in which a psychological analysis of man might profoundly affect our understanding of the nature of sin. Tillich and Niebuhr may be taken as representative examples.

Though sin does not even appear in the index to Paul Tillich's little classic *The Courage to Be*, it is clear that this is the topic with which he is really concerned. For salvation is seen as overcoming the threat of non-being, and anxiety (nominally his central topic) is defined as 'the existential awareness of non-being'.[59] Thus anxiety fulfils the role which sin does in more traditional analyses, as that which has to be overcome before salvation is secured, or as he prefers to call it, 'the courage to be': 'the courage to be is the ethical act in which man affirms his own being in spite of those elements of his existence which conflict with his essential affirmation.'[60]

One of the most interesting aspects of his analysis is the claim that different forms of anxiety have to be faced at different historical periods. At the end of ancient civilization he suggests it was ontic anxiety (anxiety in the face of death), at the end of the Middle Ages moral anxiety (anxiety in the face of moral condemnation), whereas now it is spiritual anxiety (anxiety in the face of meaninglessness). As evidence for this he gives a wealth of illustrations,[61] including Kafka's novels, Eliot's poetry and Arthur Miller's plays.

Some of it reads now as little more than a dated reflection of the neuroses of European intellectuals in the immediate post-war period (the book was published in 1952). Sometimes too he is just silly, as when he argues that the acceptance of despair is itself a positive affirmation: 'One would say that one accepts oneself as accepted in spite of one's despair about the meaning of this acceptance.'[62] But lurking behind all this is I think an important point. It is the suggestion of an intimate connection between anxiety, finitude, freedom and sin. In his major work *Systematic Theology* he puts the connection between the first three thus: 'Man is not only finite, as is every creature; he is also aware of his finitude. And this awareness is anxiety . . . Anxiety expresses the awareness of being finite, of being a mixture of being and non-being. All creatures are driven by anxiety; for finitude and anxiety are the same. But in man freedom is united with anxiety. One could call man's freedom "freedom in anxiety" or "anxious freedom".'[63]

To add an explicit connection with the fourth notion, i.e. sin, one might turn to the nineteenth-century thinker who is perhaps most appropriately regarded as the founder of Existentialism. For Kierkegaard in *The Concept of Anxiety* (German 'Angst'; English 'dread' or 'anxiety') writes: 'Anxiety is the psychological condition that precedes sin. It approaches sin as closely as possible, as anxiously as possible, but without explaining sin.'[64] One of his twentieth-century followers, Bultmann, is less cautious: 'What is the real crux of sin? What is it, if sin is unresponsiveness to the future? It is dread – the dread of the man who is unwilling to surrender to what is a mystery to him, and who wishes to cling to himself.'[65]

Whether Kierkegaard or Bultmann is nearer to the truth we shall have to consider a moment, but first it will be useful to note what Reinhold Niebuhr has to say on the issue in what I think is the most profound of the modern existentialist theologians' writings on the subject, in his very much longer classic, *The Nature and Destiny of*

Man. Unlike Tillich, here there is no shortage of reference to the term 'sin'. But this is in part to be explained by the fact that Niebuhr in these 1939 Gifford Lectures sees himself as engaged in a dialogue with Christianity's past, where the term inevitably bulks large. On the relation between anxiety and sin he takes Kierkegaard's rather than Bultmann's side: 'Anxiety is the internal precondition of sin. It is the inevitable spiritual state of man, standing in the paradoxical situation of freedom and finiteness. Anxiety is the internal description of the state of temptation.'[66] Another way of expressing this would be to say that because man is finite, i.e. limited, he experiences himself as constrained in various ways but because he is also free he experiences a desire to transcend those limits, and anxiety arises precisely because such attempts at self-transcendence involve the risk of not knowing when the limits have been reached. So Niebuhr uses a vivid simile to indicate the creative and destructive possibilities that are both equally inherent in such anxiety: 'Anxiety, as a permanent concomitant of freedom, is . . . both the source of creativity and a temptation to sin. It is the condition of the sailor climbing the mast with the abyss of the waves beneath him, and the "crow's nest" above him'[67] (the crow's nest here alluding to the possibility of intimacy with God). In other words, Niebuhr sees man as suspended vertiginously between finite and freedom, both of which he must accept if he is to have spiritual health. The vertigo expresses itself as an anxiety that is constantly tempted to escape through denying one or other of these two aspects of his nature. Man either sinks into an acceptance of his finitude with creative possibilities unacknowledged, or he keeps pushing on to demonstrate his immortality until he finally destroys himself.

Niebuhr wants to claim that what he has offered is an intelligible modern account of the nature of original sin.[68] Indeed, he insists on the inevitability of sin, though adding the comment that 'the final paradox is that the discovery of the inevitability of sin is man's highest assertion of freedom.'[69] Presumably the argument is that, if one gains freedom from anxiety by recognizing oneself as a sinner, how much more complete and lasting will such freedom be, if one discovers that one can never in this life fully overcome sin, that one always remains a sinner. There will then be no danger of anxiety expressing itself in the other form it takes, namely the dread that one's moral possibilities are infinite. Instead, man can rest assured that he is both finite and free.

As a psychological truth about one way of obtaining release from anxiety, the argument has much to commend it. Indeed the book is full of acute psychological observations. Yet I seriously doubt whether anxiety deserves as central a place as has been assigned to it by existentialist theology. Thus Niebuhr writes as though it is at the root of all sin, but it is not hard to think of counter-examples. One need only think of the careful criminal. Quite clearly, he has not simply lulled himself into acceptance of his finitude but attempted to go beyond standard conventional norms. But equally this has not produced an hubristic attempt to deny his finitude altogether. No doubt in many criminals it does, and it is their over-confidence which ensures that the law eventually catches up with them. But there are careful exceptions, and it is hard to see what their undoubted sinfulness has to do with anxiety. Again, when he defines pride as man's attempt 'to raise his contingent existence to unconditioned significance'[70] and sensuality as 'escape from the unlimited possibilities of freedom . . . by losing himself in some natural vitality',[71] one wants to protest that of course it is sometimes like that but not always. One can be proud in situations where one is all too aware of one's finitude, for instance in war, and sensuality need have nothing to do with escapism.

More problematic still, I fail to see why this existentialist analysis should be regarded as an account of original *sin*. This is not to deny its numerous intrinsic merits in pointing to features of human nature which make sin likely. But it is to observe that it shares the same basic defect as the earlier variant of the psychological approach. That is, it identifies features which can lead to sin but they are not objectively wrong, inherently sinful in themselves. One need only recall that without tension man would do nothing at all. Indeed, psychologists tells us that tension is good for us as a spur to action, and that it is only when it reaches too large proportions that it becomes a neurotic anxiety that immobilizes us from action or produces self-destructive behaviour. Bultmann was thus quite wrong in identifying sin and anxiety.

My conclusion, therefore, is that the notion of original sin is best confined to those sociological features of our existence that alienate us from God but which are outside our control. The psychological are relevant because they carry with them the potential for sin, but they are not themselves sinful.

Existentialism

We saw above with Niebuhr and Tillich the way in which Existentialism has influenced theology towards producing deep insights but also exaggerated claims about the role of anxiety. Incontestably, of all the movements in continental philosophy it is Existentialism that has exercised the most influence generally on theology. It will be helpful therefore to consider why this is so, and at the same time reflect whether there are any other aspects of its thought on human nature which might be more usefully appropriated. I shall argue that Kierkegaard's more important contribution lies elsewhere, particularly as he has been interpreted by Sartre.

Maurice Friedman, in justifying his choice of texts in *The Worlds of Existentialism*, which includes Heracleitus, the Sermon on the Mount, Marx, Nietzche and Rilke as well as more obvious authors, comments: 'Existentialism is not a philosophy but a mood embracing a number of disparate philosophies.'[72] The selection is too wide, but his choice of the word 'mood' suggests a possible way forward. For the Existentialism that grew out of Phenomenology (described earlier in this chapter) differs in emphasis from Phenomenology precisely in this, that, while both start from the subject, Phenomenology's primary interest is man's cognitive relation to the world whereas for Existentialism it is the 'mood' with which he faces that world. Nor is it hard, when put like that, to see how the one could emerge from the other. For Existentialism's greater emphasis on the emotional dimension of the subject can be seen as a consequence of its pessimism about the possibility of cognition preceding impartially without reference to the mood with which the subject views the world. This explains why Kierkegaard was seen as an obvious precursor. For, like twentieth-century existentialists he too was pessimistic about the limits of our knowledge, though in his case, as we saw in chapter 1, it was a response to Hegel's exaggerated claims for reason. Also like his modern counterparts he drew the obvious implication that, if such limits are true, then we must make our decisions on other criteria and the one most clearly to hand is the way we stand emotionally or psychologically to our world. Making this contrast also provides a clear rationale for the term 'Existentialism'. For, whereas Phenomenology in Husserl was concerned with the discovery of essences through 'eidetic intuition',[73] with the discovery of the universal in the particular, for Existentialism existence precedes essence in the sense that, so far from our having direct intuitive access to such universals, the way in which we perceive the world is entirely a function of our manner of existence. How we exist determines what structure we perceive in the world; there are no essences there in advance, waiting to be discovered.

These general remarks can be well illustrated from the writings of the twentieth-century existentialist who has had most impact upon modern theology, namely Martin Heidegger (1889–1976). His major work *Being and Time*, which intriguingly is dedicated to Husserl, dates from 1926. It is not easy to read, but he has been fortunate in his English translator, John MacQuarrie, who not only in numerous books has done much to popularize his approach and in the process established himself as the leading living existentialist theologian, but also produced an excellent guide to his thought and influence on Bultmann in *An Existentialist Theology*. In that book he notes one very important aspect of Heidegger's relation to Kant: 'Kant thought that it was a scandal to philosophy and human intelligence that there was lacking a cogent proof for the reality of a world outside ourselves. Heidegger's reply is that the true scandal of philosophy is not that such a proof is lacking, but that it was ever looked for. Man as existing is always already in a world.'[74] But despite rejection of this aspect of Kant, the introductory paragraphs of *Being and Time* which establish his methodology for the whole work can be seen as exhibiting a fundamentally Kantian turn. The question with which he opens is what we are to understand by the 'most universal' category of all, Being, but within a few pages this has been transformed into a question about man's relation to Being: 'The very asking of this question is an entity's mode of Being (*Sein*).' So, 'if we are to formulate our question explicitly and transparently, we must first give a proper explication of an entity (*Dasein*), with regard to its Being.'[75] The most obvious way of making sense of this quick transition is to assume that he agrees with Kant that the human understanding determines and constructs the form of the world which it encounters. What the world or Being in itself is like thus remains essentially unknown. All we can have access to is *Dasein* (literally 'Being-there'), our own felt relation to that world. It is one key aspect of his analysis of that felt relation that led to the account of sin we found in Tillich, Bultmann and Niebuhr.

But why of all philosophers has he exercised such influence on theology and over such a range of issues? At least three reasons can be offered by way of explanation.

The first is his basic religiosity, despite the absence of explicit religious belief. There is a fascinating chapter in MacQuarrie's Gifford Lectures, *In Search of Deity*, in which he attempts to identify Heidegger's religious position mainly from shorter or posthumously published works. Significantly an interview with the magazine *Der Spiegel* which he only agreed to have published after his death was entitled 'Only a God can save us',[76] and elsewhere he explicitly distances himself from the atheism of Sartre.[77] Admittedly, what emerges from the chapter is very different from the God of the ordinary believer, but his insistence that Being is 'wholly other'[78] than particular beings shows a marked affinity to the Platonic claim that ultimate reality is 'beyond being'.[79] Indeed it suggests that Tillich is in fundamental accord with his thought when in attempting to avoid treating God as a particular he affirms that 'it is as atheistic to affirm the existence of God as it is to deny it.'[80]

But for me the essentially religious character of his writing emerges most clearly in his most important late work, *What is Called Thinking?* There he is concerned to reinstate against modern instrumental, technological ways of thinking a non-systematic, poetic way of thought, according to which thought is conceived of as 'a gift because we incline toward it'.[81] Significantly, he connects etymologically 'think' and 'thank', declaring that 'the thought implies the thanks.'[82] Such notions pervade the work, and the most natural comparison which springs to mind for Heidegger's attitude here to Being and Thought is that of the religious believer's response of gratitude to the gift of grace. One might also add that throughout his life he retained such a strongly Lutheran conception of theology as a distinct discipline that philosophy was never really seen as a challenge to theology.[83]

Secondly, despite its strange sound to English ears, there was his use of the term 'Being'. Three features have combined to give it a special attractiveness to theologians. First, the concept had already been assigned an indispensable role within a secular philosophy. So the very first section of *Being and Time* is headed 'The Necessity, Structure and Priority of the Question of Being', and the never completed work ends with Heidegger still pointing to the question of Being as the more fundamental question to which any analysis of individual human existence (*Dasein*) must direct us: 'Something like "Being" has been disclosed in the understanding-of-Being which belongs to existent *Dasein* as a way in which it understands. Being has been disclosed in a preliminary way, though non-conceptually.'[84] It is this indispensable character of the question of Being which highlights perhaps the most basic factor in the term's popularity with theologians. When identified with God, it ensures that God cannot possibly be seen as on the margin of human concerns. Indeed, the connection is obvious, whether one speaks in the original German of *Sein* and *Dasein*, or in English of 'Being' and 'beings'. Not only that. Being is such a basic concept that when equated with God it becomes meaningless to raise the question of God's non-existence, as indeed we have already found Tillich affirming. Such an equation would of course not have much significance unless it had some basis already within the Christian tradition. The fact that it has constitutes the third important factor in the term's popularity. Macquarrie rightly asserts that 'in applying the language of "being" to God, I am, of course, taking up a very ancient tradition.'[85]

As a final reason for the popularity of the existentialist approach in theology one might mention the extent to which, unlike for example analytic philosophy, it raises theological questions naturally. Thus Heidegger's search for 'authentic existence' can, not implausibly, be interpreted as a search for salvation. Heidegger describes man as being in a situation of 'thrownness' (*Geworfenheit*), a situation in which our possibilities are strictly circumscribed – an idea which apparently forced itself upon him in the severe restrictions of First World War trench warfare.[86] These possibilities he sees as even further limited by our temptation towards conformity, to shrink into the impersonal mass of humanity, what he calls *das Man* (the neuter giving additional weight to the characterization). At one level this 'fallenness' (*Verfallenheit*) brings 'contentment' (*Beruhigung*), but at a deeper level a nagging sense of inadequacy remains, a sense of 'estrangement' or 'alienation' (*Entfremdung*) from what one might have been. But, Heidegger argues, release from this condition is possible if only one will honestly face up to these constraints, above all the temporal restraint and in particular that most definitive temporal restraint of them all, death. In contrast to *das Man* which in the face of death 'to the very end . . . always has more time',[87] authentic existence involves living in 'anticipation of this possibility' (*Vorlaufen in die Möglichkeit*).[88] Initially the phrase sounds odd, especially when it is interpreted a few pages later as 'freedom towards death'.[89] But his point is effectively summarized when he writes of death: 'Here it can become manifest to *Dasein* that in this distinctive possibility of its own self, it has become wrenched away from the "they". This means that in anticipation any *Dasein* can have wrenched itself away from the "they" already.'[90] In other words, the importance of death lies in the way in which it reveals the possibility of our independence of *das Man* ('they') – something we can realize in the immediate here and now, and so fulfil ourselves rather than social expectations of us.

That such consideration of how life can be given a meaning is not far removed from religious reflection surely cannot be denied, and so it is perhaps hardly surprising that so many theologians thought that a translation exercise was worthwhile. Where someone like Bultmann erred was not in attempting the translation, but in failing always to take adequate account of the irreducible differences that still exist. At least theologians like Fuchs and Ebeling were more moderate in their use of the later Heidegger, when they sought to interpret Jesus' parables in accord with Heidegger's attack on instrumental, analytic uses of language, and his insistence that the true thinker must receive the language event like a poet with receptive attention (*Gelassenheit*).[91] Parables were not to be seen as conveying information, but as confronting and challenging the hearer.

Heidegger makes much of anxiety in his own account of the human condition[92] but it is Kierkegaard who must take the credit or blame for securing for it such a dominant role. Significantly, his *Concept of Anxiety* is subtitled 'A simple psychological orientating Deliberation on the Dogmatic Issue of Hereditary Sin'. I have already argued that such an identification of anxiety and original sin cannot be allowed to stand. It seems to me that Kierkegaard's really important contribution lies elsewhere, one correctly identified by another famous existentialist, Jean-Paul Sartre. But first a brief word on why anxiety plays such a large role within Existentialism.

In one of his diary entries Kierkegaard confesses that 'all existence makes me anxious, from the smallest fly to the mysteries of the

Incarnation . . . My distress is enormous, boundless',[93] and it is hard not to feel that his own personal psychology has coloured his perception of others. Certainly, he makes the universal presence of anxiety definitionally true by denying that those who claim to be without anxiety are properly speaking men at all: 'That there may be men who never experience any anxiety must be understood in the sense that Adam would have perceived no anxiety had he been merely animal.'[94] But some commentators like Grossman have attempted to probe deeper by arguing that his description of the object of anxiety as 'nothing' easily lends itself to a Freudian interpretation.[95] He accepts Kierkegaard's point that anxiety is different from fear, but suggests that the only real difference is that anxiety is repressed fear. The individual is unaware of the object of his fear because it is repressed into his unconcious.

If one wanted to pursue this observation, it would not be difficult to make much of Kierkegaard's strange, broken relationship with Regina Olsen or his complex relations with his father.[96] But this cannot be the entire explanation. For his twentieth-century successors live in a post-Freudian world, but are equally insistent on the central place of anxiety. Heidegger, for example, describes it thus: 'That which anxiety is profoundly anxious about is not a definite kind of Being for *Dasein* or a definite possibility of it . . . the threat itself is indefinite.'[97] The likely explanation why Kierkegaard found an answering chord in the twentieth century has, I suspect, very little to do with the personal psychology of Heidegger or Sartre, much more with the social conditions of their time. It was an era (*c.* 1920–50) when social order and agreed conventions were in Europe noticeably breaking down and so inevitably this produced general personal insecurity. Significantly both men during the course of their careers were to lend their support to movements which had as their objective the establishment of a secure social order, in Heidegger's case Nazism, in Sartre's Marxism.

In any case Kierkegaard's more important contribution lies elsewhere. It is to be found most forcefully in the opening chapter of *The Concept of Anxiety*. There he is effectively engaged in demythologizing the story of the Fall, despite the fact that the work appeared in 1844, fifteen years before Darwin's *Origin of Species*. The net result of a literal interpretation is that 'the history of the human race acquired a fantastic beginning', with Adam 'placed fantastically outside history'.[98] He urges us instead to interpret it as saying something 'about every individual who by his own first sin brings sinfulness into the world'.[99] This means that it is no longer appropriate for the serpent to be part of the story[100] since its presence detracts from the story's universal character as an account of each man's internal development.

The core of the meaning of the myth for man now becomes that 'the prohibition awakens in him freedom's possibility.'[101] Unfortunately, this is developed in a way which is seldom easy to follow.[102] Rather surprisingly given his avowed atheism, Jean-Paul Sartre (1905–80) offers a highly perspective analysis of what Kierkegaard was probably striving to say. He draws out attention to an entry in Kierkegaard's *Journal*: 'Omnipotence . . . should make things dependent. But if we rightly consider omnipotence, then clearly it must have the quality of so taking itself back in the very manifestation of its all-powerfulness that the results of this act of the omnipotent can be independent.' From this Sartre draws the implication: 'The pre-Adamite state of innocence is the final moment of dependence. At any moment God will withdraw from his creature as the ebbing tide uncovers a piece of flotsam; and by this movement alone he creates dread – as the possibility of independence. In other words, God becomes at once the Prohibiter and Tempter . . . Dread is the internalization of this forsaken condition and it is completed by the free realisation of the sole possible future of Adam abandoned – the choice of the finite . . . The Self is chosen finitude, nothingness affirmed and delimited by an act . . . the finite is now constituted as loss of the infinite, freedom as the necessary and irremediable foundation of the formation of the Ego.'[103]

In other words, the Fall is the point at which our true freedom, real independence of God, began. It is now we who define who and what we are, not God. Sartre even says that 'everything happens as though God *needed sin* (his italics) in order that man might produce himself in front of him, as if he had solicited it in order to bring Adam out of his state of ignorance and give meaning to man.' This is to go too far. But the distancing of the Infinite, that brings with it the near inevitability of sin, was necessary if man's true humanity was to emerge. For only thus could he truly exercise his full potential for freedom, the freedom to shape his own destiny and character in conformity or otherwise to the divine will. No longer an innocent, totally dependent on God, he now possesses a radical freedom, the freedom (to revert to the style of Levinas) even to have a 'No' written on one's face.

Indeed, it is arguable that, however prominent a pessimistic preoccupation with anxiety sometimes seems, it was the defence of freedom that really was Existentialism's central concern. It is we who determine our essence, what we really are. Certainly, freedom is the dominating theme of Sartre's major work *Being and Nothingness* (1943). In the earlier *The Transcendence of the Ego* his argument for free will was that the mind cannot be made the subject of any causal analysis since the only sense in which it exists is as conscious spontaneity in relation to the world. Caws rightly objects that it is a strange form of defence to claim freedom for the mind by denying its independent existence apart from these spontaneous acts: 'The

Sartrean Ego has the elusiveness of a burst bubble, and the outcome of the analysis is an empty I.'[104] But if this argument for human freedom is bought at too high a price, some of his later arguments carry more conviction. So, for example, he notes the extent to which the way in which the world is structured into negative and positive elements is a function of the way we view the world, not any prior determination upon us. This is the point of an early illustration, the failure of Pierre to turn up for an appointment in the local café. Sartre observes: 'each element of the setting, a person, a table, a chair, attempts to isolate itself, to lift itself upon the ground constituted by the totality of the other objects, only to fall back once more into the undifferentiation of this ground; it melts into the ground.'[105] In other words, because his sole interest in entering the cafe is to meet his friend, all other objects are negated as without significance to consciousness. But, when Pierre is discovered not to be present, this negative fact becomes the sole perceived fact – 'my expectation has caused the absence of Pierre to happen as a real event.'

Again, while not denying the reality of the past, Sartre is at pains to emphasize even its malleability in relation to our future projects. He puts 'the paradox' thus: 'I can not conceive of myself without a past . . . but on the other hand I am the being through whom the past comes to myself and to the world.'[106] As illustration, he observes: 'Who shall decide whether that mystic crisis in my fifteenth year "was" a pure accident of puberty, or, on the contrary, the first sign of a future conversion? I myself, according to whether I shall decide – at twenty years of age, at thirty years, to be converted.'[107] MacQuarrie in his brief discussion of freedom in *In Search of Humanity* draws our attention to 'Sartre's aphorism: "To be free is to be condemned to be free" '.[108] But whatever Sartre's intention may have been, the overall impression created by *Being and Nothingness* is very different, of a great celebration of human freedom and the dignity it confers upon man.

In short then, my conclusion is that theology has appropriated too much of the negative side of Existentialism. What we need to do today is take more seriously its positive side. The Fall indeed brought alienation from God. But it also brought God's greatest gift to us, the freedom to be like God as creators of who we really are.

Grace

Luther and Oman

If sin is by definition man at his maximum distance from God, the obverse side of the coin must be grace, God coming close to man in his need. But, as soon as one asks how God comes close, a connection is immediately made with the theme of the previous section. For the question raises itself, how such closeness can be made compatible with an assertion of human freedom. Luther may be taken as representative of one tradition within Christianity, the logic of which eventually leads to a total denial of human freedom; John Oman as illustrative of the attempt of much twentieth-century theology, both Protestant and Catholic, to extricate itself from what can only be seen as a fundamental assault on the dignity of man. Putting the issue thus of course leaves the reader in no doubt at the outset as to the author's own convictions. But that does not mean that Luther's contribution is despised. Far from it. Any adequate theology of grace must take full account of the sort of considerations that led him (and so many others like him) to the position he held.

To begin with, it must be conceded that he has the weight of both Scripture and early church tradition in his favour. Though there are a few passages that seem to imply that the human contribution is not regarded as insignificant,[109] the balance of the New Testament, particularly with St Paul taken into account, is overwhelmingly the other way. So of the 150 occurrences of the Greek word for grace, *charis* (literally 'a kindness' or 'favour'), roughly two-thirds are in the Pauline Epistles (with only eleven in the Gospels and none in Mark or Matthew), and in St Paul it is clearly used to emphasize the totally unmerited character of divine action. For Paul his own call was an act of unmerited grace,[110] and he applies that perspective with equal force to others: 'Both Jew and pagan sinned and forfeited God's glory, and both are justified through the free gift of his grace by being redeemed in Christ Jesus.'[111] To some extent this is no more than a continuation of the Old Testament notion of God's *chesed* or loving-kindness, according to which God treats Israel far better than she deserves. The theme is powerfully illustrated in Hosea's comparison of God's love for Israel to his own love for his faithless wife, Gomer, or in Ezekiel's image of the undeserving child.[112] But Paul carries that uncontentious insight further, by insisting that the whole work is God's, and bears no relation whatsoever to human decision or merit. Most notoriously this is to be found in his image of the potter and the clay in Romans,[113] a passage that does more than enough to justify the predestinarian bias of the opening chapter of the pseudo-Pauline Ephesians. But there is no shortage of other passages to which reference could be made. 'It is God which worketh in you both to will and to do of his own good pleasure',[114] we are told, with faith itself also being seen as a divine gift.[115]

The way in which Augustine reasserted Paul's position against the British monk Pelagius is well known. Pelagius objected to Augustine's famous remark in the *Confessions*, 'Da quod iubes et iube quod vis' (Give what Thou commandest, and commandest what Thou wilt)[116] on the grounds, rightly I think, that this seemed to rob man of any real responsibility for his actions. However, in his determination to defend human free will he went to the other extreme. Having distinguished three features in human action, the power (*posse*), the willing (*velle*) and the realization (*esse*), he argued that only the first of these should be treated as exclusively a divine gift, roughly equivalent to free will itself, *posse non peccare*, the ability not to sin. He rejected any notion of inherited original sin, and preached an austere doctrine of a divine call to perfection, making much of Jesus' words in the Sermon on the Mount.[117] His views were condemned at a Council held at Carthage in 418. Another monk, John Cassian (d. 435), attempted a more moderate version of his claims in a stance that came subsequently to be labelled Semi-Pelagianism. This is the view that grace supervenes once the individual has taken the first steps towards the Christian life. Though this too was condemned at a local Council (at Orange in 529), in actual practice something like Semi-Pelagianism prevailed in the Church until Luther attempted to reassert a sterner creed.

In the most recent detailed study of his theological development Alister McGrath in *Luther's Theology of the Cross* sees Luther's theology of grace as firmly embedded in the late medieval scholastic approach known as the *via moderna* as late as 1514, a mere three years before he nailed those ninety-five theses on the church door at Wittenberg, the event that traditionally marks the beginning of the Reformation. According to the theologians of the *via moderna*, which is particularly associated with the name of the English philosopher William of Ockham (d. 1349), God's power is unconditional to do as he pleases, but he has chosen to act covenantly and so in terms of this *pactum* or *testamentum* he guarantees to grant grace whenever certain conditions are fulfilled. These are summarized in the traditional maxim: 'Facienti quod in se est, Deus non denegat gratiam' (God does not deny grace to the man who does his best). Commenting on this in his *Lectures on the Psalms* Luther writes: 'God has made himself a debtor to us through the promise of he who is merciful, not through the dignity of the human nature of he who merits. He required nothing except preparation, in order that we might be capable of receiving the gift.'[118] Even so by 'preparation' he seems to have meant no more than 'recognition of one's need for grace'.[119]

But this did not satisfy Luther. In 1545, the year before he died, he described his decisive step as the discovery of an alternative sense for Paul's phrase 'the righteousness of God'. It is exclusively a soteriological notion, rather than anything to do with common ideas about distributive justice or fairness. God accounts us righteous simply in virtue of our faith. According to MacGrath this perspective was probably initially still contained within the covenantal theology of the *via moderna*.[120] But all this had changed by the end of 1515 when faith itself came to be seen like righteousness as a work of God in man. McGrath further plausibly argues that Luther's *theologia crucis*, which was emerging from 1518 onwards, is all of a piece with this development. The *Deus absconditus*, the God who reveals himself in the 'hiddenness' of the Cross, is an attack on any natural analogy between divine and human concepts.[121] So Luther comes to see even the wrestlings and sufferings that lead up to faith as themselves part of the process of justification, all part of the exclusively divine action.[122]

This tendency to ascribe the entire work of man's salvation to God and thus leave no room for a role for the individual himself can be attacked at a number of different levels. Three in particular deserve mention.

First, there is the question of whether it really fits best with the Biblical evidence. Not only must one take seriously the contention of Biblical scholars like Stendahl and Sanders that the central concerns of the Epistle to the Romans lay elsewhere,[123] there is also the intriguing view of another Biblical scholar, Anthony Thiselton, in *The Two Horizons* that, even where the issue is before Paul's mind, he will be misunderstood unless the commentator shows a proper concern for context. Taking his inspiration from Wittgenstein's idea of language games, he suggests that the Lutheran and Catholic are both wrong in the way in which they use Scripture. The former appeals to verses like Romans 5, 1 that emphasize justification as a present reality and the latter to verses like Galatians 5, 5 that stress its future dimension. But 'each may be a valid assessment in relation to a different frame of reference.'[124] So, though he accepts the Lutheran paradox of 'simul iustus et peccator' ('counted righteous' but 'really a sinner'), he denies that there is any contradiction: 'From the historical viewpoint justification is still future, but by appropriation of the eschatological verdict it is possible to live by faith in the present experience of being justified.'[125] Again, of the supposed conflict between Paul and James[126] he maintains that they are not necessarily in conflict since they are working with a different grammatical analysis of faith: 'Whereas in Paul we see an internal or grammatical relation between faith and justification (because faith is entailed in the very concept of justification for Paul), in James we see an internal or grammatical relation between faith and works, because the very concept of faith entails acting in a certain way.'[127] In other words, Paul would not necessarily have disagreed with James that a mental state is insufficient and that one also needs a dispositional commitment to action. Rather, it is simply that from the perspective of the definitional framework in terms of which he is operating faith and works are necessarily contrasted. Faith has become part of the concept of justification and works, equally, part of the concept of law.

But, if this can do much to defuse the apparently conflicting New Testament evidence, it cannot take us all the way. Predestinarian passages like the analogy of the potter and the clay continue to challenge the legitimacy of assigning any major role to man in his own salvation. It is at this point therefore that I turn to my second level of attack, and raise the question of whether men like Paul and Augustine have not confused two very different things, their own subjective feelings with a dispassionate objective analysis of what happens. Taking up a distinction first drawn by William James in his classic *The Varieties of Religious Experience*, N. P. Williams once suggested that the different degree of stress on human sinfulness and the need for grace could be explained in terms of two very different types of personalities, the 'once-born' and the 'twice-born'. The latter, 'the sick soul . . . blessed or cursed from birth with the mysterious heritage of neural and emotional instability, whose passions have been transformed, whose communion with God and peace of mind have been won through the paroxysm of an instantaneous conversion, thinks of himself as a "brand plucked from the burning" by no effort or volition of his own.'[126] As a characterization it is hopelessly inadequate, especially when he tries to apply to the conversion of twice-born giants like Paul, Augustine, Luther and Newman the observation that it involves 'a mental and emotional explosion which diverts the greater part of the obscure energies of sex into the channel of mystical religion'.[129] Of those listed, only for Augustine did sexuality play a role, and even then it is far from clear that it played a major role. In any case, to call the once-born 'healthy-minded' simply in virtue of their character undergoing no dramatic changes would seem to say more about the Anglo-Saxon temperament than it does about human psychology *per se*!

But Williams' proposal does contain a measure of truth. My own suggestion would be that the twice-born are deceived, but that it is something entirely laudable that leads them to misperceive their situation, namely gratitude to God for their conversion. Putting the point as controversially as possible, the problem is not that they are too bad, but that they are too good. So thankful are they to God and so complete their present explicit reliance on him that they utterly fail to observe the various features in their past life that makes it entirely appropriate that God should now have so decisively spoken to them. There is not always adequate background information to make a judgement like this, but when there is, as with Augustine's *Confessions*, the truth seems obvious enough. For Augustine the decisive moment is him responding in the garden to the child's fortuitous chant of 'Tolle, lege'.[130] But the attentive reader cannot help but be aware of how so many of his previous actions have been of such a kind as to render his response to God on this occasion entirely natural and appropriate. One need only think of his first childish attempts at prayer or the way in which theft of some pears from a neighbour's tree remained firmly embedded in his mind.[131] For the truly wicked soul all such things would have long since passed from the memory. Though we know much less about the anterior history of St Paul, is it not possible that much the same explanation applies in his case as well? He himself tell us that he was leading a blameless life in respect of the Law.[132] This would make any attempt on God's part to advance him closer to himself entirely apposite. Against this stands his persecution of the infant Church, but given his avowed obedience to the Law may one not suspect the best of motives? So, though Paul only saw wickedness, God knew otherwise.

Despite his devout life as a monk, because of his over-scrupulousness Luther saw his discovery of justification by faith as a great release. Naturally this would evoke from him gratitude to God, and so part of the explanation for his position must be the same as that given above for Augustine and Paul. But two intellectual worries also played a role. So the third level of my attack on this position is to show why such worries are unfounded.

The first and less significant of the two is his concern to defend the contrast between divine justification and human justice. McGrath supports him in his rejection of the usual conceptions of justice, speaking of 'appalling theological ramifications'[135] if these are applied to God. But such rejections of fairness and so of any relevance of free will represent a total misunderstanding of the way in which free will is relevant. Theologians of the *via moderna* like Gabriel Biel had apparently claimed that man could do a great deal unaided, and against such a view Luther rightly protested. But from that he should not have concluded the opposite extreme, that no contribution is required from the individual. What one needs to say is that human conceptions of justice are still relevant, that God is not an arbitrary God but meets the individual half-way: that in proportion as we open our hearts to the working of God, to that degree does he enter into our lives in his compassion and power. That is to say, divine grace is always there taking the intiative, offering its aid if only we accept it, and that applies as much to the creation of faithful trust as to anything else. But all this is still very different from asserting that it ever overrides human free decision. In other words, human conceptions of distributive justice are still relevant, in the sense of degrees of openness to the divine initiative but not in the trite sense of qualities of goodness achieved, which is the sense which seems to have worried Luther.[134]

But one also detects a deeper worry in him, and one which I think brings us to the heart of his predestinarian theology. For he seems to have been plagued by anxieties because of the assertion of men like Biel that 'a man can never know for certain that he is doing his best' (the best that is required for God to respond to him). And little wonder since Biel interpreted this best to involve 'love of God above all things'![135] Luther's response was of course to say that God declared us righteous even while we are yet sinners. In one sense this was right, but to say it there really was no need for him to step outside the *via moderna*'s covenantal system of grace. For the only emendation he need have made was to say that God is present at each stage of the process, and that each move of ours towards him, however small, is met by a reciprocal action on God's part. His own argument carried to its logical conclusion was in fact to generate just as bad uncertainties of its own. For by 1525 in his famous debate with Erasmus on free will[136] he was maintaining that God's hidden will remains essentially unknown. His *Deus absconditus* has thus become as much part of the divine inscrutability as the way in which no rhyme or reason can be found for those whom God chooses to justify by his grace.

Putting this more controversially, the supreme irony of Luther's theology of justification seems to me to be that, despite the more moderate and more positive uses made of his basic insight by later generations, in its developed form in his own thought it remains depressingly trapped in late medieval scholastic philosophy. Central to Ockham's philosophy had been a concern to defend the divine freedom and omnipotence, and he even makes the moral law entirely subject to the divine will and choice. Luther by breaking with the restraining feature of the *via moderna*'s covenantal theology simply allowed the ultimate arbitrariness of such a God to be displayed in all its terrifying force. No doubt his motives, like Calvin's or Ockham's for that matter, were laudable ones, to defend the freedom and majesty of God. But it is done at a terrible price to the other side of the equation, the freedom and dignity of man. Yet it was all so unnecessary if only he had rested content with his earlier basic insight that God is stretching out to aid each hesitant step of faith that we make towards him. Intriguingly, even as devoted an exponent as James Atkinson cannot help occasionally slipping into using the very language which I have suggested that Luther ought to have used: 'as we keep ourselves open to his activity, we find this newly kindled divine life fed and kept strong.'[137]

John Oman (d. 1939) can be used to provide a very effective contrast to the extremes of the Reformation. As a Presbyterian minister he belonged to a church whose theology (nominally at least) is Calvinist. His earliest theological work was on Schleiermacher, whose *Speeches on Religion* he translated. Schleiermacher's influence is still evident in his 1917 classic *Grace and Personality*, and it well illustrates the extent to which Protestantism has in general moved towards a view that better

preserves the dignity and freedom of both God and man. He writes:
'An order imposed by God otherwise than through our own sense of
right, however exalted its demands, would be no true moral order . . .
Nothing is adequate to our whole moral relation to God short of the
identification, through our own insight, of our duty with his will.'[138]
Thus, though in a Schleiermacher vein he identifies religion with
dependence, he is equally emphatic that morality is a matter of
independence, of free moral decision. So the two demands can only be
reconciled by the individual freely accepting dependence on the divine.
'No succour that would be personal may ignore this central characteristic
of the moral person. Every day we are reminded of the impossibility of
truly helping people except through themselves, and of the irrelevance
for our own lives of all that does not approach us through some
personal relationship.'[139] Oman refuses to call his own position Semi-
Pelagian, but this is only because he thinks the term suggests too
precise a division of labour between the work of man and God rather
than a dynamic personal interaction. 'In a right relation of persons,
especially of father and child, the help of the one does not end where
the effort of the other begins. How is a son distinguished from a servant
if not by such perfection of help that his dependence on his father has
been the unfailing spring of his independence and mastery?'[140]

There are clearly a number of objections that could be raised against
this analysis. So let me end this section by countering two of them. Any
claim that God is always active in the production of human good is
bound to seem implausible if such action is confined to the consciously
personal level, since many good acts are performed without the agent
being in the least aware of any divine aid. But in response one may
point out that there is no reason why such aid unconsciously received
should not none the less remain a necessary condition for the
performance of any good action. To this it may be objected that there is
now the implausibility of too many divine interventions in human life,
too many 'miracles'. But, as Freudian psychology has made us all too
aware, we are constantly interacting with each other at levels other
than the purely conscious. So in suggesting that God exercises this kind
of intervention or involvement in our lives we are by no means
ascribing to him an activity of which we are unaware elsewhere. Nor
should this kind of action be seen as having anything to do with the
miraculous. Human beings in interacting with each other exercise their
free will, either directly or indirectly. Because a response is at the
unconscious level it is often thought that it must therefore not be free.
But this is quite untrue. It is we who shape our characters and so
indirectly determine the kind of response that our unconscious will
make. So Wiles is quite wrong when he argues that 'deftly administered
subconscious impulses' must 'suggest the way of the indoctrinator, of

the hidden persuader rather than the way of love'.[141] The response of our unconscious indirectly reflects our free conscious decisions.

But now a different sort of objection may arise, that such a conception of grace brings God down too much to the human level, with man almost an equal partner with God. But that was one of the implications of our earlier discussion of the divine image, that it is part of the glory of the creation that, despite the vast differences that remain, having created persons with free will means that in some sense God has placed them on the same level with himself. Nor can it be argued that it seriously detracts from the majesty of God that on this view good ceases to be his sole creation because of the indispensable human contribution. For God remains the unique source of all goodness as its first instigator and as such he has done all he lovingly can do to bring it about, compatible with respect for human freedom. Indeed, for this view nature without grace is what Karl Rahner calls a 'remainder concept' (*Restbegriff*),[142] a mere intellectual abstraction which has no independent existence. For God's grace is seen as always prevenient, and so there never can be a time or place where nature is to be found in complete isolation from it.

Foucault and freedom

One way in which a supporter of a Lutheran-type approach might respond to the above would be to argue that it is based on a misunderstanding of the true nature of freedom. Thus it may be said that my defence of what has become known as 'synergism' (the need for God and man to work co-operatively together) is based on the assumption that freedom is the absence of external restraints and so on God not predestinating how we act. But true freedom should rather be viewed positively in terms of the ability to do things, and what greater ability can we acquire than the ability to do the good that comes through God's predetermining grace? This is essentially Augustine's point, when he distinguishes between *posse non peccare* (being able not to sin) and *non posse peccare* (not being able to sin). He informs us that the 'first' liberty of the will is the former, but 'the last and greater' is the latter.[143] Elsewhere in fact it is only the latter that he is prepared properly to call 'libertas'. The former is designated *liberum arbitrium* (free will) and not regarded as very significant since in God there is no such possibility of sinning.[144] Not being able to sin is true liberty because it characterizes 'the last and greater' beatitude of Heaven, a foretaste of which we have now whenever our actions are truly spontaneous and without regret. 'Delectet te, et liber es' (Let it delight you, and you are free).[145]

In Augustine's defence it may be observed that a similar kind of contrast continues to be drawn even in modern secular thought, as in Sir Isaiah Berlin's distinction between two concepts of liberty, what he calls negative and positive freedom.[146] By negative freedom he means the absence of constraints, the freedom *from* external pressures, whereas positive freedom means the ability *to* do certain things. Berlin ended that Inaugural Lecture by remarking on the very easy way in which such a notion of positive freedom can be manipulated to say that because one's scope of liberty is being enlarged one is truly free even when coerced.[147] The object of Berlin's attack is those influenced by Hegel's ideas, but it is a criticism that can equally be levelled at Augustine's views on grace. For if grace is irresistible, what is this *libertas* of which Augustine speaks other than a hollow shell? The Augustinian response would of course be to claim that there is all the difference between being under the heavy compulsion of sin and the spontaneous goodness that charaterizes the man of grace. But spontaneity is simply a function of habit (hence the insight that virtues are habits), and so, while virtues may thus produce spontaneity, so equally can bad habits, i.e. vices. The final card up the Augustinian's sleeve is to suggest that vices could never produce true spontaneity. They will always be imbued with regret, given that such actions are not productive of happiness. But, while this is no doubt sometimes true, it seems implausible as a universal thesis.[148] In any case, one may ask how a good act can be truly spontaneous, if it is done in the knowledge that one's personal consent played no significant part in its production.

Yet spontaneity does still seem to me to have something to do with the notion of freedom. What that connection is can be most usefully explored by looking at some of the ideas of the French philosopher Michel Foucault (1926–84). To some to call him a philosopher may seem a misnomer, when his works have titles like *The Birth of the Clinic*, *Discipline and Punish* and *The History of Sexuality*. But, while it is true that he chose to pursue his ideas through a certain form of historical investigation, not only was it his intention to draw philosophical conclusions, incontestably his background was in philosophy. He held a number of appointments in philosophy, including head of the philosophy department at the University of Clermont-Ferrand. But perhaps more accurately the title he chose on election to the Collège de France in 1970 was 'Professor of the History of Systems of Thought'.

It is almost now a commonplace to describe the influence on the generation of French philosophers after 1945 and that since 1960 in terms of a contrast between the dominance of the three H's, Hegel, Husserl and Heidegger, and the three 'masters of suspicion', Marx, Nietzsche and Freud. The influence of Marx and Freud on contemporary French philosophy will concern us in chapter 5. In the case of Foucault not only did Nietzsche exercise a major influence on him, for instance in making the exercise of power a central theme, he himself also deserves that title of *maître de soupçon*[149] that Paul Ricoeur had originally coined for Marx, Nietzsche and Freud. Marx had argued that so many human commitments are in reality no more than an ideological disguise of economic interests, Freud that often they are simply an expression of very different sublimated or repressed sexual desires. Nietzsche (1844–1900) offers rather different grounds for suspicion, that what we think or do is in one way or another an expression of the will to power. In one of his most famous works, *The Genealogy of Morals*, he tells us that the morality of the *Übermensch* which he prefers is one of 'triumphant self-affirmation' but so equally is the Christianity which he despises involved in the pursuit of power. Its 'slave revolt in morals begins by rancour turning creative and giving birth to values – the rancour of beings who, deprived of the direct outlet of action, compensate by an imaginary vengeance'.[150] In other words, its real motivating force is not love but a small-minded envy of what it cannot achieve itself.

Foucault does not take up Nietzsche's attack on Christianity, but he does detect everywhere the insidious pursuit of power. However, he sees this most manifest not in the field of ethics but in questions of knowledge. Like Nietzsche he pursues a genealogy, but it is a genealogy of knowledge, not morals. One way of expressing the difference might perhaps be to say that he has given Nietzsche a Kantian turn (or Kant a Nietzschean dimension. At all events, what interests him is not as with Kant the formal conditions of our knowledge but the historical origins of that 'knowledge', the way in which what we believe we 'know' has originated through an often unconscious pursuit of power. Such a destructive programme could of course lead to extreme scepticism. And at one level that is exactly to what it does lead since he offers no new underpinning of claims to knowledge. As Alan Sheridan points out in his book *Michel Foucault* (significantly subtitled 'The Will to Truth'), Foucault is not interested in producing any overall system. His intention is to make us more aware that 'truth does not exist outside power' and so attempt to be more fully conscious of what really is going on in others and in ourselves.[151] But a positive aim is also revealed in a collection of his articles, *Power/Knowledge*. For there not only does he identify the sort of 'global totalitarian theories' against which he is reacting – Marxism, psychoanalysis, Structuralism and Phenomenology[152] – he explains why in a way which reveals the nature of his alternative commitment. Their very attempt to be inclusive is exclusive, and precludes legitimate alternative insights. So what is required is 'an insurrection of subjugated knowledges'.[153]

Discipline and Punish provides one example of this technique. The conventional view is that penal reform in the nineteenth century was inspired entirely by humanitarian motives, through horror at the severity of the tortures imposed on criminals. But Foucault presents a very different picture. He points out that imprisonment was the exception rather than the norm before this and that the complaints which led to the eventual birth of the prison as the main form of punishment were really more concerned about the ineffectiveness of the previous punitive regime. Admittedly, it punished some too severely but it also allowed too many to escape the net. So the reading Foucault suggests for the genealogy of the prison is not humanitarian, but the substitution of one form of exercise of social power by another, still more severe in its social control, if not in its cruelty. A spectacle view of punishment, in which public rituals of torture and branding demonstrated the royal power in much the same way as the publicity of a coronation, gave place to what was now intended as a detailed system for achieving social conformity and which was as much to be seen in contemporary developments in the school and workshop.

The new system was thus in effect far more of an attack on the individual than what preceded it. In fact what happened was 'the reversal of the political axis of individualisation'. Under the previous conception of society 'the more one possesses power or privilege, the more one is marked as an individual, by rituals, written accounts or visual reproductions.' But in our present situation in which society as a whole attempts to exercise control over a much wider range of activities the result is that 'the child is more individualised than the adult, the patient more than the healthy man, the madman and the delinquent more than the normal and non-delinquent.'[154] In other words, individualism is no longer seen as a mark of dignity but a problem of differentiation from the norm, that requires a solution.

Given the degree of pluralism in modern society, this may not seem obviously true. But Foucault's point is not that earlier societies were not authoritarian but that we deceive ourselves if we think that our own society is not. In particular he notes the extent to which it was only with the development of the modern penal system that society took a major interest in such things as petty crime, family matters and sexual morality.

He applies the same thesis to mental illness in another of his books, *Madness and Civilisation*. Here again we tend to view the historical development as simply a move in a more humanitarian direction, whereas according to Foucault's genealogy it was in fact indicative of a less tolerant approach. The work is subtitled 'A History of Insanity in the Age of Reason', and it is during the Classical cult of Reason in the eighteenth century that Foucault sees the decisive transition taking place. 'The constitution of madness as a mental illness, at the end of the eighteenth century, affords the evidence of a broken dialogue.' For 'in the Middle Ages and until the Renaissance, man's dispute with madness was a dramatic debate in which he confronted the secret powers of the world.'[155] As a symbol of the contrast he takes the *Narrenschiff* (the Ship of Fools), the ships which used to sail the Rhine in the late Middle Ages carrying madmen expelled from their native city to be deposited in another. 'Madness will no longer proceed from a point within the world to a point beyond, on its strange voyage; it will never again be that fugitive and absolute limit. Behold it is moored now, made fast among things and men. Retained and maintained. No longer a ship but a hospital.'[156] The extent of the change he encapsulates in the adage: 'Confinement has succeeded embarkation.' What he means is that even at the Renaissance man was still prepared to admit that he could learn something from human nature pushed to the limit into strange behaviour. But by the Age of Reason the normal or rational had come to be very closely equated, and in a way which even anticipated many of the subsequent preoccupations of psychiatry such as taking sexual deviation as a sign of irrationality.

The paradoxical result of this whole trend of equating the rational with the normal is that, as Mark Philp has put it in an article on Foucault, 'the more psychologically determined the act – that is, the more consistent it is with who and what the individual is – the more legally responsible the actor is held; while the more incomprehensible the act – the more out of character and the less determined by motive or reason it is – the more it is excused. Psychological determinism thus becomes the index both of legal freedom and of legal and moral responsibility – while to act out of character is to act unfreely.'[157] And here at last we can return to our theme of grace, freedom and spontaneity. For, though Foucault never devotes more than a passing reference to the Christian tradition, it is arguable that its notion of freedom in the Spirit provides that very openness and dialogue with 'madness' which Foucault thinks so essential to a truly liberated humanity.

What I have in mind here is the extent to which being guided by the Spirit is seen as justifying unpredictable and even strange or even 'mad' conduct. Indeed, so far as the element of unpredictability is concerned, even Luther might be enrolled in support through that strand in his thought which emphasizes that Christian freedom consists in freedom from law and so, to that degree, freedom from predictable action.[158] But what I particularly have in mind is the way in which within the Biblical period the prophet was seen as being on the margins of society challenging and de-legitimating it, while in subsequent Christian thought there is a strong tradition of saints fulfilling a similar role, being fools for Christ's sake.

So far as the Bible is concerned, several of the prophets engage in what we would regard as distinctly odd conduct, such as the odd names Isaiah gives to his children (Shear-jashub – 'a remnant shall return', or Maher-shalal-hash-baz – 'a speedy spoil, quick booty'), or Amos' use of action puns, for instance picking up a basket of ripe fruit, the Hebrew for which is very similar to the word for destruction.[159] One might also include in this category conduct like Hosea's in remaining faithful to his faithless wife. For, though intelligible today, it flew in the face of the accepted conventions of his own time. But it is Ezekiel who best supports Foucault's thesis. That his behaviour was very strange indeed can be incontestably established just from the first few chapters. Thus, in his call to the ministry recorded in chapter 2 he receives a scroll with the instruction to pronounce 'lamentations, wailings, moanings', which he thereupon immediately *eats* and declares: 'I ate the scroll, and it tasted sweet as honey.' In the following chapter he has a vision of Yahweh, as a result of which he is struck dumb, with his tongue firmly stuck to the roof of his mouth. By chapter 4 we find him lying for 390 days on his left side, and then for forty days on his right, while by chapter 5 he is anticipating present-day skinheads, shaving off first one-third of his hair, then a further third, and then the final third. Given Foucault's thesis about the lack of dialogue with the abnormal, it is therefore particularly intriguing to discover that even Biblical scholars have tended to equate Ezekiel's conduct with some form of mental illness, such as 'catalepsy', or 'schizophrenia'. The most recent major commentary, however, after surveying such explanations, comes up with what is, I think, the correct account. Zimmerli writes: 'Ezekiel was a prophet of particular sensitivity and dramatic power, for whom a metaphor could become a fully experienced event, however strange in itself this might be.'[160] In other words, so intense was his perception of the divine will for Israel that he actually symbolically lived that divine will as an individual. Naturally, such strange conduct could easily be plausibly interpreted as simply indicative of clinical madness. But religion at least provides some kind of check on any such interpretation with its insistence on the freedom of the Spirit that 'bloweth where it listeth'.[161] In Ezekiel's case it clearly produced a complete reordering of his perception of the world such that symbol was transformed into reality. But one should recall that Christ also was called a madman and that St Paul saw the following of Christ as 'foolishness to the Greeks'.[162]

Nor did the capacity for such alternative perceptions cease in the subsequent history of the Church. So, for example, if one takes the most popular saint today and reads some of the medieval lives, one discovers a very different picture of St Francis from that normally painted, one in which sanctity and 'madness' might represent two closely competing interpretations. To give but one illustration, once when he was being tempted towards material attachments, he ran out naked into the snow, and built seven snowmen, and then spent the evening treating them as his family, calling one his wife, another his daughter, and so on.[163]

The connection between 'madness' and religious insight which Plato asserts in the *Phaedrus*[164] should perhaps therefore be allowed to hold. At all events, if Christianity is to take its prophets and saints with sufficient seriousness, then it must also take seriously Foucault's contention that madness at least sometimes functions as no more than a social construct. For only then will we recognize departure from the norm into unpredictability as a true expression of the freedom of action that the Spirit brings. Certainly the inherent warning which it contains about ever treating Christianity as a completely closed conceptual system cannot be ignored. It will be an issue which recurs when we consider the status of authority within the Christian tradition in chapter 5.

But to someone like Luther such an account of the relation between the work of grace and freedom will continue to have at least one fundamental defect. It fails to encapsulate any essential reference to the work of Christ. It is to that issue that I next turn.

4

Doctrine of Salvation

The personal initiative – Atonement

Calvin and Aulén

To the perceptive reader the structure of this chapter may suggest that I have already prejudged an important issue. For by beginning with the effect on the individual of Christ's life and death, it may seem that I have already discounted the claim that it is social transformation which must come first. This is not so. It is simply that it will be easier to assess this modern perspective if we take the more traditional pattern first.

To take these two theologians, Calvin and Aulén, from two such different centuries, the sixteenth and the twentieth, may look odd; still odder that the philosophers with whom they are made to interact, Abelard and Anselm, should both come from the early twelfth century. But in fact only the Swedish theologian Gustav Aulén has made any significant contribution to thought on this issue in the twentieth century, and almost everything else can be seen as derivative from a previous age, particularly from Calvin and Abelard.

The continuing influence of Calvin's penal theory of the Atonement, what it was that made man 'at-one' with God, can be seen at both the popular and the academic level. The most common explanation within Evangelical Christianity of the necessity for Christ's death is that he bore in our place the punishment due to our sins.[1] Equally it is the theory which underlines what Barth or more recently Moltmann has had to say on the subject. In the case of Calvin it is important to recall his own legal background. It is hard not to see this as having had an effect, especially when combined with his desire to give some continuing validity to the Old Testament with all its legal imagery. At any rate, having finished his philosophical studies at Paris in 1529, he went on to study law at the then famous law faculty at Orleans. One of the professors, much admired by Calvin, was Pierre de L'Estoile, the best French jurist of the time. So one way of reading Calvin is to see him as attempting to express Christian doctrine in the language of a discipline highly prized by both himself and the culture of his time.

Calvin's God is so often misrepresented as a harsh God that it is important to recall that in his definitive expression of his view, in his major work *The Institutes of the Christian Religion*, there is no doubt that it is divine love that is central, and not divine wrath. 'God, who is the highest righteousness, cannot love the unrighteousness he sees in us all. All of us, therefore, have in ourselves, something deserving of God's hatred . . . But because the Lord wills not to lose what is his in us, out of his own kindness he still finds something to love . . . Thus he is moved by pure and freely given love of us to receive us into grace.'[2] But, if love is primary, it is none the less a love firmly bound by justice: 'Since he is a righteous judge, he does not allow his law to be broken without punishment.'[3]

Barth lies within essentially the same tradition, though there are significant differences. Two chapters[4] of *Dogmatics in Outline* provide a very effective summary of his approach. He supports Calvin's pupils' emendation of his position to the effect that Christ 'all the time of his life on earth . . . hath borne in body and soul the wrath of God against the sin of the whole human race',[5] and from this draws the conclusion that his entire life, and not just his death, reveals our condemnation: 'What is there done by men acquires its whole importance from its being done to God . . . We can only see the infinite guilt in which we stand over against God: the God who became man.'[6] The result is that 'to be a man means to be situated in God's presence as Jesus is, that is, to be the Bearer of the wrath of God. It belongs to us, that end on the gallows.'[7] Clearly, here Christ himself has become our Judge, rather than the Father, just as it is Christ who provides the means of reconciliation. 'Righteousness in the Old Testament sense', we are told, 'is not the righteousness of the judge who makes the debtor pay, but the action of a judge who in the accused recognises the wretch whom he wishes to help by putting him to rights', though significantly he adds: 'Of course not without the punishment being borne and the whole distress breaking out, but through his putting himself in the place of the guilty one.'[8] But by God putting himself in the place of man, the guilty one, the exaltation of man to the divine life, as symbolized in the Resurrection, then becomes possible.

Clearly, when put like this, judgement and forgiveness have become part of a single act in a way not envisaged by Calvin. Indeed in the *Church Dogmatics* Barth is careful to insist that God was not bound by any rules of justice: 'God would not be God if his reaction to wrong-doers could be compared to a mechanism which functions, as it were, independently of his free ruling and disposing.'[9] In the light of that freedom, God is entirely able 'to pronounce us free in passing sentence . . . to redeem and save us by our destruction.'[10] It is not always easy to interpret such Kierkegaardian paradox. But, though the language remains Calvinist, the stress does seem quite different. Christ no longer bears the punishment because someone must be punished, but because 'in the strict sense there is no knowledge of sin except in the light of Christ's Cross.'[11] In other words, it is because this is the only way of making us aware of our proper deserts.

Moltmann in *The Crucified God* also uses the language of Calvin: 'God passes judgment on himself, God takes the judgment on the sin of man upon himself. He assigns to himself the fate that men should by rights endure.'[12] But, as with Barth, there is an interesting twist. For he expresses himself unhappy with the language of expiation because of its retrospective rather than future character.[13] Instead he stresses the 'representative' nature of Christ's suffering in the way in which 'through his death the risen Christ introduces the coming reign of God into the godless present.'[14] Initially this might suggest that he has strayed very far indeed from the penal model. But he still retains from expiation the idea that 'Jesus took the place of helpless man as his representative and in so doing made it possible for man to enter into communion before God in which he otherwise could not stand and survive.'[15] Not only that, in a key section entitled 'Jesus and God: the Godforsaken',[16] Jesus' cry of deriliction from the Cross is given a legal context. For the use of Psalm 22 is interpreted as 'a legal plea . . . for the revelation of the righteousness of God who promised "not to forsake the work of his hands" '.[17] But because the Father does not act immediately, Moltmann argues that we must see the Cross as 'the theological trial between God and God. The cross of the Son divides God from God to the utmost degree of enmity and distinction.'[18] In a subsequent chapter this is expanded as follows: 'God is on the cross of Jesus "for us", and through that becomes God and Father of the godless and the godforsaken. He took upon himself the unforgivable sin and the guilt for which there is no atonement, together with the rejection and anger that cannot be turned away, so that in Christ we might become his righteousness in the world . . . God became the crucified God so that we might become the free sons of God.'[19]

Once more, as with Barth, there is the same love of paradox. But it makes a rather different point. For Barth judgement arises through the way in which the Cross convicts us of our sin. For Moltmann the point seems to be that we are all too well aware of our godforsakenness, but do not know what to do about it; so God comes to us and identifies with us as one who was pre-eminently 'godforsaken', and yet had no reason to deserve that condition. Another way of putting the difference would be to say that for Moltmann the Cross does not bring judgement, but relief from judgement in the knowledge it brings that God the Son through his Incarnation has taken man's sin against man into his own experience of suffering and shown how to transform it.

Before looking at some of the merits of this type of approach, it will be profitable to note its principal defects. First, there is what is often thought to be its main strength, its Biblical warrant. Much used to be made of *hilasterion* in Romans 3, 25, which the Authorised Version translates as 'propitiation'. But Paul is probably just recalling the fact that on the Day of Atonement the Mercy Seat was sprinkled with blood.[20] Admittedly, the problem of correct interpretation is complicated by the fact that the word seems to have originally meant propitiation of an angry god, then the sin offering when such propitiation was made, before finally the place of propitiation, i.e. the Mercy Seat or Kapporeth. If the reference is to the last, as it indisputably is in Hebrews 9, 5, Paul is simply emphasizing that Christ has effectively achieved such purification from sin as the Old Covenant could only symbolize. What this warns us against is taking metaphors too literally, and under that heading might reasonably be placed all those occasions in which Christ seems to be identified with sin. Thus we find in Paul expressions such as the following: 'in the likeness of sinful flesh'; 'condemned sin in the flesh'; 'made him to be sin for us, who knew no sin'; 'made a curse for us'.[21] Admittely, all these expressions when used of Christ could mean that Paul conceived of him being punished as 'sin' in our place. But equally they may be no more than powerful, evocative metaphors used to underline the extent to which Christ identified with our human condition – he took the same nature as sinful man and even died a form of death that the Old Testament had deemed accursed.[22]

Another difficulty is the notion of punishment which is assumed. For it is hard to see how the punishment of an innocent man is compatible with justice or how it could help the guilty, except in a way that is inimical to justice. Certainly, while we sometimes admire an innocent man going to his death on behalf of the guilty, as with Sidney Carton in *A Tale of Two Cities*, we would not admire a judge who knowingly acquiesced in such a situation. The explanation of Calvin's failure to reflect on the incongruity may lie in the fact that he is attempting to harmonize Old Testament legal language with contemporary usage. For primitive notions of the payment of 'a blood price' do not require payment necessarily from the wrongdoer; another member of his family will do just as well. But, more fundamentally, the *Lex Talionis* ('an eye for an eye' etc.) would now commonly be thought only to constitute a necessary condition for punishment, not a sufficient. That is to say, it is thought right only to punish a guilty man and even then only to the degree of seriousness of his crime when compared with other sentences being meted out. This is what the legal philosopher Herbert Hart has labelled 'retribution in distribution'.[23] That is, the defensible element in retribution is the idea of fairness in sentencing, not the necessity that a sentence be imposed. In other words, some further justification is required, such as reformation of the criminal or deterring others, before one has sufficient moral entitlement to act against the criminal, no point being served by the imposition of further suffering simply for its own sake. But, if most of us think like that in respect of the ordinary human situation, how much more so is it reasonable to expect it of a loving and forgiving God? Personally, I find such an objection conclusive against Calvin. But intriguingly, Barth moves the notion of the fitness of the punishment from the objective to the psychological realm. It is not that the Father must punish someone. It is that we become aware of our deserts through our realization of what was done to Christ. But, however much it might strengthen one's devotion to Christ the more one thought one had been 'let off', the objection remains that such an approach encourages an inadequate view of the nature and necessity of punishment and with it of God.

That brings me to my final objection, which is simply that the penal approach distorts our view of God. At least Calvin, unlike Luther, tried to give his understanding of salvation a future reference with his doctrine of sanctification[24] through the continuing work of the Holy Spirit in our lives. But even so Moltmann with his critique of expiation saw the model's central flaw, its concentration on the past rather than the future of the individual. It almost turns God into some sort of monster elephant who can never quite forgive or forget without something further being done.

But yet for many that is undoubtedly the theory's main merit, the seriousness with which it regards sin and the decisiveness of the measures it offers for eliminating our feelings of guilt. That as Christians we do need to take sin more seriously than we often do, I do not deny. In this context Barth's comments on the life of Christ convicting us of sin are entirely appropriate. The way in which paintings can remind us of this is apposite. In the twentieth century particularly evocative is Stanley Spencer's portrayal of his fellow villagers in Cookham in Berkshire planning the Crucifixion. That in view of the depths of sinfulness even in the best of us, none of us can deserve anything good of God, again cannot be gainsaid. But that is still a long way from admitting that God would therefore be morally justified in imposing upon us something bad or as horribly painful a death as the Crucifixion. To encourage people to expugn their guilt in this way could therefore only result in a very distorted view of God. But yet expugn their guilt they must, if they are to develop psychologically.

So whatever failings the penal theory has, it has at least highlighted one basic requirement of any adequate account, the need to explain how guilt can be expugned.

One person who reacted very strongly against the penal theory was the twentieth-century Swedish theologian Gustaf Aulén, whose *Christus Victor* first appeared in 1931 and has been continuously in print ever since. Jaroslav Pelikan in his Foreword to the second edition rightly describes it as 'a modern classic'.[25] Although its content is almost wholly historical, its significance lies in the way in which it tries to identify a third, more attractive alternative to the two most popular approaches in the modern world, the penal theory (or what Aulén calls 'the Latin theory' because of its alleged continuity with Anselm) and the subjective or moral approach, which I shall discuss shortly in connection with Abelard. This third, forgotten alternative he argues held almost undisputed sway for the first thousand years of the history of the Church and had a brief revival in the thought of Luther. But so much has the notion come to be identified with himself that more often than not it is simply labelled by the title of his book, though two other names are current thanks to Aulén himself. The term 'classic' encapsulates his historical claim about its original pre-eminence, while on first mention it is described as 'dramatic', presumably because of the drama of the events involved: 'This type of view may be described provisionally as the "dramatic". Its central theme is the idea of the Atonement as a Divine conflict and victory; Christ – Christus Victor – fights against and triumphs over the evil powers of the world, the "tyrants" under which mankind is in bondage and suffering.'[26]

His historical analysis could be challenged at a number of different points. For example, it could be argued that Luther's views are really a hotch-potch of different images and much nearer to the penal account than Aulen would have us believe. Likewise, later in this chapter I shall endeavour to say something in defence of Anselm's notion of satisfaction. But for the moment some assessment of this approach in its own right must be offered.

Its most obvious feature is perhaps also its most controversial, its mythological character. At least, it may be said, it takes seriously all those references in Mark's Gospel to Christ's miracles as involving the casting out of demons and the several allusions in St John to his conflict with 'the prince of this world'.[27] Again, one thinks of Paul's talk of Christ triumphing over 'principalities and powers'.[28] Later, patristic writers were to have a field-day in developing these images, particularly through considering possible implications of Mark's phrase 'a ransom for many'. Christ is envisaged as trapping the devil into accepting as a ransom for man the prize of himself which the devil is then unable to hold. Gregory of Nyssa, for example, conceives of the devil as like a ravenous fish that gulps down Christ's flesh as bait when it is offered at the end of a fishing hook.[29] But already in the fourth century his contemporary and fellow Cappadocian, Gregory Nazianzus, was expressing doubts about the appropriateness of the image. What is particularly interesting to note is that his doubts are moral and not linguistic. He objects that the devil cannot be entitled to payment because he is a robber, while the ransom cannot be paid to the Father since he is not the oppressor.[30] Even so, he fails to get to the real heart of the problem, which is the nature of metaphor. I have already suggested that the penal theory developed in part because Paul's language was taken too literally. Much the same can be said here. If I adapt Burns and describe my beloved as a red rose, I will have her general beauty or possibly the ruddiness of her complexion in mind. I certainly will not wish to suggest that everything that is true of a rose is also true of her – for example, that one gets a nasty prick every time one touches her stem/body! So in this case the image may imply no more than the costliness of the sacrifice[31] that brings release from humanity's bondage to sin.

Even with Satan not all New Testament references can have been intended literally.[32] But clearly the success of this account of atonement is going to depend in large measure on whether we can give a non-literal sense to what the New Testament and the patristic period interpreted literally as a conflict with opposing supernatural powers. For, no matter how prepared we are to acknowledge the possibility of their existence (and I certainly am), they are not central to our experience. So Christ's victory, if only interpreted in those terms, could not be seen as having much relevance to us. But there is little difficulty in the way of achieving that aim. For Jesus' story need not be told as a personalized conflict. More fundamental to it is the fact that he battles with evil in every form – the Slaughter of the Innocents, the Temptation in the Wilderness, Peter's challenge (Mark 8, 33), his confrontation with the scribes and Pharisees, Gethsemane, and finally his trial and crucifixion. In the case of the Temptations clearly what is most important is not whether they happened as portrayed but the way in which Jesus thereby overcame temptations to realize a very different sort of messiahship. Again, whether or not Jesus was aware, as Matthew suggests,[33] of supernatural powers available to him which he voluntary forgoes, the key element is not that, but what is defeated on the Cross, any hatred of those who are doing this terrible thing to him.

Such demythologization removes any objection of dualism, the claim that by acknowledging the existence of such evil supernatural powers evil is placed on a par with God. It is an objection that worried Aulén. Not only does he return to it a number of times in *Christus Victor*,[34] he even mentions the issue in a very late work, *Jesus in Contemporary*

Historical Research: 'Jesus speaks without reservation of a power struggle, but there is not the least hint that God's reign was therefore challenged or truncated. When he tells his listeners that he "by the finger of God drives out evil spirits" and that "the kingdom of God is upon you", this in itself is witness to the fact that the reign of God remains intact . . . With this in mind it becomes confusing to speak here, as has often been done, of a "dualistic" viewpoint; "antagonistic" would be a more adequate term.'[35] But in any case such worries, though often voiced, are misplaced since such 'dualism' is at an enormous distance from the relative equality assigned to good and evil in Zoroastrianism or sometimes in Hinduism with its contrast between Vishnu and Śiva.

Much more problematic is whether the appropriateness of the language of battle can survive such demythologization. It is not just that there are no longer any foes consciously plotting Christ's downfall (except perhaps towards the end of his life), it is arguable that images of battle and victory distort the very nature of Christ's response to evil. For there to be a battle there surely must be some common understanding of what weapons may be used and of what would constitute victory. But surely the whole point of Christ's ministry, particularly of his death, was his refusal to agree on terms for conflict. So, for example, when taunted, he refuses to engage in the usual cut and thrust of repartee, but answers not a word. To this it may be objected that all that is happening is that a new and profound sense is being given to the imagery of warfare, a new sense already anticipated by the way in which St John describes the Cross even before the Resurrection as a victory.[36] But this does not seem quite to answer the point. For, no matter how transformed the meaning, 'victory' still suggests some kind of triumph, whereas presumably Christ's attitude must have been, not any feeling of exultation at having defeated someone, but simply sorrow that they thought that there was a battle at all. In other words, to use the imagery suggests a smug sense of superiority, of "them against us", that is entirely inappropriate. At most, one might speak of a victory over oneself, over temptation to behave in a certain way. But this is now so far removed from the original intention of the theory as to constitute a challenge to its legitimacy.

But suppose we let that objection pass, there are still other problems to be faced. The original account was in terms of conflict with demonic forces. Sympathizers with this approach tend to think that we should look for modern equivalents, and certainly there is no shortage of theologians willing to offer possible equivalences. Tillich is one. In his *Systematic Theology* he tells us that 'in the biblical records of Jesus as the Christ . . . Jesus became the Christ by conquering the demonic forces which tried to make him demonic by tempting him to claim ultimacy for his finite nature.' A few pages later this is generalized into a definition of the demonic as 'the elevation of something conditional to unconditional significance'.[37] But I seriously doubt whether this is of much help, if only because it is all too vague about what it is to give unconditional significance to something. A criminal may well abandon his spoils if it is the only way to save a friend, while someone else might be prepared to betray his country if it is the only way of preserving a beautiful painting. But does that mean that in the one case theft has ceased to be a serious wrong, and in the other that beauty has necessarily taken on the character of the demonic? In fact, in so far as the word is used in modern English at all, the 'demonic' denotes no more (and no less) than sustained or obsessional wickedness, such as a particularly cruel crime like the Moors Murders or sustained terror like Nazism. But even supposing the term can be given a satisfactory new significance, there would still be the problem that, if Christ's 'victory' is to mean something to us, his life must have as much to say to us about the petty temptations that are our lot as about evil on the grand scale.

This brings me to a further difficulty. For, while with the penal theory there was no difficulty in comprehending how Christ's bearing of the punishment for sin was supposed to affect ourselves, it is far from clear, particularly once the process of demythologization has begun, how Christ's victory is supposed to help our own. Oscar Cullmann in *Christ and Time*[38] draws a parallel with an event like D-Day in 1944. The decisive victory was won then, though numerous mopping-up operations were still to follow. A problem with this analogy is the way in which it suggests that the contribution of those still under enemy occupation is only marginal. All the real work is being done by the newly landed, advancing army. So a better analogy might be the entry of the United States in the First World War in 1917. This offered assurance of ultimate victory to the Allied troops on the Western front but without any suggestion that their contribution was no longer essential. Yet even with this emendation something is wrong. For in the two wars we can see a necessary connection between the decisive event and the continuing war, whereas it is hard to see what justification we could have for saying that Christ's 'victory' has contributed to the success of all subsequent engagements with evil. Even if we say that an unacknowledged grace is acting on individuals to help them, we still have no reason to claim that essential to its description is some reference to the victorious Christ.

To all such objections Aulén might well reply that all he was offering was an idea, not a properly worked-out theory. Indeed, not only is he careful to talk about the 'classic idea' rather than the classic theory on the grounds that it 'has never been put forward . . . as a rounded and finished theological doctrine; it has always been an idea, a motif, a theme',[39] he attacks both the penal and subjective or moral theory for pursuing an improper 'rationalistic ideal' that 'smooths away all the oppositions (called 'contradictions' on the following page) with which the classic type abounds'.[40] But, while human explanation will inevitably fail at some point before a being as different from ourselves as God, Aulén surely gives up far too easily. For he leaves the most basic question of all unanswered, how Christ can make us 'at-one' with God. It is not enough to say that he did so for himself. So I turn to two medieval philosophers to see if they can help to resolve our present impasse.

Abelard and Anselm

The theory that most incontestably gives humanity a clear role in its own salvation is known under a number of different names, the subjective, moral, or exemplarist theory. Despite a partial anticipation by Abelard (d. 1142) it only really began to achieve popularity in the nineteenth century, presumably in large measure because of the greater emphasis in the Enlightenment and subsequent Romantic Movement on what man of himself could achieve, though another factor must also have been the pervasive sense of optimism that characterized that century. Our own age after two world wars is naturally more pessimistic, but despite this it is still probably the approach that finds the widest appeal among ordinary parishioners. Nor is it hard to understand why. Repelled by the philosophy behind the penal theory and finding the mythological motifs behind the dramatic theory too complex to decode, they are attracted by the sheer simplicity of the idea that salvation consists in responding to the example set by Christ, especially as it is a model that their secular friends will have no difficulty in comprehending.

Probably the most straightforward version of it is to be found in the writings of the nineteenth-century German theologian Albrecht Ritschl (1822–89). In his major work *Justification and Reconciliation* he follows his predecessor Schleiermacher in distancing himself from the penal theory but he adopts an alternative, much more rationalistic account than Schleiermacher with his sympathy for mysticism could ever have accepted. Sin is seen as ignorance rather than conscious opposition to God and even if it were 'active opposition to God's final end, yet persistence in such a course would make the love of God to sinners impossible only if in all cases sin were definitive and conscious opposition to his final end.'[41] Love must thus be the exclusive category in terms of which we understand what happened, and salvation becomes a matter of response to that love when known. So in respect of the two central categories with which the book is concerned he comments: 'In so far as justification is viewed as effective, it must be conceived as reconciliation, of such a nature that . . . the place of mistrust towards God is taken by the positive assent of the will towards God and his saving purpose.'[42] The love displayed by Christ and the necessity for us to make an appropriate response are thus the theory's two key features. It is an approach that earlier this century seemed almost to have achieved the dominant position within theology. Two well-argued defences of it were given in England by R. C. Moberly in *Atonement and Personality* (1901) and Hastings Rashdall in *The Idea of Atonement in Christian Theology* (1919).[43]

Moberly, Rashdall and Ritschl all see their views anticipated in Abelard.[44] But thanks to the pioneering work of Richard Weingart in *The Logic of Divine Love* (1970)[45] this is now regarded as an unjust slur on Abelard's reputation. For Weingart plausibly argues that there are elements in Abelard's account that are incompatible with a purely exemplarist approach, though it is only fair to these later theologians to note that even his most distinguished contemporary, St Bernard of Clairvaux, read him in this light: 'He holds and argues that it must be reduced just to this, that by his life and teaching Christ handed down to men a pattern of life, that by his suffering and death he set up a standard of love. Did he then teach righteousness and not bestow it; reveal love and not infuse it?'[46] The point of the objection is of course that it makes the divine contribution marginal. If our response is sufficient to secure salvation, then what happens is really up to us, not God. Not only that, if we are simply responding to an example, it is unclear why it has to be a divine one. Could not the lives of St Francis of Assisi or of Mother Theresa of Calcutta be just as effective in moving us to action, or, if it be objected that their example has in its turn been inspired by Christ, what are we to say of the lives of the Buddha or of Mahatma Gandhi? Weingart is emphatic that Abelard was not a Pelagian, and quotes one of his sermons to prove the point: 'Because it is not of our own power to accept the chalice of salvation, that is, to share by suffering in the passion of Jesus and by carrying our own cross to follow him, he himself grants this to us by his grace, by which we are redeemed.'[47] That seems clear enough, but Weingart is able to reinforce his case by further examination of the place where Abelard most extensively develops his views on atonement, in his *Commentary on the Epistle to the Romans*. So, for example, Abelard's comment on chapter 8, verse 4 significantly is that 'true love of Christ as God and of our neighbour is compelled, through that supreme benefit which he has shown to us, by condemning sin in us, that is by destroying all guilt and blame through the love that is propagated in us as a consequence of this supreme benefit.'[48] The way in which he speaks of a more than contingent connection between the demonstration of divine love and such love in us through the use of the term 'compellit' (compulsion) does argue for the view that he has more than the mere following of an example in mind. So does the way in which he speaks of love being propagated in us (caritatem . . . nobis propagatam). That it is a divine work within us of which he speaks is reinforced by his acceptance a couple of verses earlier of the medieval identification of the Holy Spirit with love. In other words, to speak of such love at work in us is already to speak of the divine. One last example of this same phenomenon would be the way in which in his commentary on chapter 5 his talk of Christ dying 'in order to propagate the true liberty of love in us' has been preceded by a paraphrase of Paul's reference to 'the Holy Spirit which is given to us' as 'the operation of divine grace being brought to us'.[49]

Yet even so there are still some reasons for lingering doubt about the strength of his commitment to the absolute centrality of such divine action within us. Thus Weingart fails to draw our attention to the fact that he has only one extended discussion of the question of the nature of redemption[50] and in it most space is devoted to attacking ransom and penal views. Indeed, it is notable that in the brief resumé of his own position with which it ends, though movingly expressed, there is still no more explicit an account of how exactly the change is effected is us. All we learn is that we are 'fired' by the divine kindness, which is 'instituted as much by word as by example'.[51] Secondly, though Weingart speaks of 'the importance attributed to the sacraments by Abelard',[52] it is astonishing to find in a medieval thinker that no serious attempt is made to use this means of linking the present transformation of the believer with the past events of Christ's life and death. Admittedly, a reference to the eucharist would have required a digression, but equally there is nothing of importance on baptism, despite Paul's extensive discussion in Romans. We know that on the question of confession he departed considerably from the general medieval view, which brings me to my third reason for doubt. For as we learn from his *Ethics* (also known as *Scito Te Ipsum*) he denied that the power of remitting or retaining sins was passed to the apostles' successors.[53] This is all of a piece with his intentional definition of sin as consent to evil.[54] For in his ethics as a whole the emphasis is very much on free, personal decision, not on any mysterious workings of divine grace. That is why in the end it seems a mistake for Weingart to speak of Abelard's 'mild synergism'.[55] I do not wish to challenge his basic contention that on the Atonement Abelard is more than just an exemplarist. But it is hard not to convict Abelard of failing to do little more than throw out hints of something more, hints that never achieve any detailed exposition and which at any rate superficially appear to be in conflict with his general theory of action.

But, if Abelard himself must be pronounced inadequate, can his general approach be emended to produce a satisfactory account of the Atonement? Certainly, there are elements from his thought that are worth retaining. The penal theory perversely sees Christ's life as only having point in his death. While the dramatic model avoids this objection, it still fails to give significance to the whole of Christ's life. What matters is victory at points of conflict and not all Christ's life can be conceived in these terms. The moral theory at least takes seriously Christ's life as a whole. Another considerable merit is the unparalleled stress placed on divine love as the motive. This must be right if only for the reason that it is impossible otherwise to comprehend such sacrificial interest in man from a being like God of vastly superior powers.

Where improvement is needed is not here but in two other respects. First, a more intimate connection must be made between that past life of Christ and the present work of salvation in us. For otherwise it makes no sense to claim that salvation is essentially a matter of what happened then, that it is a necessary condition without which no contemporary response to love can claim to be complete. But secondly Abelard's insistence on free consent must not divert us from the possibility that grace, while not denying human responsibility, might none the less work in less explicitly rationalistic ways.

To turn at this point to Anselm (d. 1109), who presents the most rational account of the Atonement yet offered, might therefore seem perverse in the extreme. But there are possibilities of development in Anselm's general approach that are seldom appreciated.[56] Before I indicate what these are, obviously something must first be said about his general approach, though without too much detail as I have already provided this elsewhere.[57]

Cur Deus Homo was written in 1097 while Anselm was in exile from England, having quarrelled with the then king, Rufus (i.e. William II) over the rights of the Church. In his Preface he explicitly asserts that his object has been to 'prove by necessary reasons' that, even if we had known nothing of Christ (remoto Christo), salvation would still only have been possible through him. On my analysis there are twenty premises before we reach the final conclusion, but for our purposes here the general structure of the argument will suffice. A concise version of the argument might run as follows: Only a man can (in the sense of 'appropriately') pay satisfaction to God's offended honour; but only God can (in the sense of 'has the power to') offer the requisite satisfaction; therefore for atonement to be effected there was a necessity for someone who was both God and man. In other words, we have an argument from a conceptual analysis of salvation to the necessity of an Incarnation. As for the two senses of 'can', the first involves the notion of appropriateness, the idea that it is fitting that the disgrace of sin should be righted through the same medium as the dishonour was perpetrated, that is, through a human nature. But at the same time in view of the amount of sin perpetrated an infinite dishonour has been done against God; so only God has the power (other sense of 'can') to provide the right degree of satisfaction.

As a formal argument it is unlikely to win much appeal today, even when set out in its full form. There are just too many contentious premises. But it is, I think, worth preserving. Aulén treated it as simply an earlier variant of the penal model, labelling both 'the Latin doctrine'.[58] But this disguises important differences. F. W. Dillistone in *The Christian Understanding of Atonement* draws an effective contrast.[59] Because of its feudal context, Anselm's version is set within the context of civil law whereas Calvin has the more severe analogue of the criminal code. In a key chapter Anselm defines sin as 'nothing else than not to render to God his due' and within the space of a few sentences this has become: 'He who does not render this honour due to God, robs God of his own and dishonours him; and this is sin.'[60] The contrast, put starkly like this, may seem to favour Calvin. After all, it may be said, at least he is working with a notion which we can all still understand and which leaves us in no doubt that sin is being taken seriously. But, if we press Dillistone's comparison further than he does, I think a very different assessment emerges.

The nearest modern equivalent to what Anselm has in mind is a suit for libel or slander, with some distinguished person's sense of honour outraged, and correspondingly large damages demanded. One small advantage of updating the analogue to modern civil law is that it reveals clearly why a substitute makes more sense in one model than in the other. For, no matter how willing an innocent man is to take the place of another, we still think it unjust that the guilty not pay the penalty, where criminal actions are concerned. But we have no such intuitions with civil law. We do not complain if someone else pays the parking fine or even large damages. But it is only a 'small advantage' because probably the major reason for this is that we view such cases less seriously. So, while it helps the analogy in one way, it weakens it in another.

But another advantage is more lasting. For 'damages' suggests reparation, 'making up', rather than punishment, and so is already to move us along rather different lines of thought from Calvin. In short, the key element is the making of amends, the expression of contrition. It is a public act of saying 'sorry' rather than retribution on an evil-doer. It was this feature which I suggest was really central to Anselm's position, and that this is obfuscated if we see him too closely against the developing confessional system of merit of his time, to which in any case he seldom refers.

But, whether historically at the heart of what Anselm is trying to say or not, it is certainly a defensible approach. Intriguingly, it is now the first line of approach in our own penal system. For first offenders of whom there is some hope of reform are now commonly sentenced to so many hours of what is called 'community service'. This normally takes a form similar to their original criminal act, for example graffiti writers painting playground walls. The objective is precisely by these means to arouse in them a feeling that they need to make such amends as they come to realize the amount of trouble and effort they have caused for others. So, paradoxically, as our own society continues to retreat from Calvin's retributive account of punishment, it moves further back in time and closer to Anselm's notion of satisfaction.

But how does this mean that we should conceive Christ's life and death? If it does not seem too trite, let us take up again that image of community service. It attempts to engender in the offender an attitude that comes naturally to most of us when we have done wrong, the desire to give concrete expression to our wish to make amends for the wrong we have done. In the context of a family it can often take quite trivial but none the less significant forms, buying a bunch of flowers or a box of chocolates or even bringing one's partner a cup of tea in bed the morning after a quarrel. Clearly, it is not the scale of the act that is important but what it is attempting to say. It is as though the verbal apology is not enough, and that some further concrete expression is required. Nor is it hard to see why. As embodied beings we feel that we have not given complete expression to our contrition until it has also been concretized in a physical form. Mere speech by itself contains the possibility of reservations, whereas an act with its gestures, its smiles and so forth is much harder to dissemble and so seems to us more fully a true reflection of our dispositions.

Even in the case of enormous crimes such as Nazism proportion in the amends is not the key thing, and so Anselm's argument that an infinite satisfaction was required for human sin is along quite the wrong lines. In the case of the two world wars significantly the 'reparations', so-called, that were sought by the victorious nations were modelled more on notions of retributive justice and were expressed impersonally in monetary terms. But true making of amends is seen most clearly in the acts of individuals doing specific concrete acts, such as helping with the rebuilding of Coventry Cathedral, where no balance of good returned against evil committed is even being attempted. Indeed, surely the major factor in the success of such acts in restoring broken relationships is the way in which the offended partner meets the guilty half-way. Had the people of Coventry simply stood back and waited for the German workers to complete the building, even supposing they were the guiltiest of Nazis (which of course they were not) and so had the most guilt to 'work off', as it were, this would not have had the desired effect but simply intensified their distance and sense of isolation from those to whom they were attempting to make amends. Exactly the same happens in family relationships. The complete success of the symbolic gesture is dependent upon at least some small participatory gesture from the offended party, even if it is only an answering smile. In saying this I am not making the trivial point that there cannot be a fully restored relationship until forgiveness is offered. That is, of course, true. My point rather is that from the guilty partner's perspective what matters is not so much the reception of that forgiveness as the way in which it is offered. So, for example, the graffiti writers are much more likely to appreciate the significance of their act and at the same time feel themselves forgiven, if the janitor of the school concerned joins in painting over the damage. Likewise, if a gang of hooligans are sentenced to community service in the form of tidying up the old-age pensioner's garden which they have vandalized, it will produce one effect if the pensioner stands aloof and watches them work; quite another, if he 'mucks in'. In the former case, they are likely to feel merely that they have 'done their time', whereas in the latter a plausible scenario is that the trade-off will cease to matter and it is the restored relationship which will assume prominence.

The application of all of this to the Atonement is not hard to see. The significance of Christ's sacrifice lies not in its infinite quality but in the way in which God as the offended party has none the less taken the initiative in making the expression of our amends for sin possible. Defenders of the penal theory rightly stress that no account of the Atonment is adequate which fails to deal with the issue of human guilt. But the solution I think lies not in any reference to punishment, but in what such a divine initiative can say to us. On the other hand, to those who are already conscious of their guilt it offers not an unreal obliteration of the past but the invitation to join with Christ in the making of amends to the Father. On the other, it challenges those who know no guilt at one and the same time both to see their guilt as revealed in the initiative taken by God as the innocent party and the way out of that guilt, through sharing in the Incarnate One's making of amends.

But what is it to share in this making of amends? An unsympathetic critic might well argue that all we have here is yet another version of the moral theory. But that would be a mistake. For, though part of what is proposed is certainly that we are envisaged as responding to what Christ has done, it is not primarily under the category of 'loving example'. Rather, we are responding to the innocent Son's participation in what ought to be essentially our task, the making of amends to his Father. Not only that. Our response is properly described as participation, not imitation, and this still further distances the model from the exemplarist theory. For it suggests that, though our consent is still required, what is really important is the divine activity in invading our lives and transforming them in the quality of our sacrificial response.

Nor is this to depart essentially from Anselm's own conception of what happens. Too many readers confine their attention to the highly logical and abstract presentation of *Cur Deus Homo* and forget the very brief but religiously impassioned account of his position in the *Meditation on Human Redemption*, written a couple of years later in 1099. There he certainly sees mystical incorporation into Christ as the only appropriate response to what he has done. He ends with the plea: 'O Lord, draw my whole self into your love . . . Let your love seize my whole being; let it possess me completely.'[61] Moreover, this is pre-eminently to be achieved through the sacrament of Communion: 'O man, let your heart feed upon these thoughts, let it chew continually upon them, let it suck upon them and swallow them whenever your mouth receives the body and blood of your Redeemer. In this life make these thoughts your daily bread, your nourishment, your provision. For through these thoughts and only through them will you remain in Christ and Christ in you.'[62]

In the next chapter we shall examine what sense can be given to this language of sacramental incorporation. But in the meantime the second half of this chapter will try to set the issue in the wider context of the social dimension of salvation as a whole. It is interesting to observe that even that most moralistic of exemplarist theologians, Ritschl, found it necessary to stress the social aspect. 'The individual can experience the peculiar effect which proceeds from Christ only in connexion with the community founded by him and on the presupposition of its existence . . . For religion is always social.'[63] But even so this is still at an enormous distance from Anselm's mystical approach, which of course dates back ultimately to St Paul himself, with Christ envisaged as our Head and us the Body of restored humanity, and is best represented in subsequent theology by Irenaeus' notion of recapitulation.[64]

But for many modern theologians even that would still not go far enough in the direction of the social. So I shall turn now to what is perhaps the best-known contemporary group within that perspective, and attempt to assess what contribution it might make to our understanding.

The social context – Salvation

Liberation Theology

The northern hemisphere has in the last decade or so become conscious of Latin America to a degree that could scarcely have been envisaged prior to the last war. Nor is this simply because it is a subcontinent in turmoil, though that is true enough. There has been an astonishing literary flowering. Not only does one think of the range of poets displayed, for example, in *The Penguin Book of Latin American Verse*,[65] of whom Pablo Neruda is of course the most famous, there is an exceedingly rich variety of talented novelists, ranging from the lively plots of the Brazilian Jorge Amado and the Peruvian Mario Vargas Llosa through the more reflective writing of people like the Mexican Carlos Fuentes or the Colombian Gabriel Garciá Márques to the frankly experimental conceptions of the Argentinian Jorge Luis Borges and the Cuban Guillermo Cabrera Infante.[66] I mention this fact because so often the growth of Liberation Theology is attributed solely to the impetus given to it by the Conference of Latin American bishops held at Medellin in 1968, the formative influence on whom in turn is seen as being the Second Vatican Council (1962–5). But, while both undoubtedly played their part, one should not discount the wider cultural framework of the growing self-confidence of this part of the world.

First, the meaning of the term must be explained. The Brazilian Hugo Assmann puts it like this in his *Practical Theology of Liberation*: 'The historical incidence of the language of "liberation" in the Latin American Church is linked to growing awareness of our situation as oppressed peoples. It began to make its presence strongly felt from 1965 onwards, when theories of development were first disclosed in their true neo-capitalist light. Underlying liberation theology is the historical experience of the actual nature of under-development, as a form of dependence.'[67] In other words, what is being rejected is an externally imposed solution to the poverty of the great mass of the people in the region, and in its place comes the suggestion that the initiative should come from the people themselves. This conception is central, and the doyen of the movement, the Peruvian Gustavo Gutierrez, even devotes an entire chapter of his highly influential *A Theology of Liberation* to drawing the contrast between liberation and development, with the former alone guaranteeing the idea of man as 'the master of his own destiny'.[68]

Despite the appropriation of the one term by guerilla movements and the ossification of the other into exclusively religious contexts, etymologically 'liberation' and redemption mean the same thing, being freed from something, and so that a particular claim is being made about the nature of salvation is not in doubt. The traditional answer about what it is one is being freed from is 'sin'. Guiterrez and his fellow liberationists use the same category, but very much move it from the area of the personal to the social. So Guiterrez writes: 'Sin is evident in oppressive structures, in the exploitation of man by man, in the domination and slavery of peoples, races and social classes. Sin appears, therefore, as the fundamental alienation, the root of a situation of injustice and exploitation . . . Sin demands a radical liberation, which in turn necessarily implies a political liberation.'[69] In chapter 3 I argued that an appropriate modern sense for original sin is to identify it with the social influences that pressurize us, often unknowingly, into doing what is objectively wrong. So to that degree I have already acknowledged a social dimension to sin. But how much further we should go along this road can only properly be answered by looking at the question of the extent to which the correlative concept of salvation should be conceived in essentially political or social terms.

Gutierrez is in no doubt. 'The liberation of Israel is a political action. It is the breaking away from a situation of despoliation and misery and the beginning of the construction of a just and fraternal society.'[70] A few pages later he tells us that 'the Exodus experience is paradigmatic. It remains vital and contemporary due to similar historical experiences which the People of God undergo.'[71] Nor is it just Liberation Theology that finds the story of the Exodus central to what salvation means. Much the same can be said of the Black Theology that it has influenced. So, for example, Allan Boesak in his book *Black Theology – Black Power* writes; 'Nothing is more central to the Old Testament proclamation than the message of liberation. God's history with Israel is a history of liberation. Yahweh's great act of liberation forms the content of the life and faith, the history and confession of Israel, and by this name he wants to be evoked for all generations to come (Ex. 3, 15). The name by which Yahweh reveals himself is YHWH – the one who is active, who is and is present, who shall free his people.'[72]

Given the frequent reference back in Old Testament writers to the Exodus as pivotal, as well as the numerous prophetic denunciations of injustice,[73] it would be hard to challenge this as a plausible reading of the Old Testament. But the New might be thought to be quite a different matter. Edward Norman certainly thought so in his 1978 Reith Lectures, *Christianity and the World Order*, in which he offers a critique of political theology, including Liberation Theology. 'In the Gospels', he declares, 'the teachings of the Saviour clearly describe a personal rather than a social morality.'[74] Gutierrez devotes a surprisingly small proportion of his book to Jesus, but he does try to redress the balance a little by, for example, arguing that Luke's absolute version of the Beatitude, 'Blessed are the poor',[75] must be accepted as having profound ramifications. 'If we believe that the Kingdom of God is a gift which is received in history . . . then we must believe that Christ says that the poor are blessed because the Kingdom of God has begun. "The time has come; the Kingdom of God is upon you" (Mark 1, 15). In other words, the elimination of the exploitation and poverty that prevent the poor from being fully human has begun.'[76] Similarly, the Mexican José Miranda finds himself using predominantly the Old Testament to bolster his case for parallels between Marxist and Biblical notions in his *Marx and the Bible*. But some interesting points are made about Jesus' teaching. So, for example, he interprets the camel and eye of a needle passage as unqualifiedly directed against 'differentiating ownership as such',[77] he argues (more plausibly than in the previous case) that the reference in the Beatitudes to 'Your reward is great in heaven' was intended to have a this-world rather than other-worldly realization,[78] and, as a final instance, he observes that 'it is striking that the precept of Lev. 19: 18 – "You must love your neighbour as yourself" – which plays such a central role in the preaching of Jesus and in the whole New Testament, is given its original vital place as a synthesis of a series of prohibitions which all concern the most rigorous justice.'[79]

But because the Exodus provides such a clear answering chord to the Latin American situation it is really only when a Liberation theologian devotes an entire book to the significance of Christ that one gets a rounded picture of how the view might be defended that Jesus' intentions were essentially social and political. In an early book, *Jesus Christ Liberator*, in which he tells us that he had to be circumspect because of the political conditions prevailing in Brazil at the time (1972), Leonardo Boff's strategy is none the less quite apparent. Jesus' teaching is seen to revolve round the notion of the Kingdom of God, which is 'not to be in another world, but is the old world transformed into a new one',[80] and this means a total and not just a personal transformation. A subsection in the chapter on the death of Jesus is headed 'Jesus is condemned as a Blasphemer and a Guerilla'. In the later Epilogue the plausibility of the accusation that he was 'a guerilla fighter' is underlined by the comment that 'his preachings and his outlook brought him close to the liberation project of the Zealots', though it is conceded that for Jesus 'the kingdom entails a more radical liberation, one that gets beyond the breakdown of brotherhood.'[81] Again, so far as later christological reflection is concerned, it is intriguing to see what Boff makes of the Infancy Narratives. The Virgin Birth is discounted. But Matthew parallels Jesus' early infancy with Moses', and so makes him 'the new Moses and the definitive liberator', while for Luke, because the shepherds, 'a despised class . . . impure before the law', are 'the first to hear the joyful message of liberation', Christ 'was sent precisely to the religiously marginalised and the classless'.[82]

Some of these themes recur in Jon Sobrino's *Christology at the Crossroads*, written in war-torn El Salvador. In his 'Theses for an Historical Christology' he stresses that Jesus' eventual condemnation for blasphemy and not heresy and his actual execution as a political rebel are but the culmination of a life in which 'the crisis of Jesus' consciousness was mediated through his external conflicts. It was embodied in his opposition to those who wielded religious, economic and social power.'[83] Perhaps the following passage may be used to summarize the nature of his argument: 'Strikingly enough, his harshest condemnations are not directed against the individual sinners . . . they are directed against the collective sins that create a situation contrary to the kingdom . . . There is poverty because the rich do not share their wealth. There is religious oppression because the priests impose intolerable burdens on people . . . There is political oppression because the rulers rule despotically. In short, the sinfulnes of these people is not something that affects only the subjective life of the individual; it is visibly crystallized in the social realm. Jesus' condemnations against these various groups of sinners clearly suggest a desire to re-create the social situation, not just the concrete individual sinner.'[84]

The general tenor of the argument should by now be clear. Obviously this is not the place to pursue the details of New Testament exegesis. That Jesus was concerned to attack private property as such, as Miranda claims, just seems to me absurd, as does Boff's attempt to extract religious significance out of the fact that Jesus was executed as a guerilla fighter (it was after all only a trumped-up charge used to secure his death). But such faults should not blind us to undoubted merits of Liberation Theology in redressing the balance in our picture of Jesus. Personal transformation may have been the primary direction of his message, but his far from deferential attitude to existing authorities and his constant reaching out to those on the margins of society certainly argue for a desire to see that personal transformation issue in what would also be a social revolution. Indeed, even Cardinal Joseph Ratzinger in his critique of the movement, *Libertatis Nuntius*, does not hesitate to concede that 'crushing poverty' is 'an intolerable violation of man's native dignity' and of the document itself he advises that 'this warning should in no way be interpreted as a disavowal of all those who want to respond generously and with an authentic evangelical spirit to the "preferential option for the poor".'[85] What he goes on to say he objects to is when that social emphasis becomes exclusive or primary. 'To demand first of all a radical revolution in social relations and then to criticise the search for personal perfection is to set out on a road which leads to the denial of the person and his transcendence.'[86] Later in this section I shall quote some rather horrific instances of this, with Christ's stress on the unique worth of each individual abandoned in favour of social goals. But that this is an inherent danger in Liberation Theology should not blind us to the fact that there is this strong social dimension to the Gospel. Practically speaking, in situations of acute oppression and poverty the individuals concerned may well be so deadened by suffering and toil that it is well-nigh impossible to effect a personal conversion without first doing something to transform their social position.

But, if in this respect Ratzinger can provide a useful corrective to one-sided emphases on the social dimension, the second half of the document's unqualified attack on the possibility of any borrowings from Marxism seems quite wrong-headed. Ratzinger puts his argument succinctly, by observing that in Marxism 'the ideological principles come prior to the study of the social reality and are presupposed in it. Thus no separation of the parts of this epistemologically unique complex is possible. If one tries to take only one part, say, the analysis, one ends up having to accept the entire ideology.'[87] It is a pity that Ratzinger's argument is pursued without the mention of any names or examples. For in practice what one finds is the very eclecticism he has pronounced impossible. Not only, for example, are Marx's ideas on materialism or the inevitability of history seldom mentioned, in terms of sources the number of references to Marx is not all that great, and later twentieth-century revisionist Marxists such as Bloch or Althusser can bulk as large, with even modern German political theologians such as Metz (who are of course themselves indebted to the Marxist tradition) sometimes achieving equal prominence.

In fact, what seems to be worrying Ratzinger is an idea which, though it can take a Marxist form, is equally insidious when it occurs in its empirical, pragmatic form, namely the notion that the 'truth' or worth of an idea is to be judged solely by its practical consequences. One need only recall the way in which in the English-speaking world the term 'theological' is used, for example by trade union leaders, as a term of abuse to denote abstruse discussions without practical relevance or, more generally, how often on any issue, even when it is conceded that such and such is true, one is then met with the response: 'But, so what? What does it matter?' Since this is an issue that affects not only our understanding of salvation but the even more basic question of how truth in religion is to be ascertained, it is a subject whose importance can scarcely be underestimated, and that therefore makes its entirely proper that we spend not only the rest of our discussion of Liberation Theology looking at this issue but also allow the question to crop up again in the subsequent philosophical section.

'In this perspective orthodoxy . . . is substituted by the notion of orthopraxy as the criterion of truth.'[88] So writes Ratzinger. But it is surprising how seldom Liberation theologians make so stark a claim about the priority of right action over right belief. Normally there are some qualifications, though I would agree with Ratzinger to this extent, that they are then not taken sufficiently to heart in what they go on to say about the nature of the Christian faith. Admittedly, Boff is not someone who exhibits such caution. He heads one section 'The Primacy of Orthopraxis over Orthodoxy', and in his Epilogue he can even write that 'the real question is who or what cause is served by a given Christology.'[89] Gutierrez, however, is much more cautious,[90] and Juan Luis Segundo's *The Liberation of Theology* represents a sustained and careful attempt to assess the nature of the relation between the two. On the one hand, he attacks traditional academic theology for pretending to impartiality when it is no more than 'conservative partiality'.[91] Indeed Rahner is even called a Pharisee for failing to appreciate this fact.[92] On the other hand, equally he does not hesitate to criticize his fellow liberationists for supposing that revolutionary commitment can arise without a prior ideology, 'whether it comes from Marx . . . or the gospel message'.[93] In fact, Segundo ends up with quite a complex position according to which, rather than *praxis* simply producing *doxa*, ideologies and *praxis* are always interacting. Faith expresses itself in different ideologies in different historical circumstances, and these perspectives are partly a product of antecedent perspectives and partly of the specific historical situation.[94] This is at any rate more plausible than the simple dogmatic assertion that orthopraxis always precedes orthodoxy.

But where Liberation Theology errs, even I suspect in its more subtle forms, is in assigning too strong a determining role to *praxis*. Indeed, in this I venture to suggest that it makes exactly the same kind of error as its conservative opposite, as in those theologians whom we noted in chapter 1 claiming that it is impossible to do theology without holiness of life. There I pointed out that, while such holiness could (and sometimes does) give rise to religious experience that produces insights not available to the great majority of us who are less open to the divine, this still does not obviate the necessity for some independent assessment of the content of these experiences. For even holiness does not guarantee intellectual rigour in giving a correct analysis of their worth or save the believer from the distorting effect of other prejudices he may have. So similarly in this case, one can still do the right action for the wrong reason. Indeed precisely because one has failed to take the issue of right belief (orthodoxy) seriously enough, one may be led to perform actions that are totally counter-productive to the desired aim. In fact, what one misses most in Liberation Theology is the recognition that it is only by maintaining the relative independence of orthodoxy and orthopraxis that theology can exercise a truly challenging and independent function. For, so long as we claim that truth is independent of action, there will always be, potentially at least, features of that truth that can exercise a critique of our current practices and commitment.

An extreme example of the failure of some Liberation theologians to allow theology to act as a critique of praxis is to be found in the conduct of the poet-priest Ernesto Cardenal, currently a member of the Sandinista government in Nicaragua. In *The Gospel in Solentiname* he describes at length his work prior to the revolution among the island community for which he was pastorally responsible. His aim was *concientización*, to make the impoverished islanders more aware of their rights, something that is being attempted throughout Latin America in small family groups, known as *commundades eclesiales de base*. But, though there was certainly much idealism present, the net impression is one of manipulation. In effect Cardenal used his superior intelligence to brow-beat the natives into a reductionist theology in terms of which they could be told things like 'God is the masses' and 'Christ forbade the sword but not the machine gun.'[95] None of this is to deny that the situation in Nicaragua was (and is) appalling[96] and that Christians may well have been justified in joining the Sandinistas in their fight for freedom. What it is to challenge is a purely pragmatic use of the Gospel, whether it be from the right or, as in this case, in order to further Marxism.

Of course, as with feminist theology, one must avoid the danger of treating instances of extremism as representative. But, as our earlier discussion of their treatment of the Biblical text demonstrated, while Liberation theologians offer a useful and important corrective to non-political interpretations, there is a constant temptation for them to overplay their hand and make the whole of the Bible conform to this pattern. Particularly welcome therefore is Jon Sobrino's statement in *Christology at the Crossroads* that 'the basic question is, of course, whether the main interest of liberation theology is Christ or liberation.'[97] Not only does what follows amply demonstrate that he is not simply equating the two, his critique of Chalcedonian christology shows a willingness to call into question all purely secular ideas. 'The crucial point about Christology is that it calls into question the very thing that the natural human being takes completely for granted. Natural human beings assume that they know what human nature is and what divine is.'[98]

If that is the critical pattern of the future, then it will no longer be possible to dismiss Liberation Theology as simply Marxist ideology in Christian dress. Instead, it will have adopted a truly corrective role without having degenerated into the same faults as its conservative opponents.

Marx to Habermas

In the previous section I have already conceded that there is an indispensable social element in any truly Christian concept of salvation. However, we saw how this was reinforced in Liberation Theology by the Marxist claim that truth is inseparable from action, that what we believe is necessarily determined by what we do and how we live. If true, this cannot but have implications for how theology is to be pursued. What I want therefore to do now is assess this claim, first in its original context in Marx's thought and then in its present development in the writings of Germany's greatest living philosopher, Jürgen Habermas.

Karl Marx (1818–83) was a student at the University of Berlin only five years after Hegel's death and, though he progressively moved away from Hegel's own position, even in 1873 he was still prepared to declare himself 'the pupil of that mighty thinker'.[99] In essense he was at the extreme limit of that movement known as Left-Wing Hegelianism that turned the original thought of Hegel on its head. Instead of the world being the locus of the dialectical realization of Spirit (as explained in chapter 2) all things divine are now viewed as human projections, the outworking of the material conditions in which man finds himself. In reaching this position Marx was particularly influenced by Ludwig Feuerbach. He had interpreted Hegel in a pantheistic direction in his early writings, but under the influence of the two Biblical critics F. C. Bauer and D. F. Strauss moved to a position of explicit atheisim in his classic, *The Essence of Christianity* (1841). In that work Feuerbach argues that man, and not God, must be seen as the ultimate subject, with the qualities once projected on to a transcendent God now to be redirected to their proper subject, man. Marx agreed, but went further. Thus in his *Theses on Feuerbach* he comments: 'His work consists in the dissolution of the religious world into its secular basis. He overlooks the fact that after this work is completed the chief thing still remains to be done.'[100] In Marx's view Feuerbach exaggerates religion's importance. He treats it as the cause rather than merely what it is, an expression of man's alienation, which can only be overcome through tackling the underlying social causes; hence the famous sentence with which the *Theses* ends: 'The philosophers have only interpreted the world, in various ways; the point, however, is to change it.'[101]

But, while the initial impetus to Marx's thought developed in this way, it would be a mistake to think that religion played any central role in his concerns. The fact that Reinhold Niebuhr in his collection *Marx and Engels on Religion* not only has to ransack numerous sources but even so has to yield the great majority to Engels should give pause for thought. While it would be pleasant to trace his vision to the lectures on Isaiah that he attended as a university student, there is in fact no evidence that religion ever exercised any fascination for him, unlike his patron and collaborator, Engels, who we know to have been devout in his youth even to the extent of composing a confirmation hymn.[102] But equally one must avoid the danger of the opposite extreme. Significantly, Lenin declared that religion is 'opium for the people',[103] whereas Marx had originally pronounced it 'the opium *of* the people'. In other words, for Lenin it was merely part of the manipulation of the people by the ruling class, whereas for Marx, though false, it is none the less a self-chosen expression of the people's despair, as the context as a whole makes abundantly clear: 'Religious distress is at the same time the expression of real distress and the protest against real distress. Religion is the sigh of the oppressed creature, the heart of a heartless world, just as it is the spirit of a spiritless situation. It is the opium of the people.'[104] But, that conceded, he immediately goes on to deny religion any objective reality: 'The abolition of religion as the illusory happiness of the people is required for their real happiness. The demand to give up the illusions about its condition is the demand to give up a condition which needs illusions.' Intriguingly, as a result the significance of the Reformation is seen in social rather than theological terms. It marks the transition between alienation as an external problem to one within the individual himself: 'Luther, we grant, overcame bondage out of devotion by replacing it by bondage out of conviction . . . He freed the body from chains, because he enchained the heart . . . It was no longer a case of the layman's struggle against the priest outside himself but of his struggle against his own priest within himself.'[105]

Though some have argued for a strong continuity in his thought,[106] the publication in 1932 of his *Economic and Philosophical Manuscripts* of 1844 is commonly thought to have revealed a Marx less committed to a deterministic view of social development and one more appealing to Christianity. So, for example, Miranda quotes them to show that Marx too saw the greatest human fulfilment in love of neighbour: 'Poverty is the passive bond which causes the human being to experience the need of the greatest wealth – the other human being.'[107] Likewise, there have been attempts on the Marxist side to detect more sympathetic features in Christianity. One particularly impressive example of this is the Czech philosopher Milan Machoveč's *A Marxist Looks at Jesus*. He acknowledges the implausibility of describing someone like John XXIII as simply 'a dispenser of opium to the people'[108] and in the demythologized account of Jesus that follows his teaching is portrayed as making 'the maximum demand on man', a demand that precludes it being spoken of as opium, though it was subsequently so used.[109] Similarly in France Roger Garaudy until his expulsion from the

Communist Party attempted various reconciling moves. Indeed, even after that point there emerged from his pen *The Alternative Future* (1972), a book roughly contemporary with Machoveč's, in which he argues for what he calls Christian Marxism. In it he sees the Marxist as committed to 'methodological atheism' rather than 'metaphysical',[110] that is, to the denial of the presence of God unless accompanied by appropriate praxis. Once again the opium passage is qualified, this time as follows: 'Religion is an "opiate" whenever, in affirming that an eternal life beyond history and beyond this life is essential, it devalues the problems of this life and the struggles of history.'[111]

But precisely because both books concentrate on the shared goal rather than the difficulties on the way, they fail to identify what I think is the heart of Marx's challenge to Christian theology. For it is one thing to concede that salvation necessarily must have a social dimension; quite another that our ability to perceive what that social dimension ought to be is likely to be systematically distorted by the conditions under which we live. For to admit the latter is to put us permanently in a position of suspicion, not only of ourselves and our own motives but also of the religious authorities on whom we rely, whether they be Bible, charismatic leader, or pope. One consequence is the way in which Boff has been led to challenge the nature of the exercise of ecclesiastical authority in his recent *Church, Charism and Power*. His alternative vision of an authority that stems from below through 'free and spontaneous acknowledgement',[112] I do not find unwelcome. But this should not deflect us from the more basic question of methodology, namely whether the assessment of a belief can be successfully disentangled from the interests with which it is held.

One recent writer to offer a pessimistic verdict is Denys Turner in his *Marxism and Christianity*. He sees the ideological false consciousness everywhere – in the authoritarian lecturer preaching anti-authoritarian ideals, in the preacher's condescension from the pulpit, the servant identifying herself only through her 'betters', and in our society's stress on tolerance as a way of suppressing real class conflicts.[113] This leads him to assert what he calls his 'identity thesis', that 'morality is Marxism'. By this he means that only in a society in which such distortions cease to exist, in which social perception and social reality coincide, could there be 'immediate, unproblematic criteria of action available'.[114] But in the meantime because there are no eternal human needs[115] no precise concrete form of that towards which one is aiming can be envisaged. So Marxism, far from being 'a rival set of answers to bourgeois moral questions', is merely 'the condition of the possibility of morality'.[116] Christianity however, is seen as 'strongly compatible' with such Marxism. Here his meaning is less clear. The explanation appears to be that Christianity also makes fundamental reference to an unrealized future, with the presence of God currently 'taking the form of his absence', that is, only a symbolic or sacramental form.[117]

But this is to concede altogether too much to Marx. In the first place, Turner writes as though 'class conflict' and 'bourgeois morality' were the obvious terms in which to analyse our society. He gives no definition of them, and yet twentieth-century Europe is very different from Marx's own day. Indeed, are not trade union leaders sometimes as manipulative as employers in using their members as fodder for political ends, as perhaps in the 1984 British miners' strike? Secondly, it is absurd to reduce all morality to Marxist-type questions of exploitation. Major moral issues can arise between equals, between friends or colleagues. Finally, it is unnecessarily pessimistic to judge everything by a future but impossible ideal. Of course, our judgements may not be as disinterested as we imagine. But that is only an argument for caveats against all we say. The provisional can still be reasonably secure, the more so if we are on our guard against distortions of our beliefs by our material situation.

A much more balanced answer to Marx's challenge is in fact given by Nicholas Lash in *A Matter of Hope*. While denying that he stands in the Marxist tradition because he finds it too much of an overall unity,[118] not only does he take Marx's challenge seriously, he argues that Marx stands somewhat closer to a position acceptable to Christianity than is commonly thought. So on the issue that concerns us here, his famous remark in *The German Ideology* that 'it is not consciousness that determines life, but life that determines consciousness',[119] he argues over two chapters[120] against the 'orthodox' interpretation that this was intended as a commitment to reductionist materialism. The 'base' conditions, rather than determines, the 'superstructure'. In other words, room is left for a human response to such pressures. Whether he is right or not in his interpretation of Marx, this does not lessen the importance he sees in Marx's challenge. For instance, it raises the question whether any revelation can be 'given and is not merely the product of human construction',[121] or in respect of the Incarnation whether 'there could exist or has ever existed an individual in whom "reality" and "appearance" wholly corresponded.'[122] He answers 'yes' to both questions, but argues that Christianity can only dare to do so for so long as it exercises a 'subversive rather than a legitimatory role' through recalling its 'iconoclastic resources',[123] the provisional character of all human images and aspirations.

Max Horkheimer (d. 1973) took a similar view. In his *Critical Theory* he writes: 'The concept of God was for a long time the place where the idea was kept alive that there are other norms besides those to which nature and society give expression in their operation . . . But the more Christianity brought God's rule into harmony with events in the world, the more the meaning of religion became perverted.'[124] Horkheimer was the only major figure in the Frankfurt School[125] to show strong sympathy to Christianity. This term (only coined in the 1950s) is used to refer to the ideas which emerged from the Institut für Sozialforschung, founded at Frankfurt in 1923. Probably the two best-known names associated with the School are Eric Fromm and Herbert Marcuse. But in terms both of general philosophical stature and of importance for theology it is Theodor Adorno (d. 1970) and Walter Benjamin (d. 1940) who spring most readily to mind. Their contribution will be discussed in chapter 6. For the moment all we need note is the general character of the School, indicated by Horkheimer's use of the expression 'critical theory'. For, while Marx is used as a starting-point, he was far from slavishly obeyed. Adorno, for instance, in *Negative Dialectics* rejects the 'primacy of practice'.[126]

Jürgen Habermas (b. 1929) can legitimately be seen as the present-day successor of that tradition, and indeed he does not hesitate to acknowledge his debt to the School.[127] Though like his predecessors he has abandoned much of the traditional Marxism, he does take the Marxist challenge about the nature of knowledge seriously. However, his response has been very different from that of Adorno. The latter retreated into pessimism. But Habermas is a very different character. His optimism has never really been shaken as over the years he has progressively built up his system of rationality to take account of the Marxist critique. I shall first outline how this has developed before going on to identify three specific areas where his response has a negative thrust against theology.

An important stage in the process, and probably still his best-known book, is *Knowledge and Human Interests* (1968). In his Introduction he tells us that even as late as Kant 'the comprehensive rationality of reason that becomes transparent to itself has not yet shrunk to a set of methodological principles', whereas now we have 'scientism', 'the conviction that we can no longer understand science as one form of possible knowledge, but rather must identify knowledge with science'.[128] The first part of the book is then concerned to demonstrate from scientists themselves and philosophers of science that science is not entitled to this august status. There is no single scientific method and in any case each inquiry is governed by some 'interest', interests that are intimately linked to questions of social life. He then turns to its despised cousin, the human sciences particularly as exemplified in the writings of Dilthey, and attempts to show that they too derive their rationale from a 'practical interest' in intersubjective understanding. Both thus need to be assessed not just in terms of instrumental success but also in terms of those interests.[129] This, it should be emphasized, does not mean that selfishness lies at the base of knowledge, but rather that what we can know is dependent on the sorts of interests we have, selfish or otherwise. The final part of the book is then devoted to one way in which self-reflection can be improved, through Freudian analysis. This is a particularly strong case of interest preceding knowledge, since 'the experience of reflection is the only criterion for the corroboration or failure of hypotheses', that is, 'the interpretation of a case is corroborated only by the successful continuation of a self-formative process.'[130] In other words, it is only the patient seeing point in the treatment that can confirm the analysis.

This synopsis may suggest a highly subjective view of knowledge. But one needs to recall that his ultimate aim is the identification of the non-instrumental underpinning of our knowledge. Interests, as the 1978 Appendix makes clear, he sees as 'grounded in deeply rooted [invariant?] structures of action and experience – i.e. in the constituent elements of social systems'.[131] Indeed, one might plausibly claim that all his writing after *Knowledge and Human Interests* is directed towards just such a universal theory of rationality. Certainly, not long afterwards it was Freud's contribution towards producing a shared social perspective that he was stressing, that is, the way in which through analysis 'insight can coincide with emancipation from unrecognised dependencies.'[132]

Habermas' more recent position may be described as having three tiers. At the most basic and perhaps most important level we have his contrast between the instrumental which merely aims at success and the more reflective activity which he calls 'communicative action', whose aim is understanding. He puts it thus in *Communication and the Evolution of Society*: 'The goal of coming to an understanding is to bring about an agreement that terminates in the intersubjective mutuality of reciprocal understanding, shared knowledge, mutual trust, and accord with one another.'[133] He takes as integral to such communicative action the idea that 'the speaker also enters into a speech-act-immanent obligation, namely the obligation to prove trustworthy (*Bewahrungsverpflichtung*).'[134] This explains his interest in the speech–act theories of the analytic philosophers Austin and Searle.

But such communication ideals can go wrong, and so the next tier of Habermas' analysis is to produce a generally theory of the acquisition of communicative competence that will not only undergird our interest in such communication but also explain how we can be deflected from such an interest. This explains the attention he devotes to the theories of Chomsky on the acquiring of linguistic competence and of Piaget and Kohlberg on moral competence. Such excursions into psychological theories enable him to identify key stages where things may go wrong, as also the characteristic forms they may take, such as defence mechanisms.[156] However, in so far as he uses such theories to bolster knowledge claims in communicative action, he has been criticized for committing the naturalistic fallacy, for supposing that non-moral facts can of themselves be used to justify evaluative ideals such as his own of universal undistorted communication. His response has been to follow Kohlberg and speak of the psychological theories confirming moral claims rather than actually justifying them.[136] He also suggests that such theories are neither strictly empirical nor transcendental but reconstructive analyses.[137] Though not open to any very straightforward empirical testing, they are none the less in principle refutable by experience.

Then at the last tier we have his theory of social evolution, which he offers as his version of historical materialism. This is a preoccupation that is particularly prominent in his most important, recent work *The Theory of Communicative Action*. There discussion of sociologists such as Weber, Mead, Durkheim and Talcott Parsons bulks large. Once again, as with the psychological theories, so here a reconstruction of the evolution of society is seen as offering further support rather than justification of the values enshrined in this knowledge that arises from free, undistorted, universal communication. It is because the entire sweep of history can be seen as having been moving in the direction of acceptance of such values that we can have greater assurance in endorsing them. But there is an additional reason for his interest in sociological theory. As he puts it in *Legitimation Crisis*: 'What is demanded is a level of analysis at which the connection between normative structures and steering problems becomes palpable. I find this level in a historically oriented analysis of social systems, which permits us to ascertain for a given case the range of tolerance within which the goal system might vary without its continued existence being critically endangered.'[138] This is an important issue for Habermas. For while he welcomes the situation in which all norms are capable of being challenged, he views our modern situation as potentially destructive as it is creative, since we can have 'no metaphysical guarantee' that it will not lead to the destruction of communicative structures.[139]

This account of Habermas' developed position may strike readers as having a more Kantian than Marxist ring with its emphasis on rationality and universalisability in the ideal speech situation. That there is this Kantian dimension cannot be denied. Indeed so much of Marx's thought is challenged that some may be puzzled why Habermas should continue to be seen as within the Marxist tradition at all. For example, he declares that 'Marx does not actually explicate the interrelationship of interaction and labour, but instead, under the unspecific title of social praxis, reduces the one to the other, namely communicative action to instrumental action.'[140] Again, in a time of considerable government intervention in all Western economies he finds Marx's economic analysis as expressed in his distinction between 'base' and 'superstructure' no longer plausible: 'It becomes inapplicable when the "base" has to be comprehended as in itself a function of governmental activity and political conflict . . . the power structure can no longer be criticized immediately at the level of relations of production.'[141] Another claim of Marx that is rejected is his view that it is socially organized labour that distinguishes man from animals; Habermas finds this also in hominids and suggests that the really crucial difference is the family structure that generates a number of different social roles.[142] As a final and more fundamental point of difference, we may take the following: 'What today separates us from Marx are evident historical truths, for example that in the developed capitalist societies there is no identifiable class, no clearly circumscribed social group which could be singled out as the representative of a general interest that has been violated.' Here his point is that 'underprivileged groups are not social classes, nor do they even potentially represent the mass of the population.'[143] With all these points of divergence it might be hard to see where his Marxist heritage lies, but fortunately Habermas states it concisely for us: 'Marx set out his theory in such a way that he could perceive and take up the trial of reason in the deformations of class society. Had he not found in proletarian forms of life the distortion of a communicative form of life as such, had he not seen in them an abuse of a universal interest reaching beyond the particular, his analysis would have been robbed of the force of justified critique . . . Like Marx's, my theoretical approach is guided by the intention of recovering a potential for reason encapsulated in the very forms of social reproduction.'[144]

Sufficient characterization of his general position has now been given for me to narrow the focus to three specific areas where his response to Marx has negative implications for theology.

The first concerns the fact that despite his search for a universal rationality all that he believes is possible is consensus, not an objectivity that guarantees correspondence with the external world. In *Theology and the Philosophy of Science* Wolfhart Pannenberg discusses the implications of this for theology. On the one hand he attacks the role Habermas assigns in *Knowledge and Human Interests* to instincts in producing communicative rationality: 'This takes no account of the fact that the instincts themselves (and not just their "interpretation") are historically mediated by the socio-cultural environment.'[145] This is a criticism that Habermas can claim to have attempted to answer by his subsequent support for psychological reconstruction theories that defend invariant features of human nature. But Pannenberg's other objection still stands: 'A pure consensus theory of truth . . . is incapable of accounting for the distinction between a consensus in truth and a prevailing convention.'[146] Why a Christian should want to say that truth is more than consensus is not hard to fathom. For we would want to say that there is a being corresponding to our belief that God exists even if no one believed us, far less there being a general consensus about the matter.

Habermas' response is to say that such correspondence theories of truth 'attempt in vain to break out of the sphere of language'.[147] Our only access to truth, he argues, is through the dialogue and argumentation that takes place within language. The effect of this is to turn truth into the approximation of an ideal in so far as consensus is reached, but Habermas is willing to accept this implication especially as life is full of other ideals, moral, political and religious, where such approximation is acceptable. In this attitude he has recently received support from an American philosopher writing within the analytic tradition. Richard Berstein argues in *Beyond Objectivism and Relativism* that much recent Anglo-Saxon philosophy is tending so much in the same direction that it is possible to speak of a convergence. Thus along with the writings of Gadamer and Habermas he examines the works of Thomas Kuhn and Richard Rorty and suggests that what they share is more significant than where they differ. All reject Cartesian foundationalism, the search for a single, secure foundation to our knowledge. But equally the result is not pure relativism. Instead, in a position 'beyond objectivism and relativism' they all accept a consensus approach to knowledge. So, for example, Rorty in Habermasian terms runs as follows: 'For him this means we must honestly accept the radical contingency of the social practices that define what we are, that our task is to cope with these and to keep open the possibility of dialogue and conversation. To say that these social practices are radically contingent does not mean that they are arbitrary.'[148] My own suspicion is that it would be more accurate to speak of a sliding scale of relativism with Habermas at the most objectivist end. But even so I think we must still protest that, even if this is the best way of discovering the truth, there is more to truth than simply human agreement. Not only is there a world independent of that consensus, there is a God independent of that world.

Schillebeeckx in his much shorter book *The Understanding of Faith* chooses to concentrate on a different problem. The Introduction implicitly endorses Habermas by declaring that 'truth is inwardly orientated towards universal consent . . . within the framework of free dialogue.'[149] But later in the book one criticism is offered, that Habermas' theory by concentrating on present consensus fails to take the past seriously enough. Following Metz, he suggests that the past has the possibility of being 'a subversive memory'.[150] The point here is that Habermas in developing his consensus theory of truth assigns no continuing creative role to the past. The consensus is to be achieved in dialogue with humanity today, not past generations. Yet clearly for theology certain events and persons in the past continue to play an indispensable role.

Another theologian influenced by Metz who explores this issue in much more depth is Helmut Peukert. In *Science, Action, and Fundamental Theology* he begins by noting the way in which so many modern theories have been 'unclosed . . . systems', giving examples such as Russell's paradox and Gödel's incompleteness theorem.[151] He then raises the question whether this may not be equally true of Habermas' communication theory, with which he is none the less in general sympathy. Where its incompleteness emerges is in its attitude to past generations. Peukert asks whether, if one accepts with Habermas 'unconditioned and universal solidarity with others . . . as the constitutive condition of one's being human . . . one can retain the memory of the conclusive, irretrievable loss of the victims of the historical process, to whom one owes one's entire happiness . . . Is this not tantamount to the betrayal of the very solidarity by which alone one is able to discover oneself?'[152] Peukert refers us to a debate between Horkheimer and Benjamin,[153] in which the latter insists that the past cannot be allowed to remain simply past but there must be what was later dubbed 'anamnetic solidarity' with those who would have otherwise suffered in vain. Peukert thinks that what this 'unclosed' element of communicative action shows is the need to raise the question of resurrection. Habermas in response admits that 'Benjamin's reflection has its place here', but seems to think 'compassionate solidarity with the despair of the tormented' is enough. At the same time he does concede that, though not fundamentally undermining his theory, it does raise the question of what are the appropriate limits to communicative discourse.[154]

As for what we are to make of all this, it surely has to be admitted that Peukert has a point. Certainly he goes too far in suggesting that such reflections must raise the question of resurrection, since one's willingness to consider this a legitimate issue does not stand on its own but depends on one's attitude to a number of other questions, for example whether one thinks survival a real possibility. But what can definitely be asserted is that Peukert has highlighted Habermas' failure to take the past seriously enough. Why should the contribution of the living alone be regarded as relevant? Why should the contribution of other generations not be seen, as in Gadamer's view of tradition, as of equal or almost equal contemporary worth?

A third area which produces conflict with theology is his recognition of only one model of communication which he believes necessarily excludes the religious. In *The Theory of Communicative Action* what emerges from his study of social developments is a highly rationalistic picture in which alternative modes of communication seem to have no place. A major theme is 'the linguistification of the sacred' (*die Versprachlichung des Sakralen*),[155] according to which 'devaluative shifts' have been taking place across the centuries with the discounting of certain kinds of reasons, first the mythical and then the 'religious-metaphysical'.[156] By contrast to religious thought which he sees as taking certain principles as simply given, the following characterization of our present situation is offered: 'Modern modes of thought do not recognise any such preserves, any such exemptions from the critical power of hypothetical thought, either in ethics or science.'[157] Earlier we noted the way in which Turner's *Marxism and Christianity* challenged whether tolerance is always a good. Tolerance is the basic value underpinning Habermas' theory. For without it there can be no personal interchange of the sort required for communicative action. Hardly surprisingly, therefore, it has been an obvious source of attack for his critics. But in this particular area I shall argue that theology has more reason to show sympathy with Habermas' position.

Certainly it must be conceded that he has a rather narrow view of how consensus might be achieved. Even his most faithful exponent in the English-speaking world, Thomas McCarthy, in his major study *The Critical Theory of Jürgen Habermas* finds himself compelled to protest at one point that there are other possible cognitive modes besides the purely rational – the 'mimetic, poetic, playful, mystical, fraternal'.[158] Raymond Geuss in *The Idea of a Critical Theory* takes a similar line to Turner and challenges whether Habermas' notion of free consent is anything more than 'a rather recent Western invention'.[159] His point is not just that previous generations did not think like that, but that we have no reason to believe that they would agree about what constitutes coercion and freedom. (This is another version of the problem of conscientization which we encountered earlier with Liberation Theology). But from the fact that the way forward may be difficult, nothing follows about it being impossible. Much the same can be said about a criticism made by both Gadamer and Alisdair MacIntyre,[160] that the attempt to identify distorted communication will produce 'epistemo-logical self-righteousness'. Certainly the danger is there, but it could be brought under control, for example by regularly and rigorously searching for it within oneself.

The problem seems to be not so much tolerance as its by-product, namely the fact that we live in a pluralist society. For this makes it impossible to maintain that as a society we are all moving in the same direction. Rather, a more appropriate model for understanding our present situation is to recognize that one group may be more advanced in one respect, more backward in another, a different group in different ways and so forth. But there is no impartial perspective from which an unbiased judgement can be made. Thus from my perspective religion is not backward and distorting, whereas from Habermas' it is, and there is no easy way towards a consensus. Indeed our pluralist society makes it all the more difficult precisely because it is not just one issue over which we are disagreeing.

But, that said, Habermas' theory can still be taken as a model for proceeding within a group where there is already some basic agreement. The Church would seem an obvious case in point, despite the bitter feuds that sometimes erupt. In this connection Peukert has some fascinating things to say. He suggests that Jesus' conflict with the Pharisees can be seen as having 'all the characteristics of a dispute about the principles of the "social construction of reality" . . . and the telling of the parables becomes a means to resolve this conflict . . . The intentions of speech action of telling parables are . . . to shake the given understanding of reality, and to disclose new possibilities of action.'[161] In other words, even Jesus can be seen as engaging in a form of communicative action, in which rather than simply authoritatively declaring his position he argues indirectly for it by encouraging his opponents to respond to the parables by recognizing themselves in them. Of course, in so far as the needy are also addressed, the parallel with Habermas' views is less close, in that they would never have seen themselves as equal partners in the dialogue. But it is still a communication in which their perception of reality is transformed, or rather can be transformed. For, as has been suggested to me,[162] the parables can be seen as open-ended communicative action in which the invitation continues to remain open to the addressees to participate in the parable and complete it through their own transformation.

But, if this was the course that the founder of Christianity pursued, it poses all sorts of perplexing questions about structures of authority in the Church. To that question I therefore now turn.

5

The Church

Identity and authority

It would be no exaggeration to say that the major Christian denominations have been undergoing something of a crisis of identity in recent years. This has been particularly true of Anglicanism and Roman Catholicism. What were once thought to be secure doctrinal frontiers have been challenged in numerous ways. In the Church of England one thinks of the denial of the Incarnation by leading Anglican theologians like Maurice Wiles, or more recently of David Jenkins' insistence on his right as a bishop to challenge traditional interpretations of the Virgin Birth and Resurrection. Nor is it hard to produce Roman equivalents. Edward Schillebeeckx's views on the Resurrection in his *Jesus* are as reductionist as those of the radical Protestant scholar Willi Marxsen,[1] while in practice the official line is repudiated by many on numerous issues not just contraception, ranging from the acceptance of non-Roman eucharists to the legitimacy of homosexual practice.

Such internal variety should certainly not be viewed entirely in negative terms. After all, the realization that often one has more in common with those of another denomination than with some within one's own communion can act as a tremendous spur to ecumenism. It has also, I believe, led to a better understanding of authority. But undoubtedly it has produced tensions. So what I want to do in this section is examine how these tensions might be contained, if not resolved!

Küng and Congar

Christian identity can be sought in a number of different ways, of which belief, worship and structures of authority are the most common. Of these it is the last that has come particularly under attack within the Roman Communion, but in a way which I think bodes well for the future of the Church. So I shall begin my discussion there.

Hans Küng (b. 1928) is probably still best known for his attack on papal authority in *Infallible?* Three years earlier in 1967 there had appeared a much more wide-ranging and more substantial book on *The Church*. Unlike its successor, it obtained a 'Nihil obstat'. Even so, his dissatisfaction with existing patterns of authority is apparent, a dissatisfaction which he finds reflected in the Second Vatican Council itself (1962–5): 'The original draft of the Constitution on the Church was to begin with the "hierarchy", the pope at its head, and only then go on to talk about the "people of God or laity". This order was rightly rejected by the Council in favour of the present order: Chapter 1, the mystery of the Church; Chapter 2, the people of God; Chapter 3, the hierarchical structure of the Church.'[2] Such questioning of authority within the Church I find a healthy development, partly because of the way in which it encourages greater respect for individual autonomy and thus for human dignity, and partly because of the encouragement it also gives towards greater flexibility and adaptability in responding to the rapidly changing features of modern society. But inevitably there are also dangers and difficulties. We need some conception of how decisions might be made in a non-authoritarian way. We need too some means of marking the limits of dissent, of distinguishing between respect for legitimate diversity and an autonomy that can only properly be exercised outside the Church if it is not to be destructive of the Church's ministry to itself and the world.

The most recent controversial discussion of the exercise of authority by the clergy has come from the Dutch Dominican Edward Schillebeeckx (b.1914). *Ministry* is in effect an attack on the last thousand years of the Roman understanding of the priesthood. Taking his cue from canon 6 of the Council of Chalcedon (451) that 'no one may be ordained priest or deacon in an absolute manner . . . unless a local community is clearly assigned to him',[3] he sees leadership of the local community as the key element. He insists that 'the history of the first millenium . . . leaves completely open the question whether the right of consecration is absolutely necessary' and that 'in the early church, presiding at the eucharist was simply the liturgical dimension of the many sided pattern of presiding in the local community.'[4] By contrast his section on 'The Second Christian Millennium' is significantly subtitled 'the notion of the church fades into the background and privatization begins'.[5] For this he blames two factors, the renaissance of Roman law with its idea of power invested in a particular person and the effect of feudalism which made the Church 'no longer a living community as before, but often simply a status symbol of secular rulers with private churches'.[6]

After his brief historical survey his conclusion is that 'on the basis of theological criteria I think that preference must be given to the first Christian millenium as a model for the future shaping of the church's ministry.'[7] This is apparently because he feels that there ought to be 'a clear expression of the New Testament datum of the priority of the community over the ministry'.[8] On this basis he then goes on to defend various illegal practices such as lay presidency at the Eucharist since 'community leaders . . . can and may ultimately do anything that is necessary for the community as the *ecclesia Christi.*'[9]

Not surprisingly his approach has encountered much criticism from fellow Roman Catholics such as Pierre Grelot's *Église et ministères.* Grelot accuses him of hermeneutic naïvety in allowing immediate practical problems to colour his reading of the evidence.[10] Certainly the shortage of priests in many countries, including the Netherlands, does make the issue an urgent one, and so Grelot is right to this extent that one should be on one's guard against simply finding retrospective theological justification for what one wants to do in any case. Principles should come first. But, that said, there are good principles to which appeal can be made.

If Schillebeeckx is well to the left of Küng, the French Dominican Yves Congar (b. 1904) is on most issues to the right of Küng. But on this matter of authority he too endorses Küng's judgement. Not only that, he gives good moral reasons for a different view of authority. In his major three-volumed work *I Believe in the Holy Spirit* he concedes that 'excessive emphasis has been given in the Catholic Church to the role of authority and . . . this has led to a distrust of expressions of the personal principle.'[11] But, partly under the influence of the charismatic renewal movement, he now sees this principle as requiring respect for personal initiative and 'an ecclesiology based on the idea of the Church as a communion of persons'.[12] Again, it seems to be this same principle that leads him to acknowledge 'centuries-long, male dominance' and so to write a very fine chapter on 'The Motherhood in God and the Femininity of the Holy Spirit'.[13] In other words, the reason why authoritarian structures are no longer acceptable is not primarily because of either of the two main factors to which Schillebeeckx points, neither the current manpower crisis in the Church nor the types of ministry the early Church had. It is basically a moral issue. The Church must respect the freedom God has given us, that makes us self-creators along with the Divine Creator. The Holy Spirit can indwell us to make us fellow sons with Jesus. But, as we saw in chapter 3, unless there is free assent to join with the Spirit, that work is without effect.

In my view, then, the Biblical and the historical evidence of alternative structures is of subordinate importance to this moral imperative. But that is not to gainsay that there is such evidence, though I doubt whether as sharp a contrast can be drawn between the first and second millenium as Schillebeeckx suggests. Notions of sacramental hierarchy were already firmly embedded in the patristic period.[14] A more plausible analysis would be in terms of an almost linear development in the increasing grip of hierarchical structures on the life of the Church. Even so, there were lay sermons as late as the twelfth century until banned by the Fourth Lateran Council, lay sacramental absolution as late as the fourteenth, and ordinations by other than bishops (Cistercian abbots) as late as the seventeenth.[15] The concentration of clerical power, of course, reaches its apogee in the declaration of papal infallibility at the First Vatican Council (1870). But before we consider the implications of that doctrine, it is appropriate to say something first about the correctives necessary to priestly power in general in the light of both the moral demand and the likely historical evidence.

Schillebeeckx in this respect seems to me a great disappointment. For to identify the priest's role as essentially that of leader of the local community is surely simply to replace one form of authoritarian hierarchy with another. Evangelical charismatic leaders can after all be just as manipulative of their followers as the cultic priest has undoubtedly sometimes been in the past. Küng offers us a very different and much better model. He notes the way in which the early Church avoided the obvious Greek words for power and chose instead the Greek for service, 'diakonia', and uses this to justify his own preferred term of 'pastor'.[16] This is surely far more apposite, when we think of the model of Christ's own life from which the Church takes its being. So often what a local community needs is not direction, but someone who can bring out the variety of gifts that may lie dormant in the community – prophets, evangelists, teachers, etc.[17] – and at the same time set an example of loving care.

But if this suggests the model of the priest as an 'enabler' rather than a leader, is it not still the case that some leaders will be required? This is an issue which can be most profitably pursued by taking the extreme case, whether there is a need for a single, supreme leader in the papacy. Much thought has gone into the question since Küng's *Infallible?* This is hardly surprising since the two issues of authority and infallibility are clearly related. For how one understands the source of papal infallibility will determine what kind of authority one believes the papacy to have. Given that Küng detects human weakness and frailty in the composition of the Scriptures and errors in General Councils,[18] it would have been astonishing if he had not brought the papacy under the same understanding. So several times he refers to the condemnation of Pope Honorius, who spoke of one will in Christ and was formally anathematized at the Council of Constantinople in 681. But his own proposal is vague and not very helpful. He draws attention to Congar's study of the concept in the Middle Ages, and his view that it meant that, though any part of the Church might err, including the pope, in the end she would remain faithful, and proposes 'indefectibility' as a better term for this. As he puts it, 'God assures the continuance of the faith and the Church, and sees that in spite of all straying and wandering it ultimately keeps direction and carries onward the truth of Christ.'[19] In theory this sounds fine, but in the previous paragraph he has already told us that the Church does not suffer from fewer or lesser errors than any other human organization. That being so, it is hard to see what practical import his suggestion can have.

More sophisticated attempts to deal with the problem have come from the American Peter Chirico in *Infallibility* (1977) and the French Canadian Jean Tillard in his *The Bishop of Rome* (1982). Chirico locates the possibility of infallibility in what he calls 'transcultural meanings'.[20] 'Such universal meanings can be infallibly grasped precisely because of their universality', though he is careful to add that this does not mean absolute human infallibility, merely the nearest man is ever likely to get to it.[21] He argues that 'the early appearance of a universal papacy would have been utterly impossible; that relatively charismatic and acephalous Churches were to be expected at first, until a community of meanings emerged and a need to unify appeared'.[22] The justification of the papacy then becomes that 'someone had to express what bound together the Churches of diverse cultures', which means that the pope 'has to become capable of an understanding as broad as that of the universal Church'.[23]

Some of what he says reads rather like trying to have one's cake and eat it. Within a few pages he talks of the Church 'blundering towards a universal morality' but denies the possibility of 'a theology that would categorise acts as good or bad'.[24] None the less his basic point seems a plausible one. For, unless someone is charged with expressing the *consensus fidelium*, what Christians of today from very different cultures and backgrounds share in common with each other and with their ancestors in the faith, it is hard to see how the temptation can be avoided of elevating one's own particular perspective and culture to universal significance. But is this not to give extraordinary power to one man? It would be if he were put in sole charge of detecting such universal meanings. But that does not seem to be Chirico's point. Admittedly, he does say that, because universal meaning may only be implicit, the pope can act as a reinforcer, stimulus and challenge.[25] But I think his main point is that the pope should reflect the understanding of the faith that has come or is coming to universal consciousness.

One way of putting this is to say that the pope functions as a symbol of the *consensus fidelium*. He expresses that unity, rather than determines it. Such an account would I think be supported by Tillard. At all events, he sees infallibility as essentially a question of genuinely speaking the mind of the Church. Not only does he note that this was the intention of Pius IX and XII when pronouncing the Marian dogmas in 1854 and 1950, he detects the view even in Vatican I with its expression 'bearing the infallibility of the whole Church'.[26] His discussion of infallibility is, however, secondary to his main concern, which is papal authority. He readily concedes the illegitimate extremes of the past such as talk of the pope as 'the vice-God of mankind'[27] and favourably contrasts Gregory the Great (590–604) with Gregory VII (1073–85), the former reluctant even to accept the title of 'universal pope'. His own preference seems to be to place the main emphasis on the local church, with 'the bishop's most fundamental task to maintain his church . . . so that every other true church may recognise herself as she meets her',[28] and it is in this context that he sees the essential move as being from the local church to universal *koinonia* rather than vice versa. But in response one wants to ask whether he has taken sufficiently into account the extreme mobility of modern society. My suspicion is that most Christians would probably find it easier with the pope than with their local bishop, if only because they commonly do not even know the latter's surname, far less his personality!

In the previous paragraph I wrote 'Christians' rather than 'Roman Catholics'. That was deliberate, because it seems to me that, though theologians are increasingly aware that within theology denominational barriers are collapsing with someone like Schillebeecx well to the left of many in the Anglican or Lutheran tradition, what they have not yet taken on board is that this also applies to the Christian community in general. This is particularly so of that sector of society with which I am most familiar, students. They quite happily flit from one denomination to another. But even the older generation which is tied more firmly to particular denominations does not use this as the decisive criterion, when their sights are set beyond their own immediate parish. So, rather than necessarily the leaders of their own tradition, it will be people like Billy Graham or Mother Teresa of Calcutta with whom they will identify, and now increasingly since John XXIII also the papacy. If it be objected that this makes no sense for those who are still not in official communion with each other, there needs to be borne in mind not only the frequency with which such rules are now broken but also the fact that sometimes the non-Catholic will feel much more ill at ease about those who nominally are of the same communion but stand at an alienating distance from him either in respect of doctrine or moral practice. I can thus see no reason why non-Catholics should not already acknowledge the pope as the symbolic expression of universal Christian values. Even points of disagreement cannot be taken as decisive, since as

Roman Catholics are now all too painfully aware many of them are also in disagreement with the pope, for example over contraception or the ordination of women.

But if priests are to be seen as enabling pastors[29] and the pope as a symbol of Christian values, how is the Church's unity to be maintained? In attacking notions of priestly hierarchy have I not effectively undermined any adequate securing of the Church's identity? Earlier I mentioned the possibility of an alternative basis in doctrine or worship. The Church of England has devoted much time of late to searching for criteria of its own identity, and this is reflected in a recent report of its Doctrine Commission, entitled *Believing in the Church* (1981). Despite the variety of position displayed, from Wright at the one end appealing for a reinstatement of doctrinal formulae like the 39 Articles to Drury at the other informing us that the atheist George Eliot's *Middlemarch* is better nourishment for the believing soul than Dean Farrar's *Life of Christ*,[30] most of them seem to believe that they have found the answer in the notion of being inspired by a common story. Significantly, however, one contribution is introduced by remarks to the effect that it is easier to give 'story' a positive significance than 'myth'.[31] For this highlights the basic problem in the approach, that appeal to story only gives a semblance of unity. For some Christians even to call the Incarnation a story is to detract from its most important aspect, its historicity, and even if agreement were reached to talk of a story, it still would not follow that one was inspired by the same story. The key question would be whether it is the same constitutive elements which fire the imagination, and clearly these will not be the same for the conservative and for the liberal. Though this is nowhere acknowledged, this perhaps explains why the report at times retreats into a liturgical framework. So Harvey: 'In our worship we hear again and again that story which is the main burden of Scripture.'[32]

A similar retreat is to be observed in the work of another Anglican, in Stephen Sykes' *The Identity of Christianity* (1984). The main body of the book is devoted to an impressive historical search for that identity in the writings of various theologians from Schleiermacher to Barth. But, having found no common core, rather than using the Wittgensteinian idea of a family resemblance as several reviewers have subsequently suggested, he resorts instead to a purely formal definition, that 'what . . . defines the Christian is the attention he gives to Jesus Christ', which, as he himself admits, is 'both banal and boring'.[33] It is presumably this that makes him fall back on the liturgy as a unifying force, and to stress that 'there can be no avoidance of the inevitable discriminations which have to be made in agreeing on what can and cannot be authorised.'[34] Only against the background of participation in such a liturgy can theologians 'have the confidence to make the necessary experiments and to risk making the necessary mistakes'.[35] There are two major objections to his position. First, it seems far too biased towards his fellow theologians and his desire to feel some sense of unity with them, however diverse their belief. For is not the unity of the pew far more practically orientated? So it is not the words of the liturgy that unite, but rather certain beliefs and the practical implications these are believed to have for one's life. Secondly, he displays an unnecessary dogmatism about liturgical stability. It is in fact intriguing to note how many radicals are conservative in liturgy. It is almost as though there is a psychological need for an anchor somewhere. But precisely because the conservative finds this elsewhere, not merely does he see no reason to resist diversity in worship, he is likely positively to welcome it.

There thus seems to me no way of escaping the search for a doctrinal consensus. This is something Congar fully acknowledges in one of his more recent books, *Diversity and Communion*. The question is pursued specifically with ecumenical relations in mind, and it is intriguing to observe how far he has moved from some of his earlier positions, for example in *Tradition and Traditions*. Following Käsemann he acknowledges doctrinal diversity even within the New Testament, but at the same time observes that diverse traditions within the subsequent history of the Church are not always as far apart as they are commonly supposed. So, for example in respect of the Lutheran Augsburg Confession of 1530 he notes that even the leading Roman Catholic theologian of the time, Johannes Eck 'found hardly anything to take up in the purely dogmatic sphere'.[36] Rather than using the once popular idea of *adiaphora* (things indifferent)[37] as a way forward, his own preference is to follow the Second Vatican Council and speak of a 'hierarchy of truths', i.e. with some more central than others. At the same time he is cautious about different language necessarily expressing different concepts. So, borrowing Niels Bohr's notion of complementarity in quantum physics, he observes of the issue of the Filioque (whether the Son proceeds from the Father and the Son or the Father alone): 'My study of the procession of the Holy Spirit in the Greek Fathers on the one hand and in the Latin tradition on the other has lead me to recognise that there are two constructions of the mystery, each of which is coherent and complete – although each is unsatisfactory at some point – and which cannot be superimposed.'[38]

This finds an echo in the American theologian George Lindbeck's *The Nature of Doctrine* (1984). He too has an ecumenical objective. In place of the two main theological approaches, what he calls the 'propositional' and the 'experiential-expressive' (the latter being exemplified in theologians like Schleiermacher and Rahner), he proposes a third approach, labelled a 'cultural-linguistic approach'.

Though not all the details and implications of this model are clear, the main point seems to be that the emphasis should fall not on the truth of individual propositions nor on the expression of particular experiences but on the context or culture as a whole and the role within it that a particular doctrine is supposed to achieve. Controversially, this leads him to deny that anything true or false about Buddhist notions of Nirvana can be said in Western religions.[39] But, more plausibly, it also leads him to suggest that doctrines are based on a deeper grammar that gives them their rationale, and so equivalences or otherwise can only be determined once this deeper grammar is taken into account. The examples he offers are Trinity, Mary and Infallibility. How far he is right need not concern us here. What is important is the principle he defends, that surface conflict is not necessarily the same thing as deep conflict.

But, while this might help to resolve some of the disputes of the past, it is hardly likely to deal with them all. Lindbeck is shrewd enough to acknowledge that 'sociological sectarianism' may well be necessary to the preservation of identity.[40] But it would be a counsel of despair to suggest that new denominational alignments are the answer. For the history of sects tends to be simply the history of further divisions. For me a more plausible answer is that we take more seriously the creative role of conflict. The prophets' critique of the established religion of Israel, the different emphases of our four Gospels, Paul's rebuke of Peter and so forth all remind us that the early history of our faith was not without its stormy passages. Nor is the later history of the Church any different. In fact it has always needed its experimenters and prophets if it was to be truly responsive to fresh divine initiatives in a constantly changing world.

But this is not to say that such 'prophets' should be accorded a central place within the community. The contrast between prophet and priest must be allowed to stand.[41] That is why Congar was so right to reject *adiaphora* as a way of achieving unity. If a community is to have a strong sense of self-identity, then its beliefs need to be, if anything, overdetermined rather than underdetermined. This is a fact which modern theologians reject at their peril. For one major reason why doctrinal innovation produces such tensions in the community of faith is that so often the innovator insists that his own viewpoint be regarded as an equally acceptable alternative, thus effectively downgrading what his opponent may hold very dear. Surely a much better model for understanding what is happening is to insist that on the issue in question the innovator is indeed at the margins of the faith and that the onus is therefore on him to persuade others that this should now form part of the *consensus fidelium*. When discussing Foucault in the previous chapter I observed how marginalized the prophet can sometimes be as with the 'madness' of Ezekiel and Francis. None the less change can be effected from the margins. St Francis is a conspicuous example of this. But if a more recent instance of this is required, one need only think of the way in which, within a century, belief in Hell as a place of eternal punishment has ceased to form part of that *consensus fidelium*.

In short, then, my answer to the question of Christian identity is that this is not to be sought in either priestly or papal authority nor in forms of worship but in credal identity, pre-eminently of course in the two great Creeds of the universal Church.[42] But this is not to exclude the 'prophet'. It is simply to stress that the onus is on him to show why his proposal should not be marginalized to the edges of the faith.[43] That way, the majority can maintain a strong sense of identity without feeling that they are living in a situation of perpetual doubt. At the same time it also allows for the possibility that these 'prophets' can change the community from within, if it really be God's will.

Lacan to Deleuze

In this section I wish to pursue further this question of the relation between authority and identity by examining the French philosopher Gilles Deleuze's strongly anti-authoritarian reaction to the psychiatrist Jacques Lacan's structuralist account of the unconscious social determinants that make us the sort of people we are. Since both exhibited considerable interest in the power of symbols, it will also provide an effective transition to our discussion of the sacraments in the next section. One reason for pursuing the subject in some detail is that this anti-authoritarian reaction to Structuralism is such a major trend in recent French philosophy. But it also contains a very salutary warning to an institution like the Church only just awakening from an extremely authoritarian past. For Lacan and Deleuze see the insidious operations of power everywhere but particularly in the unconscious reception of symbols, and one doubts whether the Church is as yet fully aware of the power of its symbolism for ill as well as for good.

Jacques Lacan (1901–81) trained as a psychiatrist in the Freudian tradition, but even in his early career he was showing wider interests, as is shown by his contributions in the 1930s to the Surrealist journal *Le Minotaure*, presided over by André Breton. The psychoanalytic movement had been rent by divisions in the past, the most famous of course being that between Freud and Jung at the beginning of the century.[44] In an address in Rome in 1953 Lacan attacked what he saw as the excessively authoritarian restraints of the Freudian school and even suggests the application of psychoanalytic techniques to the current behaviour of some psychoanalysts.[45] This led him to join a break-away group, but it was not until 1964 that he founded his own school,[46] the École freudienne of Paris. Shortly before his death he created a sensation by dissolving his own school. But, despite this and despite the notorious obscurities of his style, he remains the most influential psychiatric theorist after Freud and Jung.

At the practical level his main difference from Freud was his stress on non-intervention as the best way of helping the patient. That is to say, rather than allowing the patient to form a strong identification with the analyst through transference as in the traditional Freudian approach, he saw his role as essentially one of aiding self-discovery. But inevitably it was not his difference from Freud in practice but his different theoretical ideas that attracted such excitement when he began to teach in 1964 at Paris' most prestigious university institution, the École normale supérieure. The strength of that excitement is powerfully conveyed by one of his former pupils, Catherine Clément, in *The Lives and Legends of Jacques Lacan*, in which, intending to complement him, she describes him as a 'shaman' and 'sorcerer'.[47]

In the collection of his lectures and talks, called somewhat paradoxically *Écrits*, Lacan is at pains to insist that he is more concerned with general Freudian principles than with any slavish following of his terminology.[48] His most important innovation is undoubtedly the way in which Lévi-Strauss has influenced him to produce a structuralist account of Freud, which Robert Georgin in *De Lévi-Strauss à Lacan* goes so far as to describe as of Copernican importance.[49] Lévi-Strauss was concerned to reduce anthropology to semiology, to offer an analysis of the whole of social life in terms of the exchange of symbolic messages, and Lacan sees himself as following this insight by applying it to the unconscious.[50] Just as social life can be seen as structured like a language, so can the unconscious.

This relation has both a positive and a negative aspect. The positive aspect is that it is only through the symbolic order that a sense of individual identity is attained; the negative, the extent to which through our unconscious that symbolic order determines how we conceive that identity.

First then the positive aspect. In a much quoted phrase Lacan declares that 'language is the condition for the unconscious.'[51] What he means by this is that it is only the existence of a symbolic order that makes possible the creation of an unconscious. But more importantly it is also his view that it is only through this creation of the unconscious that individual subjectivity is produced. So, unlike Freud's rather negative views on repression,[52] for Lacan an initial primal repression is both indispensable and healthy. Anike Lemaire, who has written by far the best book about Lacan, puts the nature of the connection thus: 'In general terms, the symbolic order establishes mediate relationships between things; the relationship between man and man, between self and other is mediated, that is, by a symbol . . . It is the existence of the mediator which allows everyone to register himself in his distinct subjectivity. In an immediate relationship, on the other hand, the distinction between self and other is not clear.'[53] Applying this to the Freudian first stage of development, the so-called Oedipus Complex, Lacan suggests that initially the child identifies with whatever is the object of the mother's desire. 'He merges with the object of the other's desire and, fusing with his mother as a mere extension of her, presents himself as a nothing, as a blank.'[54] Parallel with this is the strongly imitative behaviour of young children, even to the extent of crying when they see another fall. Hence Lacan's emphasis on the importance of 'the mirror stage',[55] the point at which the child when, perhaps looking in a mirror, begins to show signs of recognizing itself as a distinct identity. But for Lacan this is pre-eminently achieved at the point of symbolic recognition, when the father is recognized as having an object of the mother's desire that the child lacks. This he terms the 'phallus'. But it is clearly only intended as a metaphor for this recognition of distinctiveness over against the child, and its desire for total identification with its mother.[56] It thus now enters the world of language and symbol in that the possibility of a gap between signifier and signified has at last been recognized. So Lacan informs us that bees cannot be described as speaking a language precisely because of 'the fixed correlation of their signs to the reality that they signify'.[57] The failure of reference has no meaning for them; they merely repeat the same act.

Mental illness is then explained as the failure to enter properly into this world of language. The psychotic is someone who has failed to make the primal repression of his desire for total identification with his mother, and so has never been able to differentiate himself from others, with the result that he has no proper conception of himself as a person. Again, the neurotic's problem is that he fails to acknowledge the gap between symbol and reality. For him the symbol has become reality.[58] By contrast, for most of us that initial entry into the world of symbolic language then inaugurates a rich and varied unconscious life, which Lacan sees characterized by two main processes, metaphor and metonymy, by which he means roughly similarity and contiguity, the linguistic equivalents of the Freudian condensation and displacement.[59] It is precisely because he sees such word association at work everywhere in our unconscious that he took such delight in his lectures in frequently resorting to word-play.[60] What we consciously express is only the tip of an iceberg, as it were. For running underneath are a whole host of word-associations, only a few of which come to consciousness.

But it is this very richness which produces the negative aspect of the relationship, the power of this symbolic domain. Lacan several times alludes to Freud's example of the child in the cot who attempts to control the absence and reappearance of his mother through a game of throwing a reel of thread and then drawing it back again, saying 'fort' (away) and 'da' (there). But for Lacan it is not ultimately we who have control over the symbols but the symbols who have control over us. More than once he criticizes Freud for failing to fully appreciate that it is 'language' or 'symbolic bonds' that gives the Church its power.[61] Significantly, he defines the unconscious thus: 'The unconscious is that part of the concrete discourse, in so far as it is transindividual, that is not at the disposal of the subject in re-establishing the continuity of his conscious discourse.'[62]

This transindividuality he expresses in his important concept of 'the Other'. What the notion stresses is the fact that because it is symbolic language that gives us our identity, it is not we ourselves who are the primary sources of meaning as for example Phenomenology would insist, but the Other that is being expressed through us. Hence his well-known formula: 'the Unconscious is the discourse of the Other.'[63] That is to say, it is only through accepting an already existing symbolic discourse in which the father is already an other to the mother that one achieves the first tentative possibility of asserting one's own identity vis-à-vis one's mother. As Lemaire succinctly puts it: 'The human being is an effect of the signifier rather than its cause . . . The young child submits to society, to its culture, organisation and language, his only alternatives being to constrain himself to it or to be ill.'[64]

But, it may be said, surely even if Lacan is right about the early stages of human development, this is no reason to extrapolate to human life in general? Lacan would I think give a two-fold response: first, that once such a pattern of response to insecurity has been established, it will continue in existence; secondly, the psychoanalyst's investigation of word-associations reveals all too clearly the extent of the influence of the Other on the unconscious. Following Freud's famous formula, 'Wo es war, soll ich werden', Lacan does accept that some freedom can be gained by following the adage 'Where it was, there must I come to be.' But he regards it as a forlorn hope that very much can be achieved. So his own formula S ($\emptyset$) expresses his conviction of the impossibility of the Subject ever dispensing with the Other.[65] Georgin observes that for Lacan the unconscious has in effect taken over the role of God as an external source of authority and meaning, and indeed quotes Lacan to that effect.[66]

However, as commentators point out, the effect of such pessimism was that Lacan neither pursued a political alternative to such domination nor indeed showed any real interest in politics at all.[67] That was left to the philosophical response which attempted to go beyond his controlling structuralist perspective, as presented in Gilles Deleuze and Felix Guattari's *Anti-Oedipus* (1972). The former is a professor of philosophy in Paris, while the latter is a psychoanalyst. The result is a rather unusual presentation. It exhibits the psychoanalyst's usual preoccupation with bodily and sexual functions, but in a way that attempts to challenge the conventional Freudian analyses, partly through the use of very explicit language that seems designed to shock one into considering alternatives. The book is subtitled 'Capitalism and Schizophrenia', and this in fact identifies well its major themes. For, on the one hand, the authors are very much concerned to attack the effects of capitalism on modern society, and, on the other, to suggest that the only appropriate response to such effects is to adopt a sort of active schizophrenia towards it all.

The underlying tendency of capitalism is contrasted with that of primitive societies. The latter are coded societies, where symbols and what they represent still have a value in their own right, and their position in social relationships is 'marked' or 'inscribed', rather than simply being an exchangeable commodity, which is the essential feature of all capitalist societies.[68] Capitalism thus inevitably leads to 'a decoding of flows' as everything gets reduced simply to its exchange value, but at the same time the absolute limit is never reached because of a phenomenon which the authors label 'reterritorialization': 'Civilised modern societies are defined by processes of decoding and deterritorialization. But what they deterritorialize with one hand, they reterritorialize with the other.'[69] The reason for the process of deterritorialization is capitalism's strive towards maximum efficiency, with exchange as the sole criterion of value. But because this produces instability in society, there is equally a pull the other way, with the reintroduction of artificially induced 'codes' that can exercise the necessary restraining influence that will prevent such instability from ever threatening the fundamental value of efficiency of exchange. 'Capitalism . . . continually seeks to avoid reaching its limit while simultaneously tending toward that limit. Capitalism institutes or restores all sorts of residual and artificial, imaginary, or symbolic territorialities, thereby attempting, as best it can, to recode, to rechannel persons who have been defined in terms of abstract quantities. Everything recurs: States, nations, families. That is what makes the ideology of capitalism "a motley painting of everything that has ever been believed".'[70]

It is into this context that their critique of Freud and Lacan needs to be placed. Significantly for our concerns here, Seem in his Introduction compares the authors' attack on psychoanalysis's use of the Oedipus Complex to Nietzsche's attack on Christianity. Psychoanalysis is described as 'a well-constituted church'[71] that legitimates a similar represssive function. Such references as there are to Christianity from the authors are not complimentary,[72] and indeed Lacan is criticized for turning Oedipus into 'a kind of universal Catholic symbol'.[73] The heart of their objection is that in assigning such a central role to an artificially coded notion like the family, 'instead of participating in an undertaking that will bring about genuine liberation, psychoanalysis is taking part in the work of bourgeois repression at its most far-reaching level.'[74] Oedipus is thus used to provide a fixed point in society, when in fact it has no such ultimate rationale. Not only is it the case that in primitive societies because of the notion of the extended family 'Oedipus . . . never manages to begin',[75] so far as modern societies are concerned, the Freudian analysis fails to take seriously the fact that 'we live today in the age of partial objects, bricks that have been shattered to bits, and leftovers.'[76] As applied to early development this means that 'it is not true that a baby experiences his mother's breast as a separate part of her body. It exists, rather, as a part of a desiring-machine connected to the baby's mouth, and is experienced as an object providing a nonpersonal flow of milk, be it copious or scanty. A desiring-machine and a partial object do not represent anything.'[77] Oedipus is thus ruled out as making no sense at that stage of development and at later stages functioning only as an artificially unifying construct.

Because all such re-coding has no secure basis the authors follow R. D. Laing in seeing schizophrenia as a natural reaction to the present state of our society, as 'one of the forms in which, often through quite ordinary people, the light began to break through the cracks in our all-too-closed minds . . . Madness need not be breakdown. It may also be breakthrough . . . The madness of our patients is an artifact of the destruction wreaked on them by us and by them on themselves.'[78] But they carry Laing's analysis much further by seeing schizophrenia not just as a by-product of a sick society but also as offering the model for escape from the restraints of that society. 'The schizo has his own system of co-ordinates for situating himself at his disposal, because, first of all, he has at his disposal his very own recording code, which does not coincide with the social code, or coincides with it only in order to parody it . . . It might be said that the schizophrenic passes from one code to the other, that he deliberately scrambles all the codes.'[79] So they can even summarize their purpose as being to 'overturn the theatre of representation into the order of desiring production: this is the whole task of schizoanalysis.'[80] This perhaps takes a bit of unpacking, but the main point should be clear, that capitalism's attempts at re-coding, at 'representation' are to be resisted through resorting to the same techniques as are found in the schizo-phrenic.[81]

What may be less clear is the reference to 'desiring production' as the alternative. Laing is criticized for his wish to continue to give a central role to the notion of personal identity, while the clinically labelled schizophrenic's refusal to use 'I' is praised.[82] Instead, man is viewed as essentially a synthesis of desiring-machines, and the positive task of schizoanalysis 'consists of discovering in a subject the nature, the formation, or the functioning of his desiring-machines, independently of any interpretations'.[83] One may doubt whether such purely 'productive', non-representational knowledge is possible, but despite the absence of practical examples[84] the intention at least is clear, with even at the personal level an almost nihilistic, anti-authoritarian celebration of the parts in preference to the whole. 'Celebration' seems the right word because elsewhere, for example in his more popular *Dialogues*, Deleuze exhibits considerable optimism about our capacity to change our situation. Thus he does not hesitate to aver that we ought to produce our own unconscious,[85] as also to entertain hopes of major changes on the world stage.[86]

In his general approach Deleuze has like Derrida[87] been much influenced by Nietzsche,[88] the most important historical figure in understanding so much contemporary French thought. But Deleuze's optimism stands in marked contrast to the third member of the trio of influential living French philosophers most influenced by Nietzsche, namely Jean-François Lyotard. In his *Economie libidinale* (1974) he shares his anti-capitalist thrust, but it is combined with a pessimistic analysis of what the revolutionary can achieve. For he sees the typical revolutionary as having an essentially religious vision, searching for the salvation of humanity with himself as the priestly figure leading his flock. But on Lyotard's analysis this 'desire for truth', as he calls it, is wrong-headed because truth cannot be had, and so the net result is that capitalism flourishes because, having no objective values, nothing stands in its way.[89]

In comparison with this Nietzchean trio of Deleuze, Lyotard and Derrida, who in order to undermine the evils of authoritarianism get rid not just of God but of truth and personal identity as well, the Church's modest moves to more democratic structures cannot but pale into insignificance. Of course, one can legitimately complain against them that they offer no clear alternative and that a certain naïvety is displayed in supposing that the proposed course of action would not in turn be subject to certain external pressures. But, that said, I do think that we must take their challenge seriously. For they are merely an extreme form of what is today a common theme, with social structures seen as oppressive and the individual's only hope of escape being to deny the identity that has been imposed upon him by society. Thus youth cults such as punks and skinheads are all essentially adopting this course, asserting their own worth despite unemployment and so forth by very publicly jettisoning social values for freshly created symbolic identities of their own.

That many aspects of their analysis are essentially correct there seems no reason for a Christian to deny. Indeed, there is an intriguing example of this from a French Christian writer, Paul Virilio. Though an architect by background, he does consciously try to respond to what Deleuze and Lyotard are saying, and they in turn feel obliged to take his ideas into account.[90] So for example in *Pure War* (1983) he accepts Lyotard's view that 'we're in the age of micro-narratives, the art of the fragment',[91] as also Deleuze's thesis of de-territorialization.[92] Where his own originality lies is in connecting this phenomenon with speed. For him 'every society is founded on a relation of speed', and he gives as examples from the past the trierarch who chartered the trireme in Athens and the 'horsemen' (equites) who were the bankers of Roman society.[93] But for us now 'history as the extensiveness of time . . . is disappearing in favour of the instant',[94] and as examples he offers the way in which reaction time to a nuclear launch is being reduced all the time with the laser beam introducing the possibility of absolute speed, travelling at the speed of light, and cities becoming 'great parking lots' in which the time between Paris and New York has become more significant than the distance between Paris and Corsica.[95] As an extreme instance of what is happening he quotes the case of the millionaire Howard Hughes who at first tried to secure an identity by having his various appartments all over the world decorated in exactly the same way and then when that failed 'ended up as a technological monk in the desert of Las Vegas, without getting out of bed'.[96]

Virilio is much better at analysing the sickness than in offering a cure. As we have seen, a major motivation for what is being said is anti-authoritarian discontent, the feeling that social norms are artificially created as a bulwark to defend alienating ends such as capitalism that make no reference to the value of the individual. That the Church also has been guilty in this respect cannot be denied, with those in positions of power within the Church in effect manipulating those committed to their charge. But even if one were forced to the pessimistic conclusion that most of the history of the Church has been like this, that does not mean that it is inherent in the nature of the Christian religion for it to be thus. Instead, a response on three distinct levels can be offered.

First, attention can be drawn to the way in which theologians are now taking up Jesus' alternative vision of authority: 'Anyone who wants to become great among you must be your servant, and anyone who wants to be first among you must be slave of all.'[97] General principles were enunciated in the previous section. But if a more practical example is preferred, one might recall from the previous chapter Leonardo Boff's *Church, Charism and Power*, with its conception of authority springing from below in the base communities. As he puts it, there must be 'the free and spontaneous acknowledgement by their subordinates of that authority'.[98]

Secondly, so far as territorialization and its opposite is concerned, Christianity can claim to offer safeguards against any attempts to absolutize such commitments, whether artificially created or otherwise. This is where its transcendent dimension becomes relevant, since it puts a question-mark against all earthly realities as in some way provisional. As the author of Hebrews puts it: 'For here we have no continuing city, but we seek one to come.'[99] The result is that even what is the object of some of Deleuze's and Guattari's most scathing criticism and where one might have expected the Church to rally to the defence, namely the family, in fact is only accorded qualified approval in the New Testament. 'If any man come to me, and hate not his father, and mother, and wife, and children, and brethren, and sisters, yes, and his own life also, he cannot be my disciple.'[100]

But clearly that cannot be the entire answer. Whether we like it or not, our life is inherently social, and so it is really no answer at all to celebrate the 'parts' of our personal 'machine' as though they were any less socially conditioned than the whole. What we surely need is an alternative social model, in which the social can be seen to form our individuality in a non-threatening and non-destructive way. It is depressing how little thought theologians have given to this question, especially when one considers how much social imagery is at the heart of the New Testament, not just the Kingdom of God but the more mystical notions of the Body of Christ and our incorporation into it in Paul and the vine and its branches in John. The reason why development of this might offer a promising response is that on the one hand the priority of the social is frankly acknowledged – it is Christ in his community that creates us, 'yet not I, but Christ liveth in me'[101] – but at the same time it is seen as a society that continues to maintain the absolute value of the individual – 'inasmuch as ye have done it unto one of the least of these my brethren, ye have done it unto me.'[102]

A recent exception to this neglect is the Greek theologian John Zizioulas' *Being as Communion* (1985). Adopting the social analogy for the Trinity he tells us that even God only 'exists thanks to an event of communion'.[103] But for our purposes here what is important is the way in which he sees the sociality of God reflected in the Christian's ecclesial identity and the symbols that go with it. He argues[104] that it will not do to think of Christ as an individual. Rather, he is a person which means that necessarily he exists in relation to his Body the Church. Indeed, we are told that 'Christ without his body is not Christ but an individual of the worse type',[105] and Christology is seen as preserving us from 'the tragedy of individualism'.[106] It does this when the Church as the eucharistic Body of Christ is correctly understood. For then 'all pyramidal notions disappear in ecclesiology: the "one" and the "many" co-exist as two aspects of the same being.'[107]

As the following pages make clear, what this means is that it is only through our free acceptance of being persons in relation and inter-dependent that the Spirit constitutes the Church as Christ's Body. This has a number of implications: that all Christians are ordained, each being assigned a particular relation in the Church;[108] that just as baptism is to enter into one such particular relation, so too is episcopacy a call to a particular community and dependent on its endorsement;[109] that apostolic succession is not an individual possession but is transmitted by the entire community.[110]

That such a vision of non-hierarchical authority and identity could come from as conservative a denomination as Orthodoxy gives great ground for hope. For the way Zizioulas argues in the normal Orthodox manner by appeal to tradition clearly demonstrates that there is an alternative vision of Christian social identity firmly embedded there, one in which the symbolic order is not seen an essentially destructive of individual freedom but rather as enhancing it. One's image of the Trinity, of Christ as more than an individual, and of the mutual interdependence of the baptized and priestly orders can thus all offer symbols of an identity that need in no sense be seen as the creation of an indifferent, alienating Lacanian 'Other'.

But how should we understand the relationship between Christ and the means through which pre-eminently this free community is created? It is to that question that I now turn.

The Eucharist

Schillebeeckx

The Swedish scholar Brilioth in his early pioneering ecumenical study listed five key aspects of what he calls the sacrament's 'many-sided glory'.[111] Even so, he failed to take account of certain features whose significance has only recently been recovered, particularly the antici-patory character of the meal, as argued in detail for example by Geoffrey Wainwright in *Eucharist and Eschatology*.[112] It will be wise therefore for us to take but one aspect here, and that the most controversial, the nature of Christ's presence in the eucharist.

Wainwright, who is a Methodist, in common with almost all Protestants finds the doctrine of transubstantiation objectionable. For him the Lord's Supper is provisional and anticipatory of the final end towards which God is leading his people, and in those terms to speak of Christ's identification with things (the eucharistic elements) is to undermine both the transcendent and personal character of this process.[113] However, it is an objection of which modern Roman Catholic theology is very much aware, and increasingly within the last thirty years alternative terminology has been sought, to reflect the sacrament as existentialist or personal encounter. This change is particularly associated with the name of Edward Schillebeeckx. As Martos writes in his popular introduction to the Catholic sacraments *Doors to the Sacred*, 'more than any other person Schillebeeckx was instrumental in showing that Catholicism could develop a theology of the sacraments which was both faithful to the insights of Thomas Aquinas and free of the minimalistic tendency of late scholasticism.'[114] In terms of influence this assessment is right, but, as we shall shortly note, the original ideas should properly be credited elsewhere.

Schillebeeckx in his key work *The Eucharist* (1968), which incidentally received an *imprimatur*, in fact exaggerates the impact of modern quantum physics on the concept of substance.[115] For why should what happens at the micro-level necessarily affect what we are entitled to say at the macro-? More plausible is his appeal that the sacraments be so defined that they be seen to be 'interpersonal encounters between the believer and Christ'.[116] Schillebeeckx fully acknowledges antecedents to his own view. However, his discussion of them is so brief[117] that these can more usefully be pursued in the most important recent book on the eucharist by a Roman Catholic theologian, M. Gesteira Garza's *La eucarista, misterio de comunion* (1983). In a section entitled 'transfinalisation and transsignification'[118] he notes how the former term was first proposed by a Protestant, F. J. Leenhardt, as an ecumenical alternative, the idea being that the sacrament should be viewed in terms of its final end decreed by God. Leenhardt argued for this in two books of 1948 and 1955,[119] but mainly because on this view too much seems to depend on the arbitrary will of God, Garza's preference is for the slightly later approach of the Catholic J. de Bacciochi in terms of transsignification, where greater stress is placed on the context. The meaning or changed significance then depends as much on what man does as on God, and not surprisingly perhaps therefore, given Schillebeeckx's stress on personal encounter, this is also his preferred way of putting it.

Schillebeeckx gives a number of examples of transsignification such as the way in which a coloured cloth can become a national flag. But perhaps the most interesting is the following because of its introduction of the language of transubstantiation. 'A Greek temple is something different for its builders, for those who worship in it and for modern tourists. Man is essentially involved in this change of relationship, but it is not completely dependent on him – the being itself of things changes when the relationship is altered. It is therefore possible to say that the temple has undergone a "historical transubstantiation" '.[120] Garza too defends the compatibility of the new terminology with the more traditional phraseology.[121] But at the same time he is insistent that this should not be thought of as some 'abstract and empty category'. Instead, using Teilhard de Chardin as a starting-point, he speaks of the eucharist as the 'anticipation' and 'prefiguation' of 'the true transubstantiation of the universe', beginning with man but including all creation.[122] So rather than stressing the initial creative word of God as with Leenhardt and Bacciochi he stresses 'the eschatological power of the risen Lord' and it is this reason that he gives for rejecting consubstantiation (the coterminous presence of Christ and the elements as in the theology of Luther), that 'it does not preserve the dimension of transition of passage towards the eschatological future which comes implied in the eucharistic transformation'.[123] Clearly in all of this there is present the claim that something objective is taking place. A similar stress is to be observed in Schillebeeckx: 'anyone who does not believe, and consequently does not see it in this way, places himself outside the reality which is *objectively* present – he is outside the order of being'[124] (his italics). What, however, this objectivity amounts to is harder to determine. But for clarity's sake the attempt must be made.

But before we do so it will be salutary to observe what meantime has been happening in Protestant theology. The writings of two Reformed theologians may be taken as illustrative. Already just before Pope John XXIII summoned the Second Vatican Council Max Thurian was writing in an eirenic spirit that 'the doctrine of transubstantiation was intended to safeguard the truth of the real presence. It was not a rational explanation of the mystery, but a categorical affirmation of the reality of Christ's presence',[125] and with that desire to preserve a full doctrine of the real presence Thurian is in complete accord. A more recent work is Alisdair Heron's *Table and Tradition* (1983). Though he rejects transubstantiation as involving too many miracles,[126] intriguingly he suggests that transsignification would probably have been acceptable to Calvin.[127] Even Pope Paul VI's condemnation of the term as inadequate is not regarded as decisive in foreclosing ecumenical dialogue since his remarks on transubstantiation are taken to mean that the 'dogma is to be understood more as an authoritative witness than as an explanation of the real presence.'[128]

Such unanimity is encouraging, but it would be wrong to use it as an excuse for avoiding important questions. First, Schillebeeckx talks of the eucharist as sign and symbol, but offers no analysis of how symbols work and what effect they might be expected to achieve. Again, Garza's placing of the sacrament in an apocalyptic context reads impressively, but one wants to know how God's acting in the here and now helps to achieve that future prospect. In other words, the first important question which presents itself is the need for some account of how symbols work, especially in the context of the sacraments. That is an issue which I shall consider in some detail in the next section, but a few remarks will be apposite here. Schillebeeckx's account strikes me as far too intellectualist and rationalist. So the way he describes his examples of the flag and the temple read very much as though he sees symbols as essentially a matter of human choice, and this seems confirmed by a footnote in which he challenges whether bread and wine are essential to the sacrament: 'Is the use of bread and wine of dogmatic significance for the concrete celebration of the Eucharist simply because Christ used bread and wine?'[129] One might contrast this with Barthes' discussion of myth as I outlined it in chapter 2. For Barthes, as with his *Paris-Match* example of the black colonial soldier saluting the French flag, it is essential to the power of the myth or symbol that one is unable to stand entirely outside of it. In other words, they reflect something that is already part of ourselves, rather than something that we choose. This seems to me a feature that must be included in any adequate analysis of the symbol of the eucharist, but which finds no echo in Schillebeeckx. Another feature that can perhaps also be explained by too rationalist an approach is his treatment of the sacrament exclusively in terms of personal encounter. This is surprising when it is so obviously contradicted by so much of our experience, when we seem totally unaware of anything in particular happening at Communion. The solution is surely not to accept this as the correct analysis, but to ponder the possibility that much in fact takes place at the subconscious and unconscious level. In the previous section we noted the stress which Lacan has placed on symbols operating at the unconscious level, and this is an issue which I think we must pursue further in the next section.

In addition to this question of the way in which symbols function, there is also another major issue which cannot be circumvented. This is the question of what it is to which the sacrament gives access. In most discussions this is treated as self-evident, the person of Christ. But what this ignores is the very feature which has created all the problems in the first place. For a phrase like 'the person of Christ' leaves it ambiguous whether it is the divinity or the humanity of Christ which is in question. If the former there is of course no problem about it being omnipresent. But, if the latter, there is. For can one still speak of a human body, if it is capable of simultaneous multiple location? Yet it was clearly just such a presence that was thought necessary to our salvation by numerous theologians of the past. Indeed, I shall argue that viewed from this perspective the principal factions at the Reformation, Luther, Calvin and Trent, have more in common than what differentiates them.

Intriguingly, in his recent magisterial defence of traditional Roman doctrines, *Synthèse dogmatique* (1985), Jean-Hervé Nicolas objects to notions like transsignification precisely on the ground that personal presence is impossible without corporeal, which of course only makes sense if it is the humanity that is in question. 'But for this presence to be real, it is still necessary that first the body as such be present in its own characteristic way, that is spatio-temporally: if the cup of tea, the gesture of offering it, the smile that accompanies the gesture are the means of a personal and real presence, it is because in the first place the mistress of the house is there corporeally.'[130] Though both the principal figures of the Reformation rejected transubstantiation, it is interesting to observe that neither denied this more fundamental concern which lay behind the doctrine, that through the eucharist we should gain access to the corporeal humanity of Christ which guarantees his identity with the Incarnate Lord. So Luther attempted to solve the problem by suggesting that through the 'communicatio idiomatum' (the interchange of attributes between divine and human nature) Christ's human nature could be ubiquitous, existing alongside the elements in the sacrament (consubstantiation). Calvin regarded this as an impossibility, because of its violation of the laws of logic of what it means to be a body: 'This is an inviolable truth about body, that it is contained by place and fixed in its dimensions.'[131] For Calvin then of necessity Christ's resurrected human body remains confined to heaven. But from this it by no means follows that he rejects any relationship with the human nature in the sacrament. On the contrary, he continues to regard it as integral. As he puts it in his *Institutes*: 'Greatly mistaken are those who conceive no presence of flesh in the Supper unless it lies in the bread. For thus they leave nothing to the secret working of the Spirit, which unites Christ himself to us. To them Christ does not seem present unless he comes down to us. As though, if he should lift us to himself, we should not just as much enjoy his presence! The question is therefore only of the manner, for they place Christ in the bread, while we do not think it lawful for us to drag him from heaven.'[132] Nor does he deny that his own position also has something of the character of the miraculous. For elsewhere he speaks of this 'bond of participation' being created by 'the secret and miraculous virtue of God'.[133]

Modern writers too easily dismiss the problem as one of excessive literalism. Thus Thurian, despite being of the same Reformed tradition as Calvin, declares that Christ 'now has a new body, assumed into the glory of his Godhead. This body cannot be defined within the limits that apply to an ordinary human body; it cannot be restricted by place or size, as Calvin expressed it.'[134] Likewise, Garza suggests that 'it was in dissociating the ecclesial body of Christ . . . from his eucharist body . . . that there began to be problems of the multilocation . . . of the individual historical body subject to the laws of physics.'[135] But in respect of the former, while the resurrected body is undoubtedly a transformed body, apparently capable of passing through doors and no longer part of our own spatio-temporal dimension, within its own heavenly dimension it must surely still occupy a limited, defined space; otherwise it makes no sense to speak of a body at all. Again, Garza's suggestion is not without its problems. For, though all Christians are part of the one ecclesial body despite their multilocation, this does not bypass the problem, since there still remains the question of the relation of all these parts to their Head, Christ. Does he himself have multilocation in the parts, or only metaphorically through his influence on 'his members'? Nor will it do simply to point to our transformed understanding of the New Testament texts. One might, for example, quote the standard authority, Jeremias' *The Eucharistic Words of Jesus*, in which he argues that Jesus intended a symbolic interpretation, 'that by eating and drinking he gives them a share in the atoning power of his death'.[136] The difficulty here is that there is still too much incorporationist and participatory language elsewhere in the New Testament, some of it obviously eucharisitic,[137] for us not to believe that something stronger than metaphor is involved here.

I turn therefore now to two very different philosophers, Aquinas and Ricoeur, in hope of further enlightenment.

Aquinas and Ricoeur

St Thomas Aquinas (1225–74) is important in this connection because he offered the first major and still the most important philosophic defence of the doctrine of transubstantiation after the introduction of the term into the official theology of the Church at the Fourth Lateran Council in 1215. This he couched in the Aristotelianism of his day that was then just beginning to rival the Platonism that had dominated the Church for the previous thousand years. The writings of Aristotle, many of which had only recently been rediscovered, have a much drier, more analytic style than Plato's[138] and reading Aquinas today on transubstantiation can easily give the impression of unnecessary technicality. But the effort is worth making, especially as behind the arid style lies a man deeply devoted to the eucharist. In fact, Pope Urban IV commissioned him to write the office for the newly instituted feast of Corpus Christi in 1264, as a result of which we have a number of hymns from his pen including 'Of the glorious Body telling'.

However, before looking at what Aquinas has to say on the subject in the relevant section of his major work, the *Summa Theologiae*, it will be as well to stress that the theological disputes which led up to Innocent III's use of the term in 1215 were like the Reformation dominated by the concern to secure access to Christ's humanity, especially as this is less obvious in Aquinas' own text. The key figure was the ninth-century Benedictine theologian Paschasius Radbertus who in his treatise *De Corpore et Sanguine Domini* offered an extreme, literalist view of the identity between Christ's eucharistic body and his earthly body that seems tantamount to physical identity. But it was only really in the following century when Berengar of Tours went to the other extreme and elicited a response from a major churchman like Lancfranc that the pressure to assert dogmatically the real presence became overwhelming. The details of this dispute need not concern us here. What is important to note is that, despite the variety of approaches in these centuries, as stressed by Gary Macy in his book *The Theologies of the Eucharist in the Early Scholastic Period*, what they do all seem to have shared is a concern that the eucharist make possible incorporation into Christ's humanity. As Paschasius himself put it: 'As Christ is in the Father through the nature of the divinity, we, on the other hand, are in Christ through his bodily nativity, and he again is believed to be present in us through the mystery of the sacraments.'[139] Given the extent of incorporationist language in the Scriptures, such a concern is perhaps hardly surprising. One should perhaps also add that in terms of Platonist metaphysics particulars only have reality in so far as they imitate or participate in the perfect exemplar, the universal Form, and this may also have played its part in determining the relation between our humanity and Christ's.

However that may be, Aquinas' defence is presented in the very different categories of Aristotelian metaphysics.[140] He admits that the body of Christ can only be localized through a miracle since 'every bodily thing that is moved from place to place must pass through all the intermediate places and there is no question of that in the present case.'[141] But the 'form' of the body of Christ, what makes it what it is in Aristotle's metaphysics, is clearly the soul since this is what makes it alive. But bread he observes[142] cannot be converted into soul. So the conversion that takes place can only be into the form of the body of Christ 'precisely in so far as it is the principle of its being a body'.[143] This in effect means that 'the change of the bread and wine does not have as its term either the godhead or the soul of Christ. Because of this, neither the godhead nor the soul of Christ is in this sacrament as a result of the sacramental sign; they are there by a natural con- comitance.'[144] But this must even apply to his quantitative dimensions, his size and appearance, since the whole of Christ is supposed to be present in each portion.[145] 'But that is not the way in which a body is localised. Hence Christ's body in this sacrament is in no way localised.'[146] 'It is always in heaven in its proper appearance and it is on many other altars under its sacramental appearance.'[147] What in effect therefore we seem to have as a result of all this argumentation is the real presence of Christ in the eucharist but one which, even in so far as it pertains to his human nature, is essentially one of concomitance. The human nature is fully present, along with the divine, in each particle of consecrated matter, and the matter is his body only in the heavily qualified sense noted above – the form of the body 'precisely in so far as it is the principle of its being a body'.

I would suggest that what really matters in all of this is the necessity of the concomitance. At all events, Aquinas finds himself forced to generate additional miracles in order to explain how the bread and wine can remain apparently unchanged. The dimensive quantity of the elements is now held to function as a subject. Rather implausibly Aquinas comments: 'everything that pertains to matter is granted to this dimensive quantity. And so, everything that could be generated from the matter of the bread if it were there, can now be generated from the dimensive quantity of the bread and wine. There is no new miracle; it all happens as a result of the original one.'[148]

One reason why Aquinas gets himself into such a complex position is that he appears to think of Christ's resurrected body and ourselves as occupying the same space–time continuum, and so it impossible for the body to be present in more than one place at once without a miracle. But, if we think of Christ's resurrection body entering another spatial dimension, then it becomes possible for us to think of it both as occupying a strictly limited dimension within that continuum and as at the same time being capable of touching our own dimension at numerous points, particularly where the eucharist is being celebrated. Indeed, one can make use of an illustration which Aquinas himself uses. As an analogy of how Christ can be fully present in each part of the broken host, he remarks: 'When a mirror is unbroken, there is only one image, but when the mirror is broken, you have a separate image in each of the parts.'[149] One might adapt the analogy and think of the relation between the two dimensions as like the numerous points of contact between the many parts of the broken mirror and the single original of the image which they are reflecting.

Alternatively one might think of the way in which even within our own space–time continuum something may be seen as a single point from within a one-dimension perspective, but as a cone linking various points spacially separated, once a further dimension is added. A rather different and perhaps more apposite illustration could be drawn from C. S. Lewis' novel *The Lion, the Witch and the Wardrobe*. For there the three children establish contact with the world of Narnia through the magic wardrobe without their spatial-temporal status on earth being at all affected. No time elapses on earth during their adventures in Narnia and their spacial location remains the wardrobe in which they have chosen to hide. In fact rather less is required in the case of the eucharist since all that is needed is a point of contact, no more – in other words, the wardrobe, not the actual transference of the children to Narnia, as happens in the case of the story.

Putting it another way, what we would then have is the idea that the bread is what takes the place of the Resurrected Body in our spatial continuum. It is the counterpart in our physical space–time dimension of the different sort of physical presence that the Resurrected Body enjoys in its different space–time continuum of Heaven. Expressed now like this, it does not seem to me that the three major Reformation positions are all that far apart. The way I have put it is nearest to the language of transubstantiation. But clearly once the notion of concomitance is taken into account this is not all that far removed from consubstantiation: the elements mark the presence of Christ's humanity in the parallel dimension. Again, Calvin can be interpreted as suggesting that through the elements we are taken beyond, into that other dimension lying alongside, which is Heaven and where Christ's glorified humanity is now to be found.

But, it may be objected, even if I have shown the intelligibility of conceiving of the eucharist in terms of such a meeting between the two space–time continua, there still remains the problem of defining what status the bread and wine have acquired in virtue of this relationship. An eirenic move might be simply to ignore the issue. But not only is that the way of cowardice, it would foreclose what I think might be important insights into the role symbols play in the Christian religion. Here the philosopher Paul Ricoeur will occupy a key role as our guide. But before using his ideas to give precision to the way in which symbols function, first we must attempt some clarification of what it is to be a symbol. This is a matter of such importance that it is worth examining in some detail before we return once more to the specific issue of the eucharist.

A primary issue is its relation to metaphor. F. W. Dillistone in *Christianity and Symbolism*, though noting the way in which the term is sometimes used as equivalent to 'faded metaphor', none the less went on to identify active metaphor as one of the two ways, along with analogy, in terms of which symbols function.[150] Intriguingly, in a book written thirty years later which acknowledges his help in the Preface, symbols are contrasted unfavourably with metaphors, precisely for this reason that, if not exactly faded, they are entrenched and so no longer properly functioning as metaphors. Thus Sallie McFague writes in *Metaphorical Theology* (1983) as follows: 'What is it about a religious metaphorical statement which makes it more powerful than a symbolical statement? . . . Most simply, a metaphor is seeing one thing as something else, pretending "this" is "that" because we do not know how to think or talk about "this", so we use "that" as a way of saying

something about it . . . Symbolic statements, on the other hand, are
not so much a way of knowing and speaking as they are sedimentation,
and solidification of metaphor. For in symbolic or sacramental thought,
one does not think of "this" or "that", but "this" as part of "that". The
tension of metaphor is absorbed by the harmony of symbol.'[151]

McFague very much belongs to the Liberal wing of the American
church. For her the metaphorical approach to theology involves being
'open-ended, tensive, secular, indirect, iconoclastic, and revolutionary'.[152] The authority of Scripture becomes 'the authority of a classic
poetic text', and traditional christology 'Jesusolatry' because incarnational language reflects none of the tension and discontinuity of
poetry.[153] It is hardly surprising, therefore, that the power of the
eucharistic words is seen to reside exclusively in their function as
metaphor: 'Jesus said, "This is my body", and instead of surprise, joy,
or disbelief, we do not even hear the metaphor.'[154]

There is much of value in what McFague has to say about the role of
metaphor in theology, particularly in respect of the way in which the
parables are intended to disconcert and shock, something that accords
well with my own remarks at the end of the previous chapter. But there
are two decisive flaws in her approach. First, she tends to caricature the
opposing view. For surely no less than this 'open-ended' theology the
conservative Christian can be overcome with wonder by what God has
done, or be disconcerted by the demands and challenges he now
perceives God to be imposing on him? Again, whatever the popular
impression may be, if my account of Aquinas on transubstantiation is
anywhere near correct, to describe this as 'symbols . . . literalized'[155] is
a long way from the truth, given all the qualifications involved. But,
secondly and more importantly, McFague writes as though metaphor
can succeed without ontological implications. At most she seems
prepared to talk of 'new quality of relationship'.[156] So for example she
praises Maurice Wiles' account of 'the parable of the cross' as involving
'a vision of God as participant in the continuing conflict with evil,
identifying himself at whatever cost with both the perpetrators and the
victims of that evil'.[157] But since both she and Wiles are non-
incarnationalists, one wants to ask what the force is of that qualifier, 'at
whatever cost'. Should we not say that, however powerful the parable
or metaphor is, unless it has referential value in a claim that God has
done something unique in this case, it remains false whether we take it
literally or metaphorically. Janet Soskice in fact takes McFague to task
on this very point in her book, *Metaphor and Religious Language*
(1985). She accuses her of ignoring the ontological dimension in
supposing that religious metaphors depict only 'the reality of human
experience and response'.[158] Though McFague is not specifically the
object of attack on this occasion, Soskice puts the point especially well

in respect of the eucharist: 'Even a conservative, catholic Christian could acknowledge that Jesus' phrase "this is my body" is, or was, metaphorical but in doing so he would make a linguistic and not an ontological point . . . The point at issue is not really whether we have metaphor here, but what the metaphor is doing . . . It is one's metaphysics, not metaphor, which is at issue. To put it another way, the question is not simply whether we have a metaphor here or not, but what, if anything, the metaphor refers to or signifies.'[159]

Thus McFague is wrong to think that in speaking exclusively in terms of metaphor she can avoid ontological issues. But this is still not yet to answer the question of what extra distinguishing feature is introduced when we speak of symbol. McFague is herself, I believe, on the right lines when she talks about 'symbolic participationism.'[160] Whether linguistic or not, they reflect reality as it is believed to be by offering dense or concentrated focal analogical representations of that reality. That is how I would suggest we should explain what we found Roland Barthes saying on the subject of myth in chapter 2. In effect, 'myth' is simply his word for symbol. But precisely for that reason we must reject McFague's claim that in the modern world symbol plays no significant role.[161] In fact, one of the most encouraging developments for the possibility of religious symbolism being treated seriously is the whole rise of semiology, the study of signs. Thus the first meeting of the International Association of Semiotic Studies took place only in 1974. But, as the Marshall Blonsky collection *On Signs* indicates, a vast range of things are now subject to such analysis – Castro's beard, a royal wedding, sexual arousal, priests and women as immune spaces, and brassière sizes.[162] Perhaps, however, McFague only intended her remarks to refer to religious symbolism. If so, she may be nearer the truth, but even so we can then call the distinguished historian of religion Mircea Eliade (1907–86) to witness that all that has really happened to modern man is merely that 'the sacred survives, buried in his unconscious'. Even this periodically bursts forth with an apparently very secular event like a motor show taking on the form of an act of worship.[163] In addition, one might in any case observe that it is very hard to draw any very firm line between sacred and secular symbolism, since both are best described as focused analogical representations of perceived reality. Equally, what image or object is perceived as 'standing in' for that reality is not something chosen as with a metaphor but something given or seen as given by the nature of things.

This is one feature of the writings of Paul Ricoeur (b. 1913) to which McFague takes exception,[164] despite the influence he has exercised elsewhere on her text. But for me Ricoeur is at his most percipient when he writes that 'the symbol gives: I do not posit the meaning, the symbol gives it.'[165] For something has only really acquired the status of a symbol when the analogical connection on which it is based is accepted as given, as integral to one's account of reality. That can perhaps largely be explained by the fact that so many symbols originate in our unconscious, where, as we saw when discussing Lacan, analogical thinking, cross-category comparisons, come naturally, and where personal choice and decision is not possible, at any rate directly.

The stress on the given in fact represents a continuing stand in Ricoeur's writings. Thus his earliest interest lay in Husserl's Phenomenology and while he translated *Ideen* into French, his own first book, *Le philosophie de la volonté I: Le voluntaire et l'involontaire* (1950), was an attack on Husserl's attempt in his reduction to give absolute priority to consciousness. Ricoeur argues that, try as we might, the 'voluntary' is limited by the 'involuntary', through unchosen motives, habits, spontaneous bodily reactions and so forth. The other major philosophic influence on him was the Catholic existentialist philosopher Gabriel Marcel, who with his emphasis on the priority of the other moved him still further away from the Cartesianism of Husserl. However, from our point of view the decisive year was 1960 when the second volume of *Le philosophie de la volonté* finally emerged in two parts, one of which was entitled *The Symbolism of Evil*. What in effect had happened was that in the process of examining the most significant restraint on the will, the fact of evil, he came to the realization that it exercised its power most effectively through the way in which it was perceived. This then raised for him the hermeneutical question both of the way in which reality is presented to us through language and symbols, and in turn our response to that reality. In *Hermeneutics and the Human Sciences* Ricoeur himself describes what happened as 'the necessity of effecting a detour via symbolism in order to account for the specific phenomenon of the evil will'.[166]

However, that turn of interest soon widened to consideration of all forms of indirect reference, including metaphor, which is studied in what is perhaps his best known book, *The Rule of Metaphor* (1975). While Ricoeur acknowledges in this work that the poet often feels himself under compulsion to use particular metaphors, he sees this as having no deeper rationale than the compulsion of creativity.[167] By contrast, symbolic language is essentially *langage lié*, 'bound language'. 'Symbolic activity', he tells us, 'lacks autonomy. It is bound activity.'[168] This is because, whether it is cosmic symbolism or oneiric (the language of dreams), the pressure is experienced as coming not from internal creativity but from the non-linguistic object itself. It is experienced as an integral given, as part of the deep structures of reality. This is not to say that metaphor cannot disclose reality. Indeed, in *The Rule of Metaphor* Ricoeur is at pains to argue against any purely reductionist view of metaphor, that it is simply an embellishment of language, capable of complete replacement at the literal level. Instead, he sees it operating at the level of the sentence to not only refer but also offer additional aspects of truth that are perhaps conveyable by no other means. But it is to claim that it offers a less profound access. Truth, he insists, is 'not only adequation but also manifestation'[169] and he does not hesitate to use the language of revelation of what is uncovered by attention to symbols. But largely through the influence of Jean Narbert the existentialist elements in his thought are modified in a more positive direction, and so instead of *Angst* before the disclosure of Being which we saw in chapter 3 as characteristic of Heidegger we have a stress on joy, as Being overflows in its unfolding to us. Hence the appropriateness of the title of Van Leeuwen's excellent survey of his thought. *The Surplus of Meaning.*[170] Symbols are invariably richer than what even our best efforts succeed in uncovering.

But how does such revelation work? Ricoeur exhibits considerable hostility to those thinkers, particularly Marx and Freud, who assign an essentially negative role of repression to symbols in the unconscious. Indeed, he labels them 'masters of suspicion'. But he is equally opposed to a structuralist like Lacan because, though Lacan assigns a positive role to at least some symbols in the unconscious, in common with most structuralists he leaves very little, if any, room for a free human response to these symbols. Instead, they are essentially seen as codes that control man. So in his discussion of Lévi-Strauss' work Ricoeur objects that 'it seems to me suspect when it sets itself up as a philosophy. An order posited as unconscious can never, to my mind, be more than a stage abstractly separated from an understanding of the self by itself; order in itself is thought located outside itself.'[171] What this represents is his conviction that symbols really only achieve their full effectiveness when they enter into conscious dialogue with the person espousing them. Otherwise, instead of the forward movement of the Spirit and a 'recollection of the sacred', all we have is a Freudian retreat to childhood and the return of the repressed'. As he puts it elsewhere in that same collection of essays: 'The two symbolisms are intermingled . . . The progressive order of symbols is not exterior to the regressive order of fantasies; the plunge into the archaic mythologies of the unconscious brings to the surface new signs of the sacred. The eschatology of consciousness is always a creative repetition of its own archaeology.'[172]

In his account of symbols Ricoeur has been much influenced by his friend and colleague at the University of Chicago, the Romanian Mircea Eliade, whom I have already mentioned in passing. Much of his writing has concentrated on primitive religion and, though most of what he describes in *The Sacred and the Profane* (with the world seen as a 'replica of the paradigmatic universe' of the gods) is now foreign to us, there do seem to be some universal natural symbols that have survived the passage of time. One such is his example of an awareness of transcendence coming through awe at the 'height' of the sky.[173] Ricoeur too accepts the existence of natural symbols: 'An essential characteristic of the symbol is the fact that it is never completely arbitrary . . . there always remains the trace of a natural relationship between the signifier and the signified.'[174] This is an important point because, if there really are such things as natural symbols, then, so far from religious language being an artificial construct, analogical language, the lateral thinking of cross-category comparison, is in fact built into the nature of things. But Ricoeur does not stop there. He has also explored the way in which symbols develop through the response of those using them, and on that basis in a recent paper[175] I have argued that this might be one profitable way in which to view the development of revelation, as involving God's dialogue with our unconscious in the creative transformation of what perhaps began as natural symbols.

So far as sacramental symbols are concerned, it does seem plausible to suggest that water as purifying is a natural symbol. For, even when water becomes destructive, its cleansing aspect surely only becomes muted, not eliminated altogether. That Scripture and in particular the rite of baptism have brought a wealth of additional associations cannot of course be gainsaid.[176] In respect of the eucharist, it is the symbolism of blood which I find most fascinating. Again, it is surely a natural symbol of life. Even today, without needing to search for the meaning, schoolboy gangs can be found making a slight cut in one of their fingers and mixing each other's blood as a symbol that their lives are now bound together by gang loyalty. Little wonder then that for ancient Israel, while the flesh of a sacrifice could be eaten, the blood was seen as belonging to God as owner of the life and therefore to be returned to him either by being poured on the ground or sprinkled on the altar. The drinking of blood was therefore regarded with peculiar horror.[177] Despite this, Jeremias suggests that Jesus used it as a startling metaphor for his own impending sacrifice.[178] That is of course possible, but our oldest text from Paul significantly uses the less direct, 'This cup is the new covenant in my blood'[179] and, though both Mark and Matthew have 'this is my blood', its metaphorical character is clearly indicated by the context through the addition of Jesus' not drinking again of the vine until he drinks it again in the Kingdom of God.[180] In fact, my suggestion would be that only in St John do we have the transformation of the symbol. For only in his Gospel[181] do we have Jesus speaking of the drinking of his blood in an unqualified way and promising with it eternal life. Significantly, this is also pre-eminently the gospel of the Incarnation, and so what I would suggest has happened is that John is drawing out fully the implications of the eucharist as he now sees them, with God himself offering to share his divine life with us in the offer of the symbol that has always in the past been seen as exclusively reserved for him alone.

Now of course the ordinary believer, even if I am right, knows nothing of this development. I mention it none the less for two reasons: first, as an illustration of the transformation of symbols that is clearly relevant here; secondly, because it is above all St John, the Gospel of the Incarnation, which has helped shape this conception of the eucharist as participation in the divine life through incorporation into Jesus' humanity.

In the process of transformation blood has clearly ceased to be a natural symbol, and becomes instead one which only makes sense in the context of a community. But that does not mean that it is now simply chosen, rather than experienced as part of the given. One can and does sometimes choose one's community, but its symbols then come as part of its account of reality. Where choice, however, does come in again is in whether one responds to those symbols. But this need not be, and indeed I suspect for the most part hardly ever is, consciously. Schillebeeckx's talk of 'personal encounter' is in fact hopelessly inadequate. Most of the time we are surely unaware of anything happening. But that does not mean that nothing is happening. Rather, as we have seen, it is characteristic of symbols to function at the unconscious level. Nor need this be seen as in any sense undermining our freedom. For though we make no decisions in our unconscious, what it does and how it responds reflects the sort of people we are at the conscious level, the sort of people we have become by our own free decisions.

Perhaps a parallel with another non-natural symbol, the monarchy, will help here. Those of us who are native-born British citizens have not chosen our community nor this, its central symbol. But we are free to respond to it or not, though we do this mostly at an unconscious level, by endorsing or otherwise the value which it represents, such as tradition, the family, social responsibility, hierarchy and so forth. Even semiologists have difficulty in giving an adequate account of how it achieves its effect. Witness their difficulty in giving an adequate description of the participatory character of a royal wedding.[182] It is a community wedding, not just the wedding of a particular family. But even that is to say too little, since for many British people the royal family is really part of their extended family, or perhaps their family as their dreams would have it be. Indeed, the parallel is such that the monarchy even provides an example of a symbol responding in its turn, since it is clear that the institution would never have survived had it not shown its adaptability to changing circumstances. But this is by no means to say that it performs simply a passive role. For example, in respect of family life or the Church it reflects an ideal image that no longer corresponds with British society as it actually is.

In calling the monarchy a symbol I intended to suggest that the monarchy encapsulates, rather than simply represents, a particular system of values. In *Ordeal by Labyrinth* Eliade recounts how he came to see the point of the icon in Orthodox spirituality by observing the way in which Bengali women treated a local lingam, a stone phallus. Realizing that it was hopelessly inadequate to speak of them as sexually maladjusted, he 'came to understand the possibility of "seeing" the symbol in the lingam. The lingam was the mystery of life, of creativity, of the fertility that is manifested at every cosmic level. And that manifestation of life was Shiva, not the anatomical member that we know. So this possibility of being religiously moved by the image and the symbol – that opened up a whole world of spiritual values to me. I said to myself: it is clear that in looking at an icon the believer does not perceive simply the figure of a woman holding a child; he is seeing the Virgin Mary and therefore the Mother of God.'[183] It is exactly that which I suggest is happening in the case of the eucharist. The nineteenth-century atheist Feuerbach is well known for the aphorism 'Der Mensch ist was er isst' (Man is what he eats). He could not have spoken a truer word of the symbolic world. For, as Paschasius remarks,[184] 'we become part of Christ because we eat him.' And, to revert one last time to the subject of the previous section, as a symbol it could scarcely be offered in a less authoritarian way. God Incarnate places himself in our hands for our unconscious to respond as we will.

Ricoeur's latest work, *Time and Narrative*, has moved in the direction of studying plot. 'Time', he informs us, 'becomes human time to the extent that is organized after the manner of a narrative',[185] and that human dimension he has studied in the writings of both historians and novelists. Of particular interest is the way in which he deals with the apparent counter-example of Europe's most distinguished contemporary historian Fernand Braudel who attempts to make geography hold the central stage. Plausibly Ricoeur responds by observing that, if individuals can really be subordinated, 'why was it necessary to conclude' his most famous work 'with such sumptuous pages on the death of Philip II'.[186]

With the subject of the next chapter, eschatology and the life to come, inevitably one of the first questions we must decide is whether the role of the theologian here is to give history a plot, or whether we have now entered the realm of the symbolic story, the realm of myth, in which case the role of the theologian may be more like that of the novelist as Michel Tournier describes his own task in his intellectual biography, *Le vent Paraclet*: 'The function of the writer is to prevent myths from becoming allegories, mere dead myths.'[187] To that issue I now turn.

6

The Last Things

In this chapter we shall find ourselves discussing a larger number of issues than might initially be suggested by the chapter's title and its two subheadings, 'Eschatology' and 'Death and Beyond'. For in the former case not only is there the question of the extent to which it is right to see the world's history as providentially ordered towards a conclusion; also raised is the status of suffering within that ordering. Again, in the case of 'Death and Beyond' the issue turns out to be not so much a matter of how the after-life is conceived as the way in which the story of Jesus challenges us to reorder the story of our past – our narrative identity – as a means of identifying with him. In addition, a subsidiary theme running throughout will be what we are to make of religious images, both in terms of their referential import and the extent to which necessarily, if at all, they have to be drawn from revelation.

Eschatology

Teilhard and Metz

'Eschatology' literally means 'account of the End' and so in theory should include what Christian doctrine wants to say about the after-life as well as what leads up to that End. But in practice because of Biblical scholars' preoccupation with New Testament expectations of an imminent end of the world the word has effectively narrowed its meaning and is now normally used simply to refer to the process that leads up to that end. In this sense it is easily confused with the closely related term, 'apocalyptic'. This has as its primary reference a particular genre of literature that offers highly symbolic accounts of the dawning of a new age. The last book of the Bible, itself sometimes called 'The Apocalypse', would be a typical example. But apart from this there is also a difference of stress. Apocalyptic tends to envisage a radical break with the past brought about by decisive divine intervention, whereas in eschatology the interest often lies in the way in which the present connects with that future prospect. At all events, that is the way in which I shall use the word in what follows.

The interest of Biblical scholars in the concept is self-explanatory, though there is no unanimity. Opinions vary from at the one extreme Schweitzer's claim that Jesus' teaching is determined as an *Interimsethik* (interim ethics) through expectation of an imminent end, or more recently Sanders' view that Jesus expected the destruction of the Temple to inaugurate the new age, to C. H. Dodd's stress on 'realised eschatology', God's kingdom now entering history, or more recently G. B. Caird's suggestion that much of the language is simply metaphorical.[1] But why should there also be a revival of interest in the notion in twentieth-century systematic theology? Part of the explanation must of course be its now perceived importance in the Biblical text. But other facts are also at play. Two in particular stand out, the question whether science's evolutionary story can be read as a Christian story and secondly the problem of the extent to which modern stress on political action within history can and ought to be incorporated as part of that story. Eschatological theology as the attempt to respond to the challenge of notions of progress in science and history can be well illustrated by the two Roman Catholic theologians of contrasted positions who are the subject of this section, Pierre Teilhard de Chardin (1881–1955) and Johannes Baptist Metz (b. 1928).

Though Teilhard's influence and reputation have now to a considerable degree faded, his views are still worth considering especially as his writings are probably the best-known works of theology since the Second World War, selling millions of copies worldwide. He himself was a trained palaeontologist. Early in his career he was one of those taken in by the Piltdown hoax[2] but he was certainly of sufficient distinction to be offered a professorship at the Collège de France in 1948, having consolidated his reputation particularly through field work in China. His most important work, *The Phenomenon of Man*, having initially been suppressed by the Vatican, finally appeared in the year of his death. It met with an enthusiastic reception from many scientists, and the humanist Sir Julian Huxley even wrote a commendatory introduction to the subsequent English edition, though the Nobel prizewinner, P. B. Medawar treated it to an extremely vitriolic review.[3]

One problem with the work is knowing the category into which it should most appropriately be set. It is an issue which Henri de Lubac considers in *The Religion of Teilhard de Chardin* with respect to his other best-known work, *Le milieu divin*. His verdict is, rightly I think, that Teilhard reveals himself as neither metaphysician nor theologian but as 'mystic'.[4] However, he is prepared to accept Teilhard's own verdict on *The Phenomenon of Man* as 'purely and simply a scientific treatise',[5] and in that I think he is wrong. Indeed, this is to invite assessment on the wrong terms, terms on which he could only fail. Rather, it is the case of a scientist reflecting on the course of evolution so far, and extrapolating its possible future direction. But it is an extrapolation for which in the nature of the case there can be no scientific evidence. For Teilhard fully accepts the fact of human freedom and so with it the possibility of things going badly wrong.[6] Admittedly, a correct understanding is not helped by the way in which his language oscillates between talk on the one hand of 'the general form in which, by analogy and in symmetry with the past, we are led scientifically to envisage the future of mankind' and on the other, two pages later, of 'a beautiful dream'.[7] A better description might be to say that he was concerned to show the reasonableness of hope for the future.

Given the fact that he was almost thirty before he became aware of the theory of evolution, he adopted it with extraordinary enthusiasm. One reason for this may well be the fact that the philosopher most influential on him and to whom he showed some of his papers was Maurice Blondel. Blondel was a major influence on Maréchal and thus on the Transcendental Thomism which we discussed in chapter 1, but here the important aspect to note is his responsibility for what Gregory Baum has labelled 'the Blondelian shift' within Catholic theology towards a stress on God as immanent within human experience.[8] Clearly Teilhard has extended this to the whole creation.

'Modern thought', he tells us, 'is at last getting used once more to the idea of creative synthesis in evolution. It is beginning to see that there is definitely more in the molecule than in the atom, more in the cell than in the molecule, more in society than in the individual . . . We are now inclined to admit that at each further degree of combination something which is irreducible to isolated elements emerges in a new order.'[9] With his fondness for special terminology he describes our present condition as the noosphere, the stage of the individual human mind. But he argues that it is reasonable to expect that it too will be transcended into a higher reality, culminating in what he calls the Omega Point. We have already noted the way in which analogy with the past direction of evolution is integral to his argument. But integral too, in understanding its presumed future direction, is his fundamental principle, that 'union differentiates'. What he means by this is that, while evolution is all the time moving towards greater complexity, it does so in a way which preserves the individual identity of the parts. So he argues that, while it is reasonable to expect the next stage to involve a transcending of human individuality, this will not carry with it as a concomitant the destruction of distinct persons. 'Thus it would be mistaken to represent Omega to ourselves simply as a centre born of the fusion of elements which it collects, or annihilating them in itself. By its structure Omega, in its ultimate principle, can only be a distinct Centre radiating at the core of a system of centres.'[10]

Teilhard then suggests that Christ fulfils the role of that 'distinct Centre'. What he means by this he strives to bring out more clearly in *The Phenomenon of Man*'s mystic complement, *Le milieu divin*: 'Across the immensity of time and the disconcerting multiplicity of individuals, one single operation is taking place . . . one single thing is being made, the mystical body of Christ . . . In a real sense, only one man will be saved: Christ, the head and living summary of humanity.'[11] Likewise, in his meditation 'The Mass on the World' he can talk of his 'overwhelming joy at being transformed into you'.[12] Before the reader dismisses all this as incomprehensible mysticism, he should recall the extent to which it is imbedded within the Christian tradition. Thus Charles Raven seems right in identifying Teilhard's ultimate source in St Paul.[13] Teilhard's mistake was not to introduce such language. It is often very movingly done. Rather, one laments his failure to pursue further his own claim that personal identity can be preserved in such a union by explaining more clearly how he conceived this possible.

But what of his general strategy? Three criticisms suggest themselves. First, he sees as the only alternative to his own position 'a self-abortive and absurd universe': 'Between these two alternatives of absolute optimism or absolute pessimism, there is no middle way because by its very nature progress is all or nothing.'[14] But, while to a contemporary of Sartre this might seem a natural inference, there is no reason why this must be so. For example, progress could be seen as more partial, with Teilhard's culmination in the Omega Point not denied but transferred to beyond the grave. This could still leave numerous areas in which progress might both be detected and hoped for, from the abolition of slavery to international co-operation. A second source of criticism, and linked to the first as a possible explanation for Teilhard's stark alternatives, is the way in which he treats evil. I have already noted his acceptance of free will. But it is never really integrated into his thought. Thus significantly evil only occurs as an appendix in *The Phenomenon of Man* and even then he is concerned to stress the contribution it makes – 'so many by-products (often precious, moreover, and re-utilisable) begotten by the noosphere on its way'.[15] But this surely is to fail to take free will seriously enough. If man really does have such radical freedom, must it not mean that he has the power to subvert, and indeed subvert ultimately, any plan God has for him?

Finally, on quite a different note one may challenge Teilhard's assumption that the rest of creation is simply a stage on the way to the culmination of human perfection. Intriguingly Raven compliments Teilhard on being very un-French in his interest in nature and in this respect at least very English. (He spent four years training to be a Jesuit at Hastings because of the expulsion of the religious orders from France in 1902.) But in response one can raise the possibility that, so far from God valuing nature simply as a means to an end, he values it in its own right as a thing of beauty, irrespective of the contribution it makes to man. In other words, it is arguable that Teilhard has not after all escaped the 'French' anthropocentric universe of which Raven complains.

Though also a Roman Catholic, Metz's theology is very different from Teilhard's. Indeed, he tells us that he prefers the atheist Jacques Monod's stress on the role of chance in nature to a Teilhardian teleology, giving as explanation the following reason: 'It is the idea of suffering that is so strongly opposed to an affirmation of the theory of reconciliation between man and nature . . . Suffering stresses the contrast between nature and history, teleology and eschatology. There can be no "objective" reconciliation and no visible and manageable unity between them.'[16] Such a contrast between nature and history is perhaps all the more surprising when one recalls Metz's extensive early contacts with Transcendental Thomism. Not only did he write one of his doctorates under Rahner, he was entrusted with extensive revisions to one of Rahner's major works.[17]

Though in that thesis he credits Aquinas with an 'anthropocentric shift' that was to culminate in the Enlightenment, he was to become increasingly dissatisfied with the failure of the Blondel–Maréchal–Rahner axis to take the implications of the Enlightenment with sufficient seriousness. The way in which Transcendental Thomism saw God as spirit immanent in every human act meant that it tended to lay all the stress on man as spirit and so demote man as enmattered. The consequence was that, despite all Rahner's stress on God as mystery, the Enlightenment's insistence on the gap between God and man was effectively lessened. Even death could be seen as a natural transition for spirit. This is, if anything, accentuated by Rahner's strong evolutionary perspective. Indeed commentators have not been slow to detect affinities with Teilhard, and one recent exposition of Rahner's thought suggests that not only do they share the same teleological perspective, it is this that leads them to a common dualism. Because man is the crown of evolution as 'conscious and free spirit', 'beyond the dogma of teleology there is another: the dogma of man's duality.'[18]

For Metz, by contrast, we do not live in a universe imbued with the sacred. There is a process of desacralization taking place, which has been intensified by the Enlightenment. But this is not something which the Christian should regret. This is the main contention of his book *Theology of the World* (1968). 'God's divinity', he tells us, 'consists in the fact that he does not remove the difference between himself and what is other, but rather accepts the other precisely as different from himself.'[19] So the 'irreversible secularisation of the world'[20] is to be welcomed as revealing the world in the colours which God intended it to have, the place where human freedom and responsibility can be exercised. 'Hence we may say that "to Christianise the world" means fundamentally "to secularise it" – to bring it into its own, bestowing on it scarcely conceived heights or depths of its own worldly being.'[21] In presenting his claim Metz likes to play on the German word for secularization, *Verweltlichung*, taking it to mean 'letting the world (*Welt*) be what it really is': 'The place where the responsibility of the Christian community starts is the world in its permanent and growing worldliness.'[22] Because he interprets the Incarnation as 'the most radical release of the world to itself' he suggests that 'the principle of incarnation' is really 'the principle of secularisation' with the independence of mankind to achieve what it can revealed proleptically 'in its eschatological character'.[23]

Many of Metz's reflections have been pursued through articles and even his books have something of this form. So it is not always easy to form a rounded picture of his ideas. But a more recent work, *Faith in History and Society*, while continuing the secularity thesis, develops another aspect of his thought in an interesting way. This is his idea of how the past can be carried into the future through the subversive character of memories. So, for example, one chapter is entitled 'The dangerous memory of the freedom of Jesus Christ', another 'The future in the memory of suffering' and yet another simply 'Memory'. Such an emphasis may seem strange in one whose primary theological interest is in the future, but that is where the qualification 'dangerous' or 'subversive' becomes relevant. So, for example, the remembrance of Jesus' identification with the oppressed 'mobilises tradition as a dangerous tradition and therefore as a liberating force'.[24] Again, his hostility to teleology is explained by his conviction that no adequate explanation can be offered of suffering in the world.[25] Instead, its meaning lies in the way in which it can be carried as a memory into the future. 'The imagination of future freedom is nourished from the memory of suffering . . . It becomes a dangerous and liberating memory over against the controls and mechanisms of the dominant consciousness and its abstract ideal of emancipation.'[26]

So far as his secularization thesis is concerned, while the stress on human responsibility is surely to be welcomed, the question remains whether this has not been bought at too high an expense. For he offers us no account of how such freedom might relate to divine grace except permissively and as future prospect, while at the other end of the spectrum nature seems to be not merely desacralized but demoted from all respect. Thus he speaks of 'a world that does not present itself as God's majestic and untouchable representative, but as the building-site and laboratory of man and his planning',[27] with the natural world seen as justifying 'cosmological atheism'.[28] This reads very oddly from a Catholic, but in fact he derives the thesis from the Protestant Friedrich Gogarten's *Verhängnis und Hoffnung der Neuzeit* of 1953, though he was apparently already beginning to work it out as early as 1926.

Richard Schaeffler in a recent book, *Was dürfen wir hoffen?*[29] has questioned whether Metz in adopting the thesis has not changed its significance, since for Gogarten it is closely tied not to the Englighten-ment but to a specifically religious doctrine, justification by faith. The argument essentially is that the Reformation by stressing faith opened works to the possibility of a purely secular achievement and at the same time put a question-mark against all attempts to divinize those achievements as normative. While accepting the caution, significantly Schaeffler as a more traditional Catholic prefers to talk of 'sacramental anticipation'.[30] Certainly we do need something to indicate continued divine involvement. Otherwise the future, so far from helping to make sense of the present, will seem to be simply a disconnected dénouement, apocalyptic in the worst sense of that term.

Of course Metz believes that he has an answer to this objection in the connections which 'dangerous memories' make from the past through the present into the future. His more recent writings have particularly stressed the way in which this is enshrined in narrative: 'The intelligibility of Christianity cannot be transmitted theologically in a purely speculative way. It can only be transmitted in narrative – as a narrative and practical Christianity.'[31] Provided referential issues (whether anything is being claimed about the external world) are not ignored, this constitutes a valuable corrective to more traditional approaches. Metz describes the philosopher Ernst Bloch's main work, *Das Prinzip Hoffnung*, as 'a great encyclopedia of "hope" stories'.[32] Since he is the main philosophic influence behind Metz and other theologians of hope like Moltmann, it will be as well to turn to the source itself for further enlightenment before attempting any further critique.

Bloch and Adorno

Just as we have been able to use Teilhard and Metz as a foil to each other despite the fact that they come from the same intellectual tradition, so what is in many ways a similar contrast can be drawn between the writings of Ernst Bloch (1885–1977) and Theodor Adorno

(1903–69) despite their common inheritance in atheistic Marxism. Bloch, like Teilhard, is supremely an optimist, while in Adorno, like Metz, we find the same suspicion of a single, closely integrated view of reality and the same pessimistic stress on the inexplicable character of suffering. Despite this, as already noted, it is Bloch and not Adorno who has deeply influenced Metz. The reason for this is not hard to find. Adorno is a thinker profoundly unsympathetic to religion. None the less both have interesting insights to offer, a fact perhaps largely explicable in another inheritance they share. They are both Jews.

One of Bloch's essays opens with the following remark: 'With this do we wish to begin, namely with the simple affirmation that it is not only at night that we dream.'[33] That might be taken as the motto of Bloch's entire philosophy. For as early as the age of twenty-two he had already written an essay with the title 'On the Category Not-Yet' and this notion of the *noch nicht*, of the way in which our dreams and hopes anticipate a future reality, was to recur throughout his long working life. So for example it is the theme of his first major work in 1918, *Geist der Utopie*, but it is equally prominent in his longest and most important work, *The Principle of Hope*, first published in the 1950s but only translated into English in 1986.[34] There he offers a fascinating range of examples – buying a new dress, images in illustrated magazines, travel brochures, antique furniture, cinema plots and so forth. In 1933 like Adorno he had to flee Germany because of his race, but unlike Adorno it was to East and not West Germany that he returned after the war. So his major work was in fact published while he held a chair of philosophy at Leipzig. However, after the 1956 Hungarian uprising things became increasingly difficult for him and with the building of the Berlin Wall in 1961 he finally fled to the West, where he was offered a chair at Tübingen, and during the student unrest of the 1960s became something of a cult figure. But he retained his commitment to his revisionary Marxism to the end.

The range of Bloch's interests may have raised once again in the reader's mind a question that may have troubled him a number of times in the course of this book, namely what it is that makes it appropriate to describe someone with such a wide range of interests as Bloch as a philosopher (or Barthes and Foucault, to mention two other obvious cases). At one level the answer is an easy one. The university appointments they have held have usually been so designated. But the deeper answer of course lies in the type of problems with which they chose to wrestle and their presuppositional or foundational character (even when anti-foundationalism is the conclusion drawn, as in Deconstructionism!). So for instance Foucault's interest in the history of such things as attitudes to sexuality, prisons and madness is in the final analysis subservient to his 'genealogy of knowledge', his attempt to identify the pursuit of power as the underlying basis to all we claim to know. So also then with Bloch; it is because for him hope exercises a similar foundational role in our relations with the world. That the main inspiration for this analysis was drawn from Marxism has already been noted.

Why he none the less retained a strong interest in religion is not hard to seek. At the personal level one may note his twenty-year-long friendship with another German Jewish thinker, whom we will discuss later in this chapter, Walter Benjamin. To this one can add the deep commitment of his first wife to Christianity. But more fundamentally there is the intellectual connection which Bloch detected between Marxism and religion. Marx offered hope for a future society in which conflicting interests are reconciled and the state withers away. But, as Heinz Kimmerle well expresses it, 'for Bloch the longer they last, the more do hope and religion become identical concepts. Religion is, as it were, the historical form of hope, and hope the present form of religion.'[35] In other words, though it may now take a secular and Marxist form, in the past hope for a better future has characteristically taken a religious form, and he interprets Marx's famous comment about religions being 'the opium of the people'[36] not as utterly condemning religion but as a recognition of the way in which covertly it points to legitimate aspirations outside of itself.

In this context of particular interest is the way in which Bloch's understanding of religion differs from the most famous atheistic reduction of the nineteenth century, that by Feuerbach, who in turn was criticized by Marx in his 1845 *Theses on Feuerbach* for not carrying his critique far enough. Feuerbach's approach is essentially reductionist in a way in which Bloch's is not. Thus for the former religion is just a matter of projection, of man ascribing to another supernatural being qualities of which he himself is fully capable in the here and now. In other words the claim is that a complete explanation and translation of what religion means can be offered without any difficulty. By contrast Bloch, though equally insisting on an atheistic content, sees its hope as having to take the same shape as religion. So equally talk of transcendence is indispensable, man transcending himself into another form of existence, and that future *humanum* is entitled to all the awe and sense of mystery traditionally ascribed to God.[37] Moltmann gets it exactly right in *Im Gespräch mit Ernst Bloch* when after observing that Bloch can sometimes appear to be merely repeating Feuerbach's monotonous 'the God-hypothesis is nothing other than . . .' continues: 'nevertheless these messianic ties of atheism allow no reduction of the religious symbols to the anthropology of man as he is at present' and so 'his atheism is not reductionist atheism.'[38] The result is that Bloch is even prepared to use the language of 'God' in his writings because of the mysterious and indefinable quality of the future hope. Perhaps inevitably as a result, in East Germany he was accused of being a pantheist rather than a Marxist.

This stance in fact leads him in one of his Tübingen works, *Atheismus im Christentum*, to a fascinating critique of Bultmann's demythologization programme.[39] Basically his argument is that too much is lost in Bultmann's reduction to an existential transformation in the present. For it is precisely through its myths that the Bible offers a *visio haeretica* of a transformed future. But, though he is right to challenge Bultmann's exclusive orientation towards the present, I seriously doubt whether even within the Christian community it is through myth as story that the future vision is preserved. Of course some stories about the future such as the parable of Dives and Lazarus[40] continue to be both meaningful and challenging, but it is surely significant that for the vast majority of Christians the Book of Revelation is now a closed book, apart from the opening chapters which refer to the present and the concluding section with its magnificent description of Heaven. The apocalyptic events on earth remain unread. Nor is it hard to understand why. Not only is the imagery too complex to make 'a good story', more fundamentally our transformed understanding of the age of our planet and its relative insignificance in the universe make it difficult to comprehend why such a decisive dénouement should be envisaged as taking place on earth. For must we not think of all generations and all forms of intelligent life as being equally significant to God?

Intriguingly, in his recently translated *Essays on the Philosophy of Music* Bloch suggests that 'music flowered when . . . God's traces in the visible world were disintegrating' and that the arts are now 'the nearest place to the house of a parousia or Second Coming'.[41] In chapter 2 I suggested that the myth of the Garden of Eden now effectively functions not as story but as single image, as in a painting. Much the same, I would suggest, has happened here. Bloch himself suggests that it is now music that for most people 'reproduces the symbols of expectancy'[42] which the liturgy of death and the eschatological stories of the Bible could once have produced on their own. Certainly for me nothing more effectively expresses 'what a fearful thing it is to fall into the hands of the living God'[43] than the *Dies Irae* of Verdi's *Requiem* with, as Bloch describes it, its 'shattering blows' and 'plummeting cries'. It leaves no belief possible than that one's survival is totally dependent on God's mercy. Equally poignant in its evocation of our ultimate ability to self-destruct in a definitive 'No' to the divine love is the conclusion to Mozart's *Don Giovanni*. Despite the pleas of Donna Elvira and Leporello that he repent and the decisive indication of approaching divine judgement in the statue of the Commendatore coming to life, Don Giovanni exercises the freedom God has given to all of us and with a sort of tragic heroism accepts the consequences of his unrepented wickedness. Nor as Christians should we be afraid of admitting that music can sometimes succeed in conveying religious truth, where the Bible is less effective or even a closed book. Peter Schaffer's play *Amadeus* powerfully imprints on the mind the paradox that the working of God's Spirit cannot be narrowly confined to the devout, with in this case the smutty-minded buffoon Mozart being his agent rather than the mediocre but pious Salieri. Indeed, even the great defender of the exclusive role of Christian revelation, Karl Barth, finds himself conceding that Mozart 'had heard, and causes those who have ears to hear . . . what we shall not see until the end of time – the whole context of providence'.[44]

But what then, it will be asked, are we to make of the central acclamations in modern versions of the eucharist: 'Christ has died, Christ is risen. Christ will come again'? Might the third acclamation not best be interpreted as proclaiming that at each and every eucharist we are offered a foretaste of what will only be fully realized in Heaven but to which we can approximate more and more, the more we allow ourselves to be incorporated into the story of that life which is recounted at each liturgy? The this-earth reference of the language thus serves a twofold purpose, in that first it is the only language we have even to describe Heaven, but secondly and equally importantly, it reminds us that even now Christ is not absent from us but available in the here and now to aid us in producing earthly approximations to that heavenly consummation.

For Bloch, of course, only a this-world consummation is possible. Two of the adages at the beginning of *Atheismus im Christentum* well summarize his position. For, if his anti-reductionist strand is encapsulated in the comment that 'only an atheist can be a good Christian, only a Christian a good atheist', equally 'decisive' for him is the maxim 'Ein Transzendieren ohne Transzendenz' (A transcending without Transcendence). What this embodies is his resistance to any attempt to objectify the symbol 'God'. 'The Bible assuredly has the future in so far as with this future it transcends without Transcendence.'[45] 'God' is an ideal term for future hope, as something which transcends ('goes beyond') the present, but, in so far as we can understand that future on the basis of present experience, all we can expect is a transformed human future. For, in what Gerhard Martin has labelled Bloch's 'central paradox', 'God disappears, when he arrives.'[46]

Leszek Kolakowski in *Main Currents of Marxism* sees his work as the nadir of a system which Kolakowski himself once embraced but now despises. Significantly the volume in which his account of Bloch occurs is subtitled 'The Breakdown' and the section on Bloch is called 'Marxism as Futuristic Gnosis', with Bloch's thought credited with 'the eventual creation of God'.[47] If this at least is a charge from which Bloch can be successfully defended, there still remains the question of what reason we could have for envisaging a transformed humanity. It all seems to hang, like Teilhard, on his understanding of the potentialities of matter. For, though he admits a looser relation between base (i.e. matter) and superstructure than in orthodox Marxism, it is to matter that he assigns the possibility of producing new forms of subjectivity in the future.[48] Hudson in his book on *The Marxist Philosophy of Ernst Bloch* rightly complains of the large number of very different senses in which the word 'matter' is used.[49] But more fundamentally one can also complain of the fault shared by all Marxist utopian visions of the future, that without some supernatural agent guaranteeing the teleology or at the very least there to effect a dénouement it is hard to see what conceivable reason there could be for such confidence. The evolution of matter perhaps, as Teilhard insists, discloses the possibility, but hardly the likelihood. This makes it all the more puzzling why his notion of God as transcendent future has been so enthusiastically endorsed in much contemporary German theology. For even with God as objective future reality and not just symbol, it still creates more problems than it solves, in particular the question of why the future should be so different if God is not found to be intimately involved in the present. For it is surely only in so far as we can identify a divine interest in the present that we gain any entitlement to speak of God's interest in man's future. This cannot thus be used as a means of avoiding the issue of the nature of divine action in the here and now.

Moltmann, though following Bloch in so much else, does take him to task on another feature which he shares with Teilhard, his supreme optimism. 'It seems to me that as in the creation narrative so in Job, the Psalms and the Lamentations of Jeremiah the new above all emerges not as the "not-yet" but exactly there in the Not itself.'[50] What he means by this is that Bloch by concentrating on the already partially present signs of hope ignores the vital issue of what to say in the face of the apparent total absence of such signs. That is presumably why he continues: 'If that is right, that would give me cause to speak of an eschatology of the Cross.'

If Moltmann's first major book, *Theology of Hope* (1965), is thoroughly imbued with the influence of Bloch, his subsequent and probably best-known work, *The Crucified God* (1973), is intended as a response to another German Marxist philosopher, Theodor Adorno,[51] and here the question of our response to the Not bulks large. But though the book is movingly and passionately written, I seriously doubt the extent to which Moltmann has in this case actively engaged with Adorno's thought. There are suprisingly few references to Adorno's writings, and it is perhaps therefore best regarded as simply an independent treatment of the problem of suffering.

Adorno's writings are in any case rather forbidding with their frequently highly complex sentences and meaning conveyed indirectly through irony. However, one of the easiest to read is in fact his attack on Existentialism, *The Jargon of Authenticity*, in which the theme of death bulks large. Heidegger's insistence on authenticity in the face of death is castigated for failing to take death seriously enough. He is accused of only being interested in the style with which one faces death and so of implicitly endorsing Nazi self-sacrifice.[52] But not only that, the true nature of death is further concealed by its being given a numinous quality: 'Death becomes the representative of God, for whom the Heidegger of *Sein und Zeit* felt himself too modern.'[53] In other words, it has become that alone to which one has a responsibility to live as one ought, that is 'authentically'. The divine freedom is even ascribed to death, since it alone escapes the conformist pressure of the impersonal 'they'. The result is that 'Heidegger's doctrine becomes an exegesis of the futile joke: Only death is free and that costs you your life.'[54] For Adorno, by contrast, there is no escaping its essential reality – 'its misery and stench', the fact that it is simply 'an animalistic kicking of the bucket'.[55]

Adorno is surely right that the stark reality of suffering and death must be taken seriously and not in any way be disguised by a false optimism. Moltmann does not consider this work, but he does offer a general response to the challenge of suffering, which is to stress the suffering nature of God. 'For this theology, God and suffering are no longer contradictions, as in theism and atheism, for God's being is in suffering and the suffering is in God's being itself.'[56] In this way he hopes to answer the 'protest atheism' of Ivan Karamazov who in a famous incident in Dostoevsky's novel 'most respectfully returns the ticket' to God for allowing a world in which a mother can witness her infant son being torn apart by dogs on the orders of her master.[57] But it is not immediately clear how this resolves the issue. In briefly alluding to Moltmann in chapter 2 I stressed how different any such divine suffering must be in virtue of the transformed understanding brought about by divine omniscience. For suffering becomes very much easier to bear when one knows for certain of a happy outcome.

What in fact seems to me to be the key issue for Adorno that is ignored both by Moltmann and by more traditional approaches to this question of theodicy is what one can say in the actual situation of the unresolved outcome. Thus at one level Auschwitz is easy to answer. God values a free human response but men have chosen to use that gift in terrible ways. As Plato said long ago, 'God is not to blame; the responsibility lies with him who made the choice.'[58] But at another level it fails completely. For, while it may give a meaning to the whole, it fails to address the awfulness of immediate experience, and if there was one thing Adorno was opposed to it was 'totality' thinking. Another way of making this point might be to say that our temporal condition needs to be taken seriously. Theodicy needs some way of addressing the unresolved present as well as the total picture, if it is to give meaning to all of human experience in the here and now.

I have known cases of clergy exhorting mourners to rejoice even at the death of a child since 'he is now with Jesus his Saviour'. One recoils from this, not because it is not true, nor because of the insensitivity of saying it (though that is true), but because it is only through the pain being first experienced as unresolved that it can then be accepted. For often nothing is worse or more soul-destroying than the suppression of this unresolved stage, the necessity for the grief to be expressed, with havoc instead being wrought in the unconscious. It is then at this point that the action of God on the Cross becomes relevant, not as one conscious of his future Resurrection but as one who in voluntary self-limitation could cry, 'My God, my God, why has thou forsaken me?' For when the Incarnation is perceived in this way, what we then have is God hallowing the unresolved present, endorsing the question that sees no meaning in the present betokening a good future. Nor is this the only example one might take. One thinks equally of the dark night of the soul of the mystics. In other words, the point I am trying to make is that Christianity needs to, and can, give significance to the unresolved present, by stressing the necessity of the temporal sequence, that there is nothing wrong with the cry of despair in the present and it needs to be lived through before its wider meaning can either be perceived or appropriated.

I have already mentioned Adorno's hostility to totality thinking. It is in fact a recurring theme of his writing. Capitalist society is seen as reducing everything to its exchange value, and he observes this reflected in philosophy itself in what he calls identity thinking, the blurring of differences and acceptance of equations in order to produce a single conceptual system. So, for example, though he was attracted to Kierkegaard, on whom he wrote his *Habilitation*,[59] because of the latter's attack on Hegel's system, he did not hesitate to accuse Kierkegaard of indulging in identity thinking in his turn. A case in point would be the way in which his identification of the 'neighbour' as all others alike ignores natural instincts and social context.[60] Again, as an exile in Oxford in 1934–7 he wrote *Against Epistemology*, which is a sustained attack on Husserl's attempt to systematize the foundations of our knowledge. But the theme continues equally after the war with the 1947 *Dialectic of Enlightenment* attacking what he sees as its totalitarian character with everything reduced to purely instrumental value. It is hardly surprising therefore that in the relatively late work, *The Jargon of Authenticity* of 1964, his objection to Heidegger on death are put in the following form: 'Identification with that which is inevitable remains the only consolation of this philosophy of consolation: it is the last identity.'[61]

So convinced is Gillian Rose of the decisive influence of Nietzsche on Adorno that she takes the latter's ironic adaptation of Nietzsche's phrase 'the gay science' as the title of her own book on Adorno, *The Melancholy Science*. She notes that even as central a concept as *Verdinglichung* (reification), the process of objectification that makes identity thinking possible, may owe more to Nietzsche than to Marx.[62] But for our purposes here of more interest is the fact that Adorno unlike Bloch shares Nietzsche's hostility to religion. He thinks that religion necessarily involves identity thinking. Thus, for example, Cartesianism, including Husserl's, is taken to be attempting 'to reproduce out of itself the Christian cosmos'[63] or again in *Minima Moralia* he informs us that 'it is no accident that catholicism is the Greek word for the Latin totality.'[64] Thus in so far as he does indulge in utopian thinking it is hardly surprising that it is not to religion that he turns but to the Arts, particularly music.

He himself was an accomplished musician, having studied under the composer Alban Berg in Vienna, and his *Philosophy of Modern Music*, in which he championed the music of Schoenberg against that of Stravinsky, exercised a considerable influence after the war. What seems to have particularly attracted him to Schoenberg's twelve-note technique was its resistance to being turned into yet another form of commodity exchange and so its resultant ability to comment on society simply in virtue of this contrast. But it is not just the resistance in itself that attracts him, but what makes that resistance possible, the formal features of the new music. It is imageless thinking, and what especially traps us into reification is images. True thought, he tells us, 'is no picturing of reality . . . The clarifying intention of thought, demytho- logisation, extinguishes the picturing nature of consciousness. What is bound up with a picture remains deluded in mythological idolatry.'[65] Significantly in the light of this, he attacks Georg Lukács (the best- known twentieth-century defender of something like orthodox Marxism) for failing to appreciate that literature achieves its critique not through narrative but through various formal techniques, such as irony.[66]

Art thus on Adorno's view indirectly suggests an alternative, a 'utopia', through there lurking in the form' a hidden "it should be otherwise" '.[67] Given the inevitable allusiveness of the subject of Christian theology and the resultant need to resort to analogy to describe such a non-embodied being, this cannot but find some answering chord among theologians. Indeed, at one point in *Negative*

Dialektik Adorno even suggests that all he is really doing is carrying the Jewish prohibition on images to its legitimate conclusion.[68] But at the same time there is need for caution, since at the heart of the Christian faith lies the assertions that God has in fact offered a perfect image of himself in Jesus.

Indeed, even within the Jewish context one can challenge whether it is ever form of itself which achieves the distorting, 'utopian' effect and not rather the dynamic interchange between form and content, with the content (the 'image') often making the decisive contribution to this relationship. Bloch illustrates the inadequacy of any purely formal analysis when he notes the way in which Bach can use the same melody that was once attached to a folk love song to express the chorale 'O sacred head sore wounded', or now to express hypocrisy, now the *Kyrie* in the *Mass in G*.[69] But let me add two examples of my own, still from within this same Jewish context. The German poet Paul Celan lost both his parents in the Holocaust and he himself committed suicide in 1970. His best-known poem is *Todesfuge* ('Death Fugue'),[70] a reflection on Auschwitz. The intriguing thing about it is that it achieves its effect precisely through the poignant contrast that is brought about when the beauty of its language and structure is set against the horrific nature of what is being described. In that case, despite the essential contribution from the content, it is clearly the form which makes the decisive contribution. But an example of a case where the decisive contribution comes from the images can in fact be offered from Adorno's favourite composer, Schoenberg himself.

The theme of his masterpiece *Moses und Aron*, written in 1932 but not produced until after his death in 1957, is the impossibility of expressing God in images. Thus the opera opens with an emphatic declaration from Moses that God is quite beyond perception and representation, and the intended shape of the plot was that, though his brother Aron compromised in order to secure the allegiance of the people, the final act would show Moses triumphant and Aron dead through his folly. But that final act was never set to music in the twenty years which elapsed before his death, and so the opera as performed has a very different structure. But not only that. Aron is accorded music of such lyrical beauty in contrast to Moses' spoken part that one's sympathies cannot help but be drawn to Aron rather than Moses, a sympathy that is only further reinforced when Moses breaks the tablets of the Law in response to Aron's declaration that they also are only images ('. . . die nur ein Bild'). It is a fascinating comment from a Jew of deep religious commitment, and musicologists have not been slow to point out that his failure to complete the third act may in itself be a recognition of the ultimate sterility of making the form, imageless thinking, its own *raison d'être*.

Death and beyond

Jüngel

Eberhard Jüngel, like Moltmann and Küng, is a professor of theology at Tübingen. From there he continues to propagate the Barthian tradition, his first important work being a study of Barth's theology of the Trinity, first published in 1964. Though he himself describes it as a 'paraphrase' of Barth,[71] significantly the German title, *Gottes Sein ist im Werden*, has a Hegelian ring – 'God's Being is in Becoming' – and while the limits of the content of his theology remain firmly Barthian, the form of their expression takes on an increasingly Hegelian stamp. That Barthian framework emerges with, if anything, increased vigour in his longest work to date, *God as the Mystery of the World* (1977), in which we are treated to a sustained attack on philosophical attempts at justifying belief in God. What cogency this has we shall examine shortly, but first note must be taken of the position to which this leads him. 'For responsible Christian usage of the word "God" ', he tells us, 'the Crucified One is virtually the real definition of what is meant with the word "God".'[72] The implications of this he regards as involving not only a radical questioning of traditional attributes including the exclusion of possibility from God,[73] but also, and more relevant to our purposes here, the view that it is only through this death that we can have access to the life beyond.

It is a position for which a short earlier work, *Death: the riddle and the mystery*, had already laid the ground. There he comes out emphatically against the immortality of the soul, which he identifies as the classical Christian view.[74] What he finds wrong with this is the way in which it treats as absolute something which the Bible only acknowledges, if at all, in relationship. The Old Testament attitude he observes is that 'the name is something which belongs to the living. And the name of the dead person can live on only through the living.'[75] The result is that 'Israel's God is the God of the living, not of the dead. The dead are cut off from his hand.'[76] From this he takes the chief characteristic of death for the Old Testament to be 'relationlessness',[77] an event in which an individual is conceived as being not only cut off from his fellow human beings but even from God. All this changes with the new life made possible by Christ, so much so that for the New Testament 'life and death are . . . no longer the criteria which define man's relationship to God. Jesus Christ and faith in him is the one criterion for defining that relationship.'[78] The consequence is that death is now seen as no more than a natural end, not a breaking-off,[79] and the real threat of the breaking off of the relation, 'the curse of death', is seen as already passed in this life with the arrival of faith.[80] Hence the reason presumably why Paul can use the language of death and resurrection of the beginnings of Christian life in baptism and John speak of eternal life as beginning in the here and now.[81]

As an account of the Biblical view this is very fair, though much less so in respect of those who stress the role of the soul since orthodox versions of this have always insisted that the life of the soul remains incomplete without a resurrected body.[82] Here too there is thus a dependency on divine grace for a full and worthwhile survival. But so concerned is Jüngel to accentuate grace that anything at all that draws attention away from God's action on the Cross and our justification by faith through it is immediately ruled out of court. Indeed, such attitudes, which he labels 'theism', are held responsible for the rise of atheism, and his claim in *God as the Mystery of the World* is that 'atheism can be rejected only if one overcomes theism.'[83] Descartes is seen as the source of the problem with his attempt to prove divine existence starting from the indubitable certainty of human subjectivity in his famous *Cogito* ('I think, therefore I am').[84] Indeed, his introduction of the possibility of a deceiver God in the course of his argument is described as 'monstrous' and this whole tradition of Cartesianism, of attempting to found our knowledge on something other than God, is labelled 'the dictatorship of metaphysics'.[85] For Jüngel, by contrast, there can be only one starting-point that avoids all attempts at self-justification, and that is the Cross. That way we avoid the 'methodological will to atheism',[86] the necessary calling of his existence into doubt in order to prove his existence. Instead, it is God who first addresses us in the weakness and suffering of the Cross. In a way that recalls Moltmann, though it is actually to a rather controversial interpretation of Hegel's 'speculative Good Friday' that he appeals,[87] theodicy is thus he believes at the heart of our knowledge of the divine existence, not its periphery.

There are at least four criticisms which can be made of his stance here. First, though the way in which he is thus led to stress divine attributes such as love and passibility is clear enough, the rationale behind some other forms of expression is obscure, if not downright unintelligible. So, for example, he does not hesitate to speak of the death of God and of the necessary connection between divinity and perishability in the Crucifixion.[88] Behind this talk lies a Hegelian dialectic, with a stage implied beyond this meeting of opposites, but what is left unresolved is what such language really means. For it is one thing to say that suffering could be part of the divine nature; quite another death itself. This is not to say that the notion could not be rendered intelligible, merely that Jüngel offers no aid.

This is in large part explained by his resistance to any borrowing of terminology from philosophy that is clearly non-biblical. Hegel escapes only because he is seen as endorsing the Biblical picture. J. B. Webster in an otherwise largely sympathetic treatment of Jüngel suggests that the fault lies in 'a confusion between ontological and epistemological issues. That is to say, he does not distinguish between the claim that God is *contingent* upon the world and the claim that *knowledge* of God is dependent upon *knowledge* of the world.'[89] This may well be part of the problem. But at its heart seems to me to lie the question of self-justification versus divine justification. It is held that only if God is our starting-point can we avoid the fault implied in the former. But this is to misconstrue what philosophers or anyone who indulges in apologetics is trying to do. To admit that something is more fundamental epistemologically is by no means to endorse that it be given greater weight in one's life, anymore than it follows from an admission that artistic creativity is impossible without enough to eat, that eating is thereby accorded more value than art or literature.

None of this is to deny that Jüngel provides a very effective challenge to any philosopher who thinks that our account of God must be produced by natural theology or not at all. But Jüngel is equally mistaken in thinking that appeal to revelation can bypass questions of justification that just as much place God at the end or conclusion of an argument. Thus in depicting his suffering God Jüngel stresses the cry of dereliction from the Cross. But why should we take that verse from Mark as definitive rather than, say, the great cry of triumph with which he dies according to St John's Gospel?[90]

Finally, it is hard to see how such rigid and exclusive concentration on divine justification can avoid the accusation that in effect what is being asserted is the ultimate worthlessness of human existence. For on this view God appears to value us only if we deny ourselves and those whom we love all intrinsic value. That then makes it all the more puzzling why God should wish for the extension of such lives beyond death, since they have no value in their own right, only in the artificial value God has accorded them through justification by faith. A much better explanation of this doctrine, I would suggest, is that God's love for us is already infinite even at our lowest base; so what appropriation of this, as demonstrated on the Cross, means is the realization that nothing we do can add to our value in God's eyes. There is thus no need to prove ourselves. But from this it by no means follows that anything further that we do is without value, any more than one when added to infinity loses its numeral value, though it in no way increases infinity. Putting it another way, looked at as a whole each life is of the same infinite value, but looked at in its parts some are of more value than others. But because the whole is infinite it is not possible nor permissible for us to judge someone's worth simply in virtue of his parts.

It seems to me that it is precisely because the parts do matter and have value that the narrative of our lives is of such significance for our future destiny. Jüngel does insist that temporal sequence must continue after death if our identity is be preserved,[91] but unfortunately in his discussion of narrative he confines his attention to 'the Humanity of God as a Story to be Told'.[92] His stress on divine justification has blinded him to the fact that faith is not just appropriation of another's story, that of Jesus, but also the reordering of one's own past such that its parts too can have value in God's eyes. Jüngel twice mentions Benjamin in the course of his discussion. He too is primarily concerned with the way in which story shapes communal identity. So with that better understood we should also be able to answer more effectively our question about individual identity.

Benjamin

Walter Benjamin (1892–1940) published only two books during his lifetime, and neither made much impact at the time. However, since his suicide while trying to escape occupied France his reputation has steadily increased, so much so that George Steiner has described him as 'the most important aesthetician and literary critic of this century'.[93] Part of the problem was his style. Like Adorno he had difficulty in obtaining his *Habilitation*, and it is not hard to see why, since even Steiner finds himself describing it as 'one of the most impenetrable pieces of prose in German'.[94] But balanced against that is the lucidity of his shorter writings, many of which have been usefully assembled in a volume entitled *Illuminations*, and which can be used as a way of access to his longer writings.

One of these, a discussion of the nineteenth-century Russian short story writer Leskov, and simply called 'The Storyteller', is full of illumination on the theme of narrative. He opens controversially: 'Familiar though his name may be to us, the storyteller in his living immediacy is by no means a present force. He has already become something remote from us and something that is getting even more distant.'[95] This is because his art depends on a corporate oral tradition, and Benjamin argues that this is inevitably breaking down because of the speed of change in the modern world. The result is that the novel has usurped its place, for this is essentially the product of 'the solitary individual', whereas the story is not. 'The storyteller takes what he tells from experience – his own or that reported by others. And he in turn makes it the experience of those who are listening to his tale.'[96] Its position in the communal memory is he believes what explains its lack of psychological analysis and its openness to various interpretations. For even within a shared framework of assumptions, it still needs compactness and freshness in order to retain its status.[97] But, more surprisingly, this also he suggests explains the story's relation to death, and points to one part of the reason for its decline. 'Death is the sanction of everything that the storyteller can tell. He has borrowed his authority from death.'[98] What he means by this is, first, that it is only at death that a person's life is released to the story-teller as open to a definitive intepretation, a definitive telling, and, secondly, that each such story because of the communal character of story offers us a way of seeing our own life in death. But decline in the public experience of death has meant that this is now a less central concern and so all the novel offers us is something that firmly remains someone else's fate. Indeed, in another essay[99] he uses Proust's notion of the *mémoire involuntaire* to suggest that all the novelist can do is recapture, from the unconscious, fragments of what was once the corporate experience on which story-telling was based.

These comments cannot but be of relevance to what has become known as Narrative Theology. Yet, though several of its exponents refer to Benjamin, it cannot be claimed that he is the major intellectual force behind it. Indeed, one of the most influential writers on the subject, Hans Frei of Yale, does not even mention Benjamin in his *The Eclipse of Biblical Narrative* (1974). But narrative theology and Benjamin do, it seems to me, need to be brought into creative dialogue with each other since, though the former does acknowledge the breakdown of narrative identity, it fails to take it with the seriousness upon which Benjamin insists.

For Frei the problem has been with us since the rise of Biblical criticism. On the traditional reading the Bible was treated as an integrated narrative with the meaning only discoverable in the inter-relations of the whole, not in isolatable units. So even non-literal readings such as typology had no difficulty in finding their place since they had an obvious rationale in reinforcing the unity of the narrative as a whole. But with the rise of Biblical criticism meaning came instead to be identified with reference, with the question of whether a particular unit or even word corresponded with objective reality. The result was that feeling for the unity of the narrative as a whole was lost, with liberal and conservative alike assuming that the key issue was that of reference.[100] Even Schleiermacher's hermeneutics should not, Frei suggests, be seen as a reversal of this process since what is stressed is continuity in the consciousness of the author not in the interrelation of characters and events which he is describing, i.e. in the narrative itself.[101] Frei is concerned to offer a history of this 'eclipse', not provide a solution. But he acknowledges his debt to Barth and the way in which he sums up this 'great reversal' leaves us in no doubt that he would favour a solution along Jüngel's lines: 'interpretation was a matter of fitting the biblical story into another world with another story rather than incorporating the world into the biblical story.'[102]

A particularly valuable feature of George Stroup's *The Promise of Narrative Theology* is the way in which he tackles this question of the relation between the individual's narrative and the community's. Taking up some suggestions of Reinhold Niebuhr's brother, Richard, that 'revelation includes the appropriation of external events at the level of internal history and that this "appropriation" necessarily assumes the form of a story, what Niebuhr referred to as "the story of our life" ',[103] he argues that not only should we think of revelation as narrative but also as itself an invitation to rewrite our own narrative histories in accordance with it. This he suggests is precisely what happened in the case of Augustine[104] with the events of his past now given a fresh interpretative framework. Alienation and self-deception, on the other hand, are what happens when the individual is faced with conflicting stories of his identity.[105]

Stroup acknowledges the existence of competing narrative loyalties even in Christians,[106] but, so far as I can make out, he seems to regard the appropriate resolution of this conflict simply in terms of a proper incorporation into the Biblical narrative. At all events, his reading of St Mark as a narrative designed to identify Jesus in such a way that 'in so doing it raises the question of whether the reader is truly a disciple of him'[107] seems intended to further just such an end. But matters are surely much more complex than that. Not only are the Gospels seldom read at a single sitting in the way that is demanded by Stroup's suggestion, much more difficult to correct is the fact that, the more secularized the individual's culture, the harder he will find access to the appropriate religious categories that would make appropriation of the story possible.

This fragmentation of culture is certainly something which Benjamin took with the utmost seriousness. This is his view of our own age, but, rather surprisingly he found 'remarkable analogies'[108] in the apparently much more devout age of seventeenth-century baroque. These are developed, implicitly rather than explicitly, in his *Ursprung des deutschen Trauerspiels*. He argues that precisely because of the uniformity of belief and increasing absolutism of monarchs[109] their age was as distant from the transcendent as our own. Instead, melancholy was the result, so much so that Benjamin suggests that despite surface appearances the Renaissance should be seen as the age more open to religion's transforming power, to 'apocalyptic': 'Whereas the painters of the Renaissance know how to keep their skies high, in the paintings of the baroque the cloud moves, darkly or radiantly, down towards the earth. In contrast to the baroque the Renaissance does not appear as a godless and heathen period, but as an epoch of profane freedom for the life of faith, while the Counter-Reformation sees the hierarchical strain of the middle ages assume authority in a world which was denied access to a beyond.'[110] This he finds reflected in the way in which plays of the time centred on the inevitability of fate, from a dramatist of international statue like the Spaniard Calderón[111] to Benjamin's own immediate concern, the *Trauerspiele* or 'mourning plays' of the minor and now forgotten German tragedians of the age. For despite the difference in denomination they were just as much subject to a 'grim belief in the subjection of man to fate', accentuated by the Lutheran doctrine of justification by faith as a result of which 'human actions were deprived of all value.'[112]

Thus, though the reasons are very different (fragmentation of culture in our case and claustrophic uniformity in theirs) both ages have confronted the artist with a similar problem of how to communicate something new – how to get beyond the fragmentation or uniformity. What Benjamin suggests makes that age like our own is the way in which both have had to resort to shock tactics. In the case of the seventeenth century there was the use of allegory and the appearance of allegorical figures on stage. In our own day we have from art Duchamp's moustached *Mona Lisa* and numerous other examples from Dadaism and Surrealism, while in drama he takes the case of Brecht's use of unexpected interruptions.[113] Both, however, are equally remote from story where the new is still capable of emerging without disruption from tradition. That is why both can be described as ruins of culture even if in the case of baroque he talks of 'carefully constructed ruins'.[114]

The relevance of all this to the possibility of Christian narrative is surely not hard to find. The renewal and reordering of one's life in the light of story is not something that comes naturally in our present world. Even Christians tend to treat the Bible as a book of reference rather than as a recurring source of fresh and not necessarily entirely consistent inspiration for continual restructuring of the narrative that we wish to tell of our lives. That said, the difficulties become even more acute when we reflect on communicating the significance of the Bible to those outside the community of faith. Significantly, it is as much the religious as the non-religious who in the modern world have resorted to shock tactics. One need only think in music of Schoenberg's use of twelve-note technique or Messiaen's mode of limited transposition, or in art of Kandinsky's resort to pure colour or Mondrian's to pure form in order to convey the spiritual. But to be shocked into a sense of the spiritual is not of course the same thing as to be initiated into the peculiar power that story can exercise, when properly appropriated. It is surely here that secular narrative can find a legitimate role. For it sometimes provides a useful medium for initiating the reader into a realization that the Bible's essential role is not just that of communicator of facts (though it does that as well). So, for example, in understanding atonement not just as doctrine but as liveable experience a novel like Ken Kesey's *One Flew over the Cuckoo's Nest* can exercise a useful translation and mediating role, especially as the religious symbolism in the novel is so mute. Again, at the end of the last chapter we quoted the French novelist Michel Tournier to the effect that 'the function of the writer is to prevent myths from becoming allegories', and in this he succeeds admirably with his novel *The Four Wise Men*, with its tale of the fourth wise man in search of Turkish Delight. It sounds flippant, but it forces the reader to the conviction that the essential point in the story of the Magi is about the transformation of values and lives, irrespective of whether it has an historical base or not.[115] Despite our fragmented world means of initiation into the transforming power of this story are thus still available though it should be noted that because the appropriation will almost inevitably be mediated in one way or another, the agent of mediation cannot help but also affect the interpretation. But this need be no bad thing since, as I have already argued, it is impossible to confine the workings of the Spirit narrowly to revelation.

But how exactly does one narrative affect another, the story of Jesus change the narrative we are prepared to tell about our own lives and in turn affect our life beyond the grave? The short answer is that the narrative we tell determines our moral and spiritual identity. For what we make of our past, the significance we assign to one event and not another, expresses who we really are or want to be. In such a restructuring process the temporal segments will of course not all be accorded the same significance, and so, while the order of events must remain the same (otherwise it would not be the narrative of the same life), what becomes crucial in determining identity is which events are highlighted, which demoted. A striking example of this from within the Bible is the way in which it summarily dismisses the reign of King Omri despite the fact that secular narrative clearly saw him as Israel's greatest king after David and Solomon.[116]

The contrast between ordinary or calendar time and redemptive or messianic time is a recurring theme in Benjamin's writings. Thus from his last important essay, 'Theses on the Philosophy of History', there emerges a strong hostility to a teleological view of history.[117] 'History', we are told, 'is the subject of a structure whose site is not homogeneous, empty time, but time filled by the presence of the now.' A secular example is then given, the way in which for Robespierre ancient Rome was 'eine mit Jetztzeit geladene Vergangenheit' (a past laden with the 'now'), which 'he blasted (heraussprengte) out of the continuum of history'.[118] This example might suggest that all Benjamin meant by *Jetztzeit* (the 'now') is the way in which the past is brought into the present. This is certainly part of the truth, and in this sense it is closely related to his notion of the 'aura' of past literary works, their ability to speak at once to us in the present and beyond it.[119] But equally important are the connections which are made. In this case we now have a story that connects ancient Rome and the French Revolution. But a more telling example is given in an earlier essay on Kafka. There, in the course of arguing that 'it will be the Messiah's mission to set right someday . . . the distortions of our time', he tells the story of a group of people discussing what wish they would want granted, given a choice. After a number of conventional answers a beggar replies by saying that he would like to have been a king who has been overthrown and has only managed to escape in the few rags he has now.[120] The point of course is that the ability to tell a different story about the past is really far more effective in giving one a new identity than any dreams about the future.

The same I suggest will be true about our future. What matters is not our actual calendar past, but our willingness to reorder that past into a narrative in conformity with the story of Jesus. This will mean demoting events which we now regard as landmarks in our lives, and exalting others which are apparently insignificant. Nor is it a process which is likely to cease with death. For our lives, like society, are fragmented and not a consistent narrative. So there will be a need after death to integrate into one consistent narrative those events in our lives which we have so far failed or been unwilling to integrate. Since narrative and the construction of narrative identity are both essentially temporal processes, it would seem strange to suppose that the further reordering that must take place after death could also be anything other than temporal. That being so, this seems to afford some justification for a doctrine of purgatory, at least in the sense that what we have here is both a transitional temporal process and one which cannot but be painful given the nature of the self-discovery involved.[121]

But beyond purgatory there is Heaven, something of which Benjamin makes no mention despite his use of the language of redemption. Commentators are in fact sharply divided about where his real commitment lay, to religion or Marxism. For example, Roberts and Eagleton see him in essentially Marxist terms, while Gershom Scholem in *The Story of a Friendship* strongly defends the continuity of his commitment to Judaism.[122] For me his image of theology as the hunchback pulling the puppet strings of historical materialism[123] leaves it in no doubt where his sympathies lay, though Wolin is of course right that this need not imply commitment to 'a suprahistorical redeemer'.[124] But significantly not only has Wolin given a religious title to his book on Benjamin, *An Aesthetic of Redemption*, the illustration on the front cover is of Benjamin's favourite painting, Paul Klee's *Angelus Novus*. Benjamin interpreted the painting as being of an angel blown from

Paradise into an unknown future, unknown because the wind is too strong for him to be able to turn round.[125] That I think summarizes well his attitude to God. It is not that there are no redemptive signs in the present, but that we can have no idea of what the total pattern will be in the future. Thus, though Scholem insists on his belief in God, he notes that for Benjamin it is also a highly unknown God: 'God is the unattainable centre of a system of symbols intended to remove him from everything concrete and everything symbolic as well.'[126]

One might contrast this with Jüngel's emphatic rejection of Luther's *Deus absconditus*, the possibility that God has a different character behind that disclosed in revelation.[127] He tells us that 'to grasp God as love . . . explodes the thesis of the unspeakability of God' and so *finitum non capax infiniti* ('the finite is incapable of grasping the infinite') must give place to *caritas capax verbi* ('love makes speech possible').[128] No other choice is possible, it seems to me, for anyone who takes revelation seriously. But that does not mean the complete abandonment of the former principle. For clearly our understanding is limited, whereas God's is not. So, though there is much about God about which we can be confident in this life, much remains to be discovered in the next life and even then we will never completely grasp the infinite riches of such a Being. So one way to think of Heaven is to think of it as an exploration into the Ultimate Mystery, but an exploration which can have no end, since there is no end to the resources of God, neither in respect of his own being nor of the relations with each other into which he can initiate us.

But precisely because this Mystery that is our ultimate destiny is so rich and all-encompassing, for theology to turn in on itself and ignore the contribution of other disciplines such as philosophy is already effectively to deny that richness. That is one reason why this book has been written.

Notes

Introduction

1 My policy on quotations has been, wherever possible, to offer translations other than my own. The reason for this is twofold. First, it gives a bit more variety of style in the text. But, secondly and more importantly, it directs the student to available translations for what can sometimes be very different originals, for example Lacan or Adorno. So far as bibliographical details are concerned, place of publication is always given, except where this is London.

Chapter 1   Theological Method

1 K. Ward, *The Concept of God* (Fount, 1977), p. 53.
2 Ibid., p. 117.
3 F. Schleiermacher, *On Religion: speeches to its cultured despisers* (Harper Torchbook, New York, 1958), p. 36. For some pantheism is the central feature of Schleiermacher's thought. Richard Brandt in *The Philosophy of Schleiermacher* (Greenwood Press, Westport, Conn., 1941) goes so far as to argue that, partly under the influence of the post-Kantian philosopher Schelling, Schleiermacher did intend to identify God with the universe as a whole. Cf. esp. pp. 96ff, including long footnote on pp. 104ff.
4 P. Tillich, *Systematic Theology* (Nisbet, 1953), vol. I, pp. 67ff. Intriguingly, W. Härle and E. Herms in their survey of German Protestant theology since the Second World War, 'Deutschsprachige protestantische Dogmatik', list second among shared features a new concern for the issues, if not the methods, of natural theology, of which Tillich would be typical. 'Furthermore a clear point of convergence is that this christological concentration (their first point of common interest) serves no longer as a motive for the exclusion of Natural Theology from Dogmatics but on the contrary for the integration of its

problems into the work of Dogmatics' (*Verkündigung und Forschung*, 1982, Heft 2, pp. 2–100 and 1983, Heft 1, pp. 1–87, esp. p. 83).

5 *Systematic Theology*, Vol. I, pp. 193ff.

6 Ibid., p. 272.

7 Ibid., p. 271.

8 Ibid., p. 227. For Tillich's negative judgment on the 'hybris' of Hegel cf. e.g. P. Tillich, *Perspectives on 19th and 20th Century Protestant Theology* (SCM, 1967), p. 118. For the acknowledgement of his debt to Schelling, ibid., pp. 141ff.

9 P. Berger, *A Rumour of Angels* (Penguin, Harmondsworth, 1971), pp. 70ff.

10 Ibid., p. 90.

11 F. Schleiermacher, *The Christian Faith* (T. & T. Clark, Edinburgh, 1928), p. 16.

12 Made in Hegel's preface to H. F. W. Hinrich's *Die Religion im inneren Verhältnisse zur Wissenschaft*. Cf. *Hegels Berliner Schriften* (ed. J. Hoffmeister, 1944 repr.), pp. 346ff.

13 K. Rahner, *Christology at the Crossroads* (Burns and Oates, 2nd corr. imp., 1977), p. 15. Cf. M. Heidegger, *Existence and Being* (Vision Press, 1949), p. 364 for the same image used of boredom in a metaphysical context. Rahner studied under Heidegger and so, though the epistemology is that of Transcendental Thomism, the terminology often has, like Tillich's, a Heideggerian ring. It is interesting to observe that, despite the undoubted great differences, it is also to Schleiermacher and Tillich that George Vass turns for obvious parallels in his recent survey of Rahner's thought: *Understanding Karl Rahner* (Sheed and Ward, 1985), vol. I, p. 124.

14 K. Rahner, *Foundations of the Christian Faith* (Darton, Longman & Todd, 1978), p. 32. Not all German academics would agree in attaching such significance to Rahner's argument. Wilhelm Weischedel in his survey of philosophical theology, *Der Gott der Philosophen* (Wissenschaftliche Buchgesellschaft, Darmstadt, 1979) dismisses Rahner in a couple of paragraphs, whereas a major section is devoted to 'The renewal of natural theology with Pannenberg' (vol. II, pp. 74ff). Yet Pannenberg's argument is not all that dissimilar from Rahner's, especially in anthropology and meaning, though less philosophically based.

15 Kant, *Critique of Pure Reason* (Dent Everyman Library, 1934), Preface to 2nd Edition, p. 18. For a discussion of the significance of the *Opus Postumum*, mentioned in a subsequent paragraph, cf. C. C. J. Webb, *Kant's Philosophy of Religion* (Oxford University Press, 1926), esp. pp. 199–201; for a different view, more concerned to stress continuity in Kant's thought, K. Ward, *The Development of Kant's View of Ethics* (Basil Blackwell, Oxford, 1972), pp. 160–4.

16 Lonergan acknowledges Maréchal's influence in the Introduction to his major philosophical work, *Insight* (Longmans, Green, 1957), p. xxii.

17 J. Maréchal, *Le point de départ de la métaphysique*, 2nd edn (L'Édition Universelle, Brussels, 1949), vol. V, p. 33.

18 Ibid., p. 573. For a detailed discussion of Transcendental Thomism, see O. Muck, *Die transzendentale Methode in der scholastischen Philosophie der Gegenwart* (Felizian Rauch, Innsbruck, 1964).
19 R. Walker, *Kant* (Routledge and Kegan Paul, 1978), pp. 171ff.
20 B. Mitchell, *The Justification of Religious Belief* (Macmillan, 1973); R. Swinburne, *The Existence of God* (Oxford University Press, Oxford, 1979). America's most distinguished analytic philosopher of religion, Alvin Plantinga, is pursuing a rather different position, with belief in God treated as a 'basic belief' not requiring further justification. Cf. *Faith and Rationality*, ed. A. Plantinga and N. Wolterstorff (University of Notre Dame Press, Notre Dame, Ind., 1983).
21 K. Barth, *From Rousseau to Ritschl* (SCM, 1959), p. 349. Cf. p. 352. But it is important to note that, despite the severity of some of his judgements on Schleiermacher, Barth never denied the challenging importance of his thought. For a history of the nature of the relationship as Barth sees it, cf. esp. 'Concluding unscientific postscript on Schleiermacher', in K. Barth, *The Theology of Schleiermacher* (T. & T. Clark, Edinburgh, 1982), pp. 261–79.
22 T. Altizer, *The Gospel of Christian Atheism* (Collins, 1967). It is worth noting that L. Gilkey in *Naming the Whirlwind* (Bobbs-Merrill, Indianapolis, 1969, esp. part I, chs 3 and 4) holds Barth in part to blame for the development of the Death of God school. As one of them, W. Hamilton, succinctly puts it, it is 'a short step . . . to move from the otherness of God to the absence of God' (quoted on p. 117).
23 Cf. my *The Divine Trinity* (Duckworth, 1985; Open Court, La Salle, Ill., 1985), ch. 1, esp. 'The redundancy argument', pp. 10–18.
24 K. Barth, *The Epistle to the Romans* (Oxford University Press, 1933), pp. 330 and 331.
25 K. Barth, *Church Dogmatics*, 2nd edn (T. & T. Clark, Edinburgh, 1975), vol. I, 1, p. 238. For his discussion of analogy, cf. pp. 227–47, esp. pp. 238–40 and 243–4, and p. 437. In vol. III, 2, p. 220 he even goes so far as to deny an *analogia entis* in respect of the human nature of Christ: 'This is not a correspondence and similarity of being, an *analogia entis*. The being of God cannot be compared with the being of man.'
26 Ibid., vol. II, 1, p. 634.
27 Ibid., vol. III, 3, pp. 297–9, esp. p. 298.
28 K. Barth, *The Humanity of God* (Fontana, 1967), p. 39.
29 *From Rousseau to Ritschl*, p. 354.
30 His emphasis on the moral content of Jesus' teaching is striking, as is the demotion of eschatology on the grounds that this is not a feature unqiue to Jesus. A. Harnack, *What is Christianity?* (Williams & Northgate, 1901), pp. 52ff.
31 V. A. Harvey, *The Historian and the Believer* (SCM, 1967), p. 159.
32 E. Troeltsch, *Gesammelte Schriften* (Mohr/Paul Siebech, Tübingen, 1913), vol. II, pp. 729–53.
33 Joshua 10, 13.
34 T. S. Kuhn, *The Structure of Scientific Revolutions* (Chicago University Press, Chicago, 1962). This question is examined in more detail in part I

of *The Divine Trinity*, and with particular reference to historical issues on pp. 62–6.

35 *Gesammelte Schriften*, pp. 754–68, esp. p. 756.

36 *The Encyclopedia of Philosophy*, ed. P. Edwards (Macmillan, 1967), s.v. Kierkegaard.

37 W. Lowrie, *A Short Life of Kierkegaard* (Princeton University Press, Princeton, NJ, 1970), p. 254. For a detailed analysis of his attitude to Hegel, see N. Thulstrup, *Kierkegaard's Relation to Hegel* (Princeton University Press, Princeton, NJ, 1980).

38 Barth, *The Epistle to the Romans*, p. 279.

39 *Fear and Trembling* (Princeton University Press, Princeton, NJ, 1983), pp. 54–67.

40 E.g. A. Hannay, *Kierkegaard* (Routledge and Kegan Paul, 1982), pp. 75ff.

41 *Concluding Unscientific Postscript* (Princeton University Press, Princeton, NJ, 1968), p. 55. For another illustration of 'paradoxical passion' taking over the role of a powerless Kantian reason, cf. *Philosophical Fragments* (Princeton University Press, Princeton, NJ, 1962), p. 49.

42 *Concluding Unscientific Postscript*, p. 178.

43 Genesis 28, 20–1; Habakkuk 3, 17–19.

44 *Training in Christianity* (Princeton University Press, Princeton, NJ, 1967), p. 143.

45 *Philosophical Fragments* (Princeton University Press, Princeton, NJ, 1962), p. 29.

46 *The von Balthasar Reader*, ed. M. Kehl and W. Löser (T. & T. Clark, Edinburgh, 1982), p. 94.

47 To date, vols I (1982), II (1984) and III (1986) have appeared, but so far the intention seems to be to translate only the seven volumes of the first part of the trilogy.

48 H.U. von Balthasar, *The Glory of the Lord* (T. & T. Clark, Edinburgh, 1982), vol. I, Foreword.

49 ibid., pp. 45ff, esp. pp. 47–8.

50 Ibid., pp. 70ff, esp. p. 72.

51 Ibid., p. 29.

52 Ibid., p. 32.

53 Ibid., p. 31.

54 For the former, *The von Balthasar Reader*, pp. 135ff, esp. p. 138; for the latter, pp. 220–5 and pp. 276–7.

55 E.g. *The Glory of the Lord*, vol. I, p. 39.

56 Ibid., p. 23.

57 *The von Balthasar Reader*, p. 393.

58 G. Wainwright, *Doxology* (Epworth, 1980); A. Louth, *Discerning the Mystery* (Oxford University Press, Oxford, 1983).

59 Wainwright, *Doxology*, pp. 57–8.

60 Ibid., pp. 48ff.

61 Ibid., pp. 205ff, esp. p. 209.

62 For the influence of von Balthasar on Louth, cf. e.g. A. Louth, *The Origins of the Christian Mystical Tradition* (Oxford University Press,

Oxford, 1981), pp. 200–1. For a particularly good example of the identification of God with beauty cf. esp. Pseudo-Denys, *De divinis nominibus* IV, 7; and for the continuing influence of this transcendent view of beauty, R. Assunto, *Die Theorie des Schönen im Mittelalter* (DuMont Buchverlag, Cologne, 1982).

63 *Discerning the Mystery*, pp. 96ff.

64 H.-G. Gadamer, *Truth and Method*, 2nd edn (Sheed & Ward, 1979), p. 164. Gadamer's judgement now needs some correction in the light of Heinz Kimmerle's edition of *Schleiermacher's Hermeneutics: the hand-written manuscripts* (Scholars Press, Missoula, Mont., 1977). This includes some previously unpublished material and indicates that, while Gadamer's remark is true of the later Schleiermacher, his earlier position very much stressed linguistic context.

65 The text explains the most common use of the term, but, confusingly, it is also used to describe the interaction of whole and parts, i.e. of words and sentence or text and context, in determining meaning.

66 *Truth and Method*, p. 264. The closeness of Gadamer's relationship to both Bultmann and Heidegger is well described in his pen sketches of his contemporaries in *Philosophical Apprenticeships* (MIT Press, Cambridge, Mass., 1985), esp. pp. 45–60.

67 *Truth and Method*, p. 262.

68 Ibid., p. 245.

69 Ibid., p. 248.

70 'The hermeneutic claim to universality', in J. Bleicher (ed.), *Contemorary Hermeneutics* (Routledge and Kegan Paul, 1980), p. 207.

71 J. Habermas and N. Luhmann, *Theorie der Gesellschaft oder Sozial-technologie – Was leistet die Systemforschung?* (Suhrkamp, Frankfurt, 1971), pp. 120ff, 239ff, 246ff.

72 *Truth and Method*, pp. 264–5.

73 H.-G. Gadamar, *Reason in the Age of Science* (MIT Press, Cambridge, Mass., 1981).

74 A. MacIntyre, *After Virtue* (Duckworth, 1981).

75 *Truth and Method*, p. 266.

76 *Reason in the Age of Science*, p. xix; J. H. Newman, *An Essay on the Development of Christian Doctrine* (Penguin, Harmondsworth, 1973), p. 100.

77 See A. Grafton, 'Prolegomena to Friedrich August Wolf', *Journal of the Warburg and Courtauld Institutes*, 1981, pp. 101–29, esp. pp. 119ff.

78 The English translation by John Marsh was not published until 1963 (Basil Blackwell, Oxford), which is perhaps an indication of the slowness with which the method was accepted in England, though Vincent Taylor was already a moderate advocate by 1933.

79 On adultery, contrast Mark 10, 11 with Matthew 5, 32; on the woman divorcing her husband, the additional verse in Mark – 10, 12.

80 R. Bultmann, *Faith and Understanding* (SCM, 1966), p. 132.

81 Ibid., p. 138.

82 *Kerygma and Myth* (Harper & Row, 1961), p. 41.

83 J. MacQuarrie, *An Existentialist Theology* (Penguin, Harmondsworth, 1973), p. 173.

84 *Jesus Christ and Mythology* (Charles Scribner's Sons, New York, 1958), p. 15.

85 J. Barr, *Escaping from Fundamentalism* (SCM, 1984).

86 This model is expounded in detail in chapter 2 of *The Divine Trinity*. For the importance of freedom to Christian theology, see chapter 3 of this book.

87 See, for example, his lecture 'Structuralism and linguistics' in D. Robey (ed.), *Structuralism: an introduction* (Oxford University Press, 1973), pp. 9–10.

88 This is the qualification required to teach philosophy in a French school.

89 C. Lévi-Strauss, *Tristes tropiques* (Penguin, Harmondsworth, 1976), p. 71.

90 C. Lévi-Strauss, *Myth and Meaning* (Routledge & Kegan Paul, 1978), pp. 25–33. These radio lectures are probably the best introduction to his thought.

91 C. Lévi-Strauss, *Structural Anthropology* (Basic Books, New York, 1963), pp. 62 and 71.

92 C. Lévi-Strauss, *The Savage Mind* (Weidenfeld & Nicolson, 1972 edn), p. 247.

93 'The struggle with the angel', in F. Bovan (ed.), *Structural Analysis and Biblical Exegesis* (Pickwick, Pittsburg, Pa, 1974).

94 E. G. McKnight, *Meaning in Texts* (Fortress Press, Philadelphia, Pa, 1978), p. 245.

95 Ibid., pp. 275ff; D. Patte, *What is Structural Analysis?* (Fortress Press, Philadelphia, Pa, 1976).

96 For the former, *What is Structural Analysis?*, pp. 35–52 and pp. 76–83; for the latter, ibid., pp. 59–76.

97 F. Kermode, *The Genesis of Secrecy* (Harvard University Press, Cambridge, Mass., 1979), pp. 84–95. Cf. also p. 105, with its strange claim that 'reality-effects' are more common in fictional than in factual narrative.

98 'Structuralism in social anthropology', in D. Robey (ed.), *Structuralism*, p. 54.

99 J. Derrida, *Writing and Difference* (Routledge and Kegan Paul, 1978), p. 112 and p. 73.

100 J. Derrida, *Of Grammatology* (Johns Hopkins University Press, Baltimore, Md, 1976 edn), pp. 14 and 13.

101 Ibid., p. 15.

102 Ibid., p. 8.

103 Ibid., p. 14.

104 *Writing and Difference*, pp. 79–153, esp. p. 133.

105 As his argument is partly pursued in the periodical *Glyth*, the best point of access is probably J. Culler's synopsis in his *On Deconstructionism* (Routledge and Kegan Paul, 1983), pp. 110ff.

106 T. Altizer (ed.), *Deconstructionism and Theology* (Crossroad, New York, 1982), p. 31.

107 M. C. Taylor, *Erring: a postmodern a/theology* (University of Chicago Press, Chicago, 1984), quoted on p. 6. The quotation comes from J. Derrida, *Positions* (University of Chicago Press, Chicago, 1981), p. 40.
108 Taylor, *Erring*, pp. 177 and 182.
109 Ibid., pp. 158ff.
110 P. Lacoue-Labarthe and J.-L. Nancy (ed.), *Les fins de l'homme* (Paris, 1981), pp. 526–9.
111 Cf. J. G. Merquior, *From Prague to Paris* (Verso, 1986), p. 233.
112 F. Kerr, 'Derrida's wake', *New Blackfriars*, 1974, pp. 449–60; T. Eagleton, 'Decentring God', ibid., 1976, pp. 148–51.

Chapter 2   Doctrine of God

1 P. Hodgson and R. King (eds), *Christian Theology: an introduction to its traditions and tasks* (SPCK, 1983). E.g. the first four contributions all open on a very negative note.
2 R. R. Ruether, *Sexism and God-Talk* (SCM, 1983), p. 61.
3 C. Christ, 'Why women need the Goddess', in C. Christ and J. Plaskow (eds), *Womanspirit Rising: a feminist reader in religion* (Harper & Row, San Francisco, 1979), pp. 273–87; Starhawk, (pseudonym for M. Simos), *The Spiral Dance: the rebirth of the ancient religion of the Goddess* (Harper & Row, New York, 1979).
4 *Sexism and God-Talk*, p. 39.
5 Ibid., p. 45.
6 Ibid., p. 21.
7 Cf. e.g. ibid., p. 48.
8 E. S. Fiorenza, *In Memory of Her* (SCM, 1983), p. 133.
9 Ibid., p. 138.
10 Ibid., p. 332.
11 Ibid., p. 161.
12 Cf. Ruether, *Sexism and God-Talk*, pp. 157–8; Fiorenza, *In Memory of Her*, pp. 140–1 and p. 344.
13 Though Fiorenza weakens her case by refusing to concede Jesus' rejection of divorce, cf. p. 143.
14 E.g. ibid., p. 217.
15 Jesus wrongly ascribes Deuteronomy to Moses and the Psalms to David – cf. Mark 10, 3–4; Mark 12, 35–7.
16 Paul's implicit denial is in 1 Corinthians, 15, 5; Fiorenza's brief discussion, pp. 50–1.
17 Ibid., p. 47. Both are mentioned in Romans 16. The problem with Phoebe is that the Greek word *diakonos* is frequently translated differently here from when it refers to a man.
18 Isaiah 42, 14.
19 For Jesus' use cf. Fiorenza, *In Memory of Her*, pp. 130–40.
20 Acts 1, 14. For Fiorenza's demotion of Mary in the passages she does discuss cf. pp. 146–7 and 326–7.

21 Plato, *Republic* 479a.

22 What effect the slippery character of *einai*, 'to be', and its derivatives has on Plato's argument is well exposed by G. Vlastos, 'Degrees of reality in Plato', in R. Bambrough (ed.), *New Essays in Plato and Aristotle* (Routledge and Kegan Paul, 1965), pp. 1–19.

23 In *Republic* 477ff. Plato argues that the sensible world as the object of brief is intermediate between existence and non-existence.

24 Cf. *Parmenides* 158b–d. God is so described in *Republic* 509.

25 Plotinus, *Enneads* VI, 9.

26 J. Hopkins and H. W. Richardson (ed. & trans.), *Anselm of Canterbury* (SCM, 1974), vol. I, p. 36; *Monologion*, ch. 22.

27 The problem is even more acute if divine intervention is denied. See D. Brown, *The Divine Trinity* (Duckworth, 1985), pp. 24–6.

28 N. Pike, *God and Timelessness* (Routledge and Kegan Paul, 1970); R. Swinburne, *The Coherence of Theism* (Oxford University Press, 1977), pp. 210ff; A. Kenny, *The God of the Philosophers* (Oxford University Press, Oxford, 1979), pp. 38–48.

29 Cf. Plotinus, *Enneads* VI, 9; Anselm, *Monologion*, ch. 17, translation cited above, p. 26.

30 *Phaedo* 78.

31 *Philosophical Investigations*, I, 47.

32 J. Moltmann, *The Crucified God* (SCM, 1974), p. 229.

33 Malachi 3, 6.

34 *The Crucified God*, p. 205.

35 Ibid., p. 230.

36 Ibid., p. 274.

37 For a more detailed discussion, see *The Divine Trinity*, pp. 252–7.

38 So Genesis 1, 6–7 and even more graphically in 7, 11 with the Flood being caused by the sluices of the heavenly vault being opened (what the A.V. calls 'the windows of heaven').

39 Though this is not to discount a general influence. For it has been argued that it is the emphasis in Christian theology on the contingency and order of the universe that made possible the rise of modern science. Cf. P. E. Hodgson, 'The Judeao-Christian origin of science', in *Ampleforth Journal*, 1974; S. L. Jaki, *The Road of Science and the Ways to God* (Scottish Academic Press, Edinburgh, 1978).

40 Quoted in Paul Davies, *God and the New Physics* (Dent, 1983), p. 171. For a useful detailed discussion of the principle, see 'Anthropic principle, world ensemble, design' by J. Leslie in *American Philosophical Quarterly*, 1982, pp. 141–51.

41 *Proverbs* 8, 27–31.

42 T. F. Torrance, *Theological Science* (Oxford University Press, 1969), cf. pp. 31 and 329–30 on Schleiermacher and Bultmann respectively.

43 Ibid., p. 30.

44 Ibid., p. 55.

45 Ibid., cf. esp. pp. 8–10.

46 Ibid., p. 138.

47 Ibid., p. 309.

48 Ibid., p. 265.
49 Ibid., pp. 273–4.
50 Ibid., p. 33, cf. also p. 174.
51 Ibid., p. 135.
52 A. R. Peacocke, *Science and the Christian Experiment* (Oxford University Press, 1971), pp. 12–28.
53 Ibid., pp. 23–4.
54 A. N. Whitehead, *Process and Reality* (Cambridge University Press, Cambridge, 1929), p. vi.
55 Quoted in ibid., pp. 97–8.
56 Ibid., p. 130.
57 Ibid., pp. 131–3.
58 Ibid., p. 488.
59 E.g. W. Mays, *The Philosophy of Whitehead* (Muirhead Library of Philosophy, 1959).
60 S. Ogden, *The Reality of God* (SCM, 1967), p. 59.
61 *Process and Reality*, pp. 267–71, esp. p. 268; cf. also Ogden, *The Reality of God*, p. 57.
62 *Process and Reality*, p. 72. Cf. also p. 486.
63 Cf. e.g. C. Hartshorne, *The Logic of Perfection* (Open Court, La Salle, Ill., 1962), pp. 119–27 and 138–40.
64 *The Reality of God*, p. 49.
65 E.g. G. M. Jantzen, *God's World, God's Body* (Darton, Longman & Todd, 1984). For an excellent presentation of arguments against divine embodiment, cf. T. Tracy, *God, Action and Embodiment* (Eerdmans, Grand Rapids, Mich., 1984), esp. chs 6 and 7.
66 *The Reality of God*, pp. 177–8.
67 Ibid., p. 37.
68 W. Kaufmann, *Hegel: a reinterpretation* (Notre Dame, Ind., 1978). Interestingly, at one point (p. 156) he notes that Whitehead is close to Hegel's dialectic, in his acceptance of contradiction as a legitimate stage in argumentation.
69 Ibid., p. 27.
70 Ibid., pp. 147–8.
71 Ibid., p. 273.
72 Ibid., p. 41.
73 Ibid., p. 38.
74 E. L. Fackenheim, *The Religious Dimension in Hegel's Thought* (University of Chicago Press, Chicago, 1982 edn), p. 77.
75 Ibid., p. 81.
76 Ibid., pp. 85–86.
77 Ibid., p. 153.
78 Hegel, *Begriff der Religion*, ed. G. Lasson (Leipzig, 1927), p. 148.
79 Hegel, *Phenomenology of Spirit*, trans. A. V. Miller (Oxford University Press, Oxford, 1977), p. 111; para. 178.
80 Ibid., p. 114; para. 187.
81 Ibid., pp. 467–8; para. 775.
82 Kaufmann, *Hegel*, gives a long list: pp. 252–3.

83 C. Taylor, *Hegel* (Cambridge University Press, Cambridge, 1975), p. 209.

84 As with *Taking Leave of God* (SCM, 1980).

85 L. Feuerbach, *The Essence of Christianity*, trans. George Eliot (Harper & Row, New York, 1957), p. 12 (ch. 1, sec. 2). For a collection of readings from the first generation to be influenced by Hegel, including Feuerbach and Marx, see *The Young Hegelians*, ed. L. S. Stepelevich (Cambridge University Press, Cambridge, 1983); for a detailed history of the period, J. E. Toews, *Hegelianism: the path towards dialectical humanism*, *1805–41* (Cambridge University Press, Cambridge, 1980).

86 K. Barth, *From Rousseau to Ritschl* (SCM, 1959), p. 304; P. Tillich, *Perspectives on 19th and 20th Century Theology* (SCM, 1967), p. 118.

87 Cf. Anselm's distinction between the necessary and the appropriate, discussed in J. Hopkins, *A Companion to the Study of St. Anselm* (University of Minnesota Press, Minneapolis 1972), pp. 48–51.

88 SCM, 1963, with Tillich's phrase used as the title of his third chapter, with its emphatic declaration that 'God is not "out there" ' but 'in the midst of our life' (p. 47).

89 W. Pannenberg, *Jesus: God and man* (SCM, 1968), p. 182.

90 Ibid., p. 320.

91 Augustine, *Confessions*, Book XI, 13.

92 *Jesus: God and man*, p. 69.

93 *The Divine Trinity*, pp. 127–9.

94 *Jesus: God and man*, p. 320.

95 Ibid., pp. 283ff.

96 Ibid., p. 285.

97 Ibid., pp. 334ff.

98 Ibid., p. 340.

99 Ibid., e.g. pp. 321–3.

100 Ibid., p. 339.

101 In *The Divine Trinity* (pp. 238–9) I interpreted Pannenberg in terms of (b). However, I am now of the opinion that his position is probably nearer (a) or (c).

102 *The Divine Trinity*, pp. 245–71.

103 F. Loofs, s.v. 'Kenosis', in *Encyclopaedia of Religion and Ethics* (T. & T. Clark, Edinburgh, 1908).

104 *¡Hola!*, Christmas number, 29 December 1984, p. 6.

105 M. Wiles, *The Remaking of Christian Doctrine* (SCM, 1974), p. 38.

106 Ibid., p. 33.

107 Quoted in B. Reardon, *Hegel's Philosophy of Religion* (Macmillan, 1977), p. 85.

108 Quoted in J. Hick, *The Myth of God Incarnate* (SCM, 1977), p. 153.

109 Ibid., cf. p. 161.

110 Ibid., p. 162.

111 Ibid., p. 165.

112 S. Sontag (ed.), *Barthes: selected writings* (Fontana, 1983), p. 474.

113 R. Barthes, *Camera Lucida* (Fontana, 1984), pp. 26ff.
114 R. Barthes, *Mythologies* (Granada, 1973), p. 25.
115 Ibid., p. 21.
116 Ibid., p. 25.
117 Ibid., p. 109.
118 Ibid., p. 123.
119 Ibid., e.g. pp. 116, 118, 124.
120 Ibid., p. 129.
121 Ibid., p. 128.
122 Ibid., p. 141.
123 Ibid., p. 146.
124 N. Frye, *The Great Code: the Bible and literature* (Ark Edition, Routledge and Kegan Paul, 1983), pp. 5–16.
125 Ibid., p. 23.
126 Ibid., p. 47.
127 Ibid., pp. 39ff.
128 Ibid., pp. 100–1.
129 Ibid., p. 227ff.
130 Ibid., p. 42.
131 Ibid., cf. pp. 171ff.
132 For example in the Report of the Doctrine Commission of the Church of England, *Believing in the Church* (SPCK, 1981). It is perhaps significant that Wiles too uses this term in his more recent book, *Faith and the Mystery of God* (SCM, 1982).
133 *The Great Code*, p. 32.
134 J. Moltmann, *The Trinity and the Kingdom of God* (SCM, 1981), p. xvi.
135 Ibid., p. 1.
136 Ibid., p. 6.
137 For Barth, ibid., p. 141, cf. p. 63; for Rahner, p. 144.
138 Ibid., p. 145. For the likely response of Rahner, cf. *Theological Investigations* (Darton, Longman & Todd), vol. XIII, p. 127–9.
139 *The Trinity and the Kingdom of God*, p. 155.
140 Ibid., p. 174.
141 Ibid., cf. pp. 58, 99.
142 *The Divine Trinity*, pp. 276–80.
143 *The Trinity and the Kingdom of God*, p. 148.
144 *De Trinitate* 5, 10.
145 Ibid., 10, 18.
146 They are pursued in *The Divine Trinity*, pp. 281–3.
147 As Augustine himself notes in *De Trinitate* 9, 17.
148 The best guide to Middle Platonism is J. Dillon, *The Middle Platonists* (Duckworth, 1977).
149 H. A. Wolfson, *The Philosophy of the Church Fathers*, 3rd edn (Harvard University Press, Cambridge, Mass., 1970), p. 203.
150 A. H. Armstrong, *Platonian and Christian Studies* (Variorum Reprints, London, 1979), V, 48.
151 *De Principiis* 1, 6.
152 *Enneads* V, 4, 1. Translation used from quotation in A. O. Lovejoy, *The*

Great Chain of Being (Harvard University Press, Cambridge, Mass., 1936), p. 62.

153 Wisdom 7,25. Cf. e.g. Origen, *De Principiis*, 1,2,5; 1,2,9.

154 *Contra Academicos* 3,18; *Confessions* VII, 9, 13; *The City of God* VIII, 6 and 7.

155 *Plotinian and Christian Studies*, XXIII, 86.

156 Ibid., XXIII, 82.

157 *De Trinitate* XV, 42.

158 Ibid., XV, 44.

159 Ibid., XV, 48.

160 Dionysius the Areopagite, *The Divine Names*, trans. C. E. Rolt (SPCK, 1940), XIII, 3, pp. 187–8.

161 Acts 17, 34.

162 D. B. Burrell, *Aquinas: God and Action* (Routledge and Kegan Paul, 1979), p. 143.

163 Ibid., p. 18.

164 Ibid., pp. 13–14.

165 Ibid., p. 69.

166 For a German example, cf. J. Pieper, *The Silence of St. Thomas* (Faber and Faber, 1957), esp. pp. 67–70 and 91–4 and Essay II as a whole. The best-known French example is probably the writings of Stanislas Breton. Intriguingly, Richard Kearney accords him a philosophic status comparable with Ricoeur, Levinas, Marcuse and Derrida in his *Dialogues with Contemporary Continental Thinkers* (Manchester University Press, Manchester, 1984), pp. 89ff. He also notes that his negative views on God have led to accusations of atheism (pp. 98–9).

167 *Aquinas: God and Action*, p. 67.

168 J. M. Rist, *Plotinus: The Road to Reality* (Cambridge University Press, Cambridge, 1967), p. 217.

169 So J. A. Weisheipl, *Friar Thomas D'Aquino* (Basil Blackwell, Oxford, 1975), p. 219.

170 P. Brown, *Augustine of Hippo* (Faber, 1967), e.g. pp. 245–6.

171 Plotinus, *Enncads* VI, 9, 11 (trans. S. MacKenna, Faber, 1969).

172 It is particularly common in his discussion on virtue I, 2.

173 *Theaetetus* 176B (trans. F. M. Cornford, *Plato's Theory of Knowledge*, Routledge and Kegan Paul, 1960).

Chapter 3   Doctrine of Human Nature

1 Genesis 1, 26.

2 Genesis 9, 6.

3 K. Barth, *Church Dogmatics* (T. & T. Clark, Edinburgh,), vol. III, 1, p. 196.

4 Wisdom 2, 23 (*Jerusalem Bible* translation).

5 Genesis more directly through reflection on the obvious fact of human power; Wisdom more indirectly, but as the passage as a whole makes

clear, through reflection on the way in which the unjust receive this life's rewards, and so the need for an alternative answer.

6 Colossians 1, 15.
7 1 Corinthians 15, 49.
8 For this cf. 2 Cor. 3, 18; Rom. 1, 23.
9 1 Cor. 11, 7ff.
10 Cf. verse 10.
11 This is the best interpretation of *Adversus Haereses* 5, 6, 2 and 3, 18, 1, when taken together.
12 Ibid., 4, 4, 3 (*Library of Ante-Nicene Fathers* translation).
13 *De Trinitate* 14, 4, 6. A connection with immortality is also made in the passage.
14 This is particularly clear in *Adversus Haereses* 5, 16, 2.
15 *Summa Theologiae*, 1a, 93.
16 2 Peter 1, 4 glosses 'partakers of the divine nature' as 'escaping the corruption that is in the world'. For Athanasius cf. *De Incarnatione* 4–5.
17 Gregory Palamas, *The Triads*, III, iii, 68 (Classics of Western Spirituality, SPCK, 1983, p. 69).
18 V. Lossky, *In the Image and Likeness of God* (Mowbrays, 1975), p. 139.
19 Calvin, *Institutes*, III, vii, 6.
20 Barth, *Church Dogmatics*, vol. I, 1, p. 273.
21 Ibid., vol. III, 1, p. 184.
22 Ibid., on the same page.
23 Ibid., vol. III, 1. pp. 189ff.
24 Barth may have confused himself about the actual versus potential character of this aspect of the image by his use of the term 'real man' where in fact he means ideal man. Cf. ibid., vol. III, 2 (44,3) and p. 198.
25 Ibid., vol. III, 4, p. 166.
26 *Cartesian Meditations*, trans. D. Cairns (Martinus Nijhoff, The Hague, 1960); *Ideas*, trans. W. R. Boyce Gibson (Collier Edition, Macmillan, 1962).
27 So Herbert Spiegelberg in his definitive historical study, *The Phenomenological Movement* (Martinus Nijhoff, The Hague, 1982), p. 126.
28 *The Crisis of European Sciences and Transcendental Phenomenology*, trans. D. Carr (Northwestern University, Evanston, Ill., 1970). The original lecture is conveniently available in E. Husserl, *Phenomenology and the Crisis of Philosophy*, trans. Q. Lauer (Harper Torchbook, New York, 1965), pp. 149ff.
29 The interest roused by the letter is described by Merleau-Ponty in *Signes*, trans. R. C. McCleary (1964), part II, 3, p. 107.
30 Cf. Spiegelberg, *The Phenomenological Movement*, pp. 79–80. In addition, Louis Dupré in *A Dubious Heritage* (Paulist Press, New York, 1977, p. 79) notes that once in conversation when asked what he thought to be the fundamental problem in philosophy, Husserl replied: 'The problem of God, of course.'
31 *Ideas*, II, 5, 49, p. 138.
32 E. Pivćević, *Husserl and Phenomenology* (Hutchinson, 1970), p. 82.
33 M. Scheler, *The Nature of Sympathy*, trans. P. Heath (Archon Books,

Shoe String Press, Hamden, Conn. 1970), part III, pp. 213ff, esp. p. 250. For John Paul II's acknowledgement of his debt to Scheler, cf. esp. K. Wojtyla (John Paul II), *The Acting Person* (*Analecta Husserliana*, vol. X, Reidel, Dordrecht, Holland, 1979), p. xiii and p. 308 n. 8. There is also an early work which was entitled 'The possibility of the foundations of Christian ethics on the philosophy of Max Scheler'. The two most conspicuous features of *The Acting Person* are its stress on acting rather than thinking as what gives human identity and a strong social emphasis which none the less insists on the irreducible transcendence of the human person. For an example of the use of Phenomenology within English-speaking theology, cf. E. Farley, *Ecclesial Man: a social phenomenology of faith and reality* (Fortress Press, Philadelphia, Pa, 1975), and idem, *Ecclesial Reflection* (Fortress Press, 1982).

34 English translations of both are available: *Totality and Infinity*, trans. A. Lingis (Duquesne University Press, Pittsburgh, Pa, 1969); *Other than Being and Beyond Essence*, trans. A. Lingis (Martinus Nijhoff, The Hague, 1980).

35 'Beyond intentionality', in A. Montefiore (ed.), *Philosophy in France Today* (Cambridge University Press, Cambridge, 1983), p. 108.

36 'Violence and metaphysics', in J. Derrida, *Writing and Difference* (Routledge and Kegan Paul, 1978). The deconstructionist turn in Derrida's argument in this case is the claim that 'Levinas' metaphysics . . . presupposes . . . the transcendental phenomenology that it seems to put in question' (p. 133). He contends (not very plausibly) that Levinas needs the relative difference of Husserl's 'analogical appresentation' in order to prevent his own stronger claims from degenerating into meaninglessness (cf. esp. pp. 124 and 129).

37 Quoted in ibid., p. 91 without page reference from Levinas, *Le temps et l'autre*. One might compare here the way in which he chooses to draw the contrast between his own position and that of Existentialism. He informs us that the key issue in life is not facing up to death but avoiding committing murder (cf. *Totality and Infinity*, p. 47).

38 *Writing and Difference*, p. 314 n. 37.

39 M. Buber, *I and Thou* (T. & T. Clark, Edinburgh, 1958), p. 62.

40 Ibid., p. 65.

41 Ibid., pp. 66–7.

42 E. Levinas, *Totalité et infini* (Martinus Nijhoff, The Hague, 1961), p. 77. In a recent work, *Transcendance et intelligibilité* (Éditions Labor et Fides, Centre Protestant d'Études, Geneva, 1984), he has expressed sympathy with the Christian idea of kenosis, though admitting that it has got him into trouble with his fellow Jews (cf. pp. 56–7).

43 'Beyond intentionality', p. 111.

44 Romans 5,8.

45 So in the common phrase, 'publicans and sinners' (e.g. Matt. 11, 19). It is even used on occasion as equivalent to 'Gentiles'; thus in Mark 14, 41 the intended reference is clearly the Roman soldiers.

46 'Paraptoma' and 'hamartia'.

47 Romans 3, 23.

48 The Authorised Version of Romans 5, 12 retains the problem present in the original: 'Wherefore, as by one man sin entered into the world, and death by sin; and so death passed upon all men, for that all have sinned.' The Greek that is translated by 'for that' is most naturally expanded to mean 'for this reason that', with the resultant implication that death is a consequence of our own sins. But the Latin translation Augustine used had 'in quo', thus referring the responsibility back to Adam.

49 Cf. e.g. the title of one of his chapters in *The Institutes*: 'Ex corrupta hominis natura nihil nisi damnabile prodire' (Only damnable things come forth from man's corrupt nature) – *Institutes*, 2, 3.

50 N. P. Williams, *The Ideas of the Fall and of Original Sin* (Longman, 1927), p. xiii. He pursues the point further on pp. 43–4 and pp. 49–50.

51 *Jerusalem Bible* translation. In a footnote the Hebrew version is translated as follows: 'God put him in the hand of his own inclination and handed him over to the power of his enemy.'

52 D. Whiteley and R. Martin, *Sociology, Theology and Conflict* (Basil Blackwell, Oxford, 1969), p. 64. D. Jenkins, 'Responsibility, freedom and the Fall', in *Man: fallen and free*, ed. E. W. Kemp (Hodder & Stoughton, 1969), p. 14.

53 V. White, *God and the Unconscious* (Fontana, 1952), p. 95 and p. 96 n. 17.

54 Ibid., p. 99.

55 Ibid., p. 192.

56 R. S. Lee, *Freud and Christianity* (Penguin, Harmondsworth, 1967), pp. 68–9.

57 Ibid., pp. 49–50.

58 Ibid., p. 84.

59 P. Tillich, *The Courage To Be* (Fontana, 1962), p. 44.

60 Ibid., p. 15.

61 Ibid., pp. 140ff.

62 Ibid., p. 170.

63 P. Tillich, *Systematic Theology* (James Nisbet, 1957), vol. II, p. 39.

64 S. Kierkegaard, *The Concept of Anxiety*, ed. and trans. R. Thomte (Princeton University Press, Princeton, NJ, 1980), p. 92.

65 R. Bultmann, 'The understanding of man', in *Essays: philosophical and theological* (SCM, 1955), p. 81.

66 R. Niebuhr, *The Nature and Destiny of Man* (Charles Scribners' Sons, New York, 1964), Vol. I, p. 182.

67 Ibid., p. 185.

68 Cf. ibid., ch. IX.

69 Ibid., p. 263.

70 Ibid., pp. 186–207.

71 Ibid., p. 186.

72 M. Friedman (ed.), *The Worlds of Existentialism* (University of Chicago Press, Chicago, 1964), p. 3.

73 The notion is described for example (under the heading 'essential insight') in *Ideas*, 1, 3 (pp. 48–50).

74 J. MacQuarrie, *An Existentialist Theology* (Penguin, Harmondsworth, 1973), p. 38.
75 M. Heidegger, *Being and Time*, trans. J. MacQuarrie and E. Robinson (Basil Blackwell, Oxford, 1962), p. 27.
76 J. MacQuarrie, *In Search of Deity* (SCM, 1984), p. 155.
77 As MacQuarrie explains, ibid., pp. 163–4.
78 Quoted ibid., p. 159.
79 Plato, *Republic* 509B (where the Form of the Good is so described).
80 P. Tillich, *Systematic Theology* (James Nisbet, 1953), vol. I, p. 263.
81 M. Heidegger, *What is Called Thinking?* (Harper & Row, New York, 1968), p. 4.
82 Ibid., p. 139.
83 See especially his 1927 paper 'Phänomenologie und Theologie' and the brief 1964 letter which is printed as an appendix to it in M. Heidegger, *Wegmarken*, 2nd edn (Vittorio Klostermann, Frankfurt am Main, 1978), pp. 45–77. He also seems to have had a strong early interest in St Paul, cf. O. Pöggeler, *Der Denkweg Martin Heideggers* (Pfullingen, 1963), p. 37.
84 *Being and Time*, p. 488.
85 *In Search of Deity*, p. 172.
86 So MacQuarrie, *An Existentialist Theology*, p. 79.
87 *Being and Time*, p. 477.
88 Ibid., p. 306.
89 Ibid., p. 311.
90 Ibid., p. 307.
91 This later influence is explored by A. C. Thiselton, *The Two Horizons* (Paternoster Press, Exeter, 1980), pp. 327–47.
92 E.g. *Being and Time*, p. 310.
93 Quoted in *The Concept of Anxiety*, p. 170.
94 Ibid., p. 52. Cf. also pp. 42, 157.
95 R. Grossman, *Phenomenology and Existentialism* (Routledge and Kegan Paul, 1984), pp. 73ff.
96 For Regina Olsen cf. W. Lowrie, *A Short Life of Kierkegaard* (Princeton University Press, Princeton, NJ, 1974), pp. 135–43; for his father, ibid., pp. 16–30.
97 *Being and Time*, p. 232.
98 *The Concept of Anxiety*, pp. 25 and 26.
99 Ibid., p. 34.
100 Ibid., p. 48.
101 Ibid., p. 44.
102 Though Hannay makes a valiant effort. Cf. A. Hannay, *Kierkegaard* (Routledge and Kegan Paul, 1982), pp. 177–90.
103 J.-P. Sartre, 'Kierkegaard: the singular universal', in *Between Existentialism and Marxism* (Verso, 1983), p. 159.
104 P. Caws, *Sartre* (Routledge and Kegan Paul, 1984), p. 58.
105 J.-P. Sartre, *Being and Nothingness* (Methuen University Paperback, 1969), pp. 9–10.
106 Ibid., p. 496.

107 Ibid., p. 498.
108 J. MacQuarrie, *In Search of Humanity* (SCM, 1982), p. 20; Sartre, *Being and Nothingness*, p. 129.
109 E.g. Romans 2, 1–11.
110 Cf. Galatians 1, 15.
111 Romans 3, 23–4 (*Jerusalem Bible* trans.).
112 Hosea 1–3; Ezekiel 16.
113 Romans 9, 14–21.
114 Philippians 2, 13.
115 E.g. Phil. 1, 29.
116 *Confessions* X, 29. A less literal but clearer translation might run: 'Give me the grace to do as you command, and command me to do what you will!' (Penguin trans.).
117 He placed special emphasis on Matthew 5, 48, with its call to perfection.
118 Quoted in A. E. McGrath, *Luther's Theology of the Cross* (Basil Blackwell, Oxford, 1985), p. 87.
119 So at any rate McGrath, ibid., p. 89.
120 Ibid., p. 118.
121 Ibid., pp. 158–9.
122 Cf. ibid., p. 151.
123 K. Stendahl, *Paul among Jews and Gentiles* (SCM, 1977), cf. esp. pp. 2–4 and 28–9; E. P. Sanders, *Paul and Palestinian Judaism* (SCM, 1977), pp. 442–7 and 474ff.
124 A. C. Thiselton, *The Two Horizons* (Paternoster Press, Exeter, 1980), p. 420.
125 Ibid., p. 421.
126 Cf. esp. James 2, 18–26.
127 *The Two Horizons*, p. 424.
128 N. P. Williams, *The Ideas of the Fall and of Original Sin* (Longman, 1927), pp. 169–70.
129 Ibid., p. 331.
130 *Confessions* VIII, 12.
131 Ibid., I, 9 and II, 4.
132 Philippians 3, 6.
133 *Luther's Theology of the Cross*, p. 112; cf. p. 140.
134 So in his 1545 account of his theological development he speaks of his worries about not being able to be confident that God would be pleased with his 'satisfaction' (*satisfactio*). The word recalls crude medieval practices of quantifying amends.
135 Translated from the Latin quotation given by McGrath, *Luther's Theology of the Cross*, p. 110 n. 39.
136 So in *De Servo Arbitrio* Luther tells us that God has not 'set bounds to himself by his Word, but has kept himself free over all things'. The result is that though in his Word he does not will the death of a sinner, 'he wills it by his inscrutable will' (*The Bondage of the Will*, trans. J. I. Parker and O. R. Johston, James Clarke, Cambridge, 1957, p. 170). Even McGrath's normally admiring attitude to Luther balks at this (cf. *Luther's Theology of the Cross*, pp. 166–7).

137 J. Atkinson, *Martin Luther: prophet to the Church Catholic* (Paternoster Press, Exeter, 1983), p. 112. For a recent German attempt to give a more positive sense to Luther's notion of freedom, cf. 'Marcuses Kritik an Luthers Freiheitsbegriff', in O. Bayer, *Umstrittene Freiheit* (J. C. B. Mohr/Paul Siebeck, Tübingen, 1981), pp. 13–38.

138 J. Oman, *Grace and Personality* (Fontana, 1962), p. 54.

139 Ibid., p. 47.

140 Ibid., p. 81.

141 M. Wiles, *The Remaking of Christian Doctrine* (SCM, 1974), pp. 96–7.

142 K. Rahner, 'Concerning the relationship between nature and grace', in *Theological Investigations* (Darton, Longman & Todd, 1961), vol. I, pp. 297–317, esp. p. 302.

143 *De Corruptione et Gratia* 12, 33; *Patrologia Latina* 44, 936.

144 *Opus Imperfectum contra Julianum* 6, 11; *Patrologia Latina* 45, 1521.

145 *Homilies on St John* 41, 8, 10; *Patrologia Latina* 35, 1698.

146 I. Berlin, 'Two concepts of liberty', in *Political Philosophy*, ed. A. Quinton (Oxford University Press, 1967), pp. 141–52.

147 Ibid., pp. 150ff.

148 That is to say, there seems no reason why comparisons between individual vices and virtues in terms of happiness should not sometimes go in favour of the vices. The most that the eudaemonist (someone who believes that virtue and happiness are connected) seems committed to is the claim that when the two lives are compared overall, then the balance will fall in favour of the virtuous life.

149 Ricoeur, who first employed the term in 1965, has used it many times since, e.g. *The Conflict of Interpretations* (Northwestern University Press, Evanston, Ill., 1974), p. 331. V. Descombes is one of those who makes the contrast between the 1945 and the 1960 generation, cf. *Modern French Philosophy* (Cambridge University Press, Cambridge, 1980), p. 3.

150 F. Nietzsche, *The Genealogy of Morals* (Doubleday Anchor, New York, 1956), I, 10; p. 170.

151 A. Sheridan, *Michel Foucault: the will to truth* (Tavistock, 1980), pp. 220–3.

152 M. Foucault, *Power/Knowledge*, ed. C. Gordon (Harvester Press, Brighton, 1980), cf. esp. pp. 80–1, 114, 116.

153 Ibid., p. 81.

154 M. Foucault, *Discipline and Punish: the birth of the prison* (Penguin, Harmondsworth, 1979), pp. 192–3.

155 M. Foucault, *Madness and Civilisation: a history of insanity in the Age of Reason* (Tavistock, 1971), pp. xii and xiv.

156 Ibid., p. 35. The adage is to be found on the following page.

157 M. Philp, 'Michel Foucault', in Q. Skinner (ed.), *The Return of Grand Theory in the Human Sciences* (Cambridge University Press, Cambridge, 1985).

158 Cf. e.g. the following argument in 'The freedom of a Christian': 'If he has no need of works, he has no need of law; and if he has no need of the law,

surely he is free from the law' (M. Luther, *Three Treatises*, 2nd edn, Fortress Press, Philadelphia, Pa, 1970, p. 284).
159 Isaiah 7, 3 and 8, 3; Amos 8, 1–2.
160 W. Zimmerli, *Commentary on Ezekiel* (Fortress Press, Philadelphia, Pa, 1979), vol. I, p. 20.
161 John 3, 8.
162 John 10, 20; 1 Corinthians 1, 23.
163 'The Life of St. Francis', in *Bonaventure* (Classics of Western Spirituality, SPCK, 1978), 5, 4; pp. 220–1. John Sayward pursues the history of the influence of the idea of 'fools for Christ's sake' in his book *Perfect Fools* (Oxford University Press, Oxford, 1980).
164 *Phaedrus* 244ff.

Chapter 4   Doctrine of Salvation

1 A good example of scholarly Evangelical Christianity of this type would be Leon Morris, *The Cross in the New Testament* (Paternoster Press, Exeter, 1976).
2 J. Calvin, *The Institutes of the Christian Religion*, ed. J. T. McNeill (Westminster Press, Philadelphia, Pa, 1960), II, xvi, 3 (vol. I, pp. 505–6).
3 Ibid., II, xvi, 1 (p. 504).
4 K. Barth, *Dogmatics in Outline* (SCM, 1949), chs 15 and 17.
5 Ibid., p. 101.
6 Ibid., pp. 105–6.
7 Ibid., p. 107.
8 Ibid., p. 119.
9 K. Barth, *Church Dogmatics* T. & T. Clark, Edinburgh, 1956), vol. IV, 1, p. 221.
10 Ibid., p. 222.
11 *Dogmatics in Outline*, p. 119.
12 J. Moltmann, *The Crucified God* (SCM, 1974), p. 193.
13 Ibid., p. 183.
14 Ibid., p. 185.
15 Ibid., p. 183.
16 Ibid., pp. 145–53.
17 Ibid., p. 150.
18 Ibid., p. 152.
19 Ibid., p. 192.
20 Cf. Leviticus 16, 15–16.
21 Romans 8, 3–4 (first two quotations); 2 Corinthians 5, 21; Galatians 3, 13.
22 Galatians 3, 13 is based on Deuteronomy 21, 23: 'he that is hanged is accursed of God.'
23 H. Hart, *Punishment and Responsibility* (Oxford University Press, 1968), pp. 9ff.
24 For relation between sanctification and justification, cf. *Institutes*, 3, 11, 6.

25 G. Aulén *Christus Victor*, 2nd edn (SPCK, 1970), p. xi.

26 Ibid., p. 4.

27 John 12, 31; 14, 30; 16, 11; cf. also 8, 44–52.

28 Cf. Colossians 2, 10–15.

29 The phrase is from Mark 10, 45. Gregory of Nyssa develops the image of the fish in his *Great Catechism*, ch. 24.

30 Gregory Naziazus, *Oration* 45, 22.

31 Cf. 1 Corinthians 7, 23.

32 E.g. Luke 10, 18.

33 Matthew 26, 63–4 and 27, 14.

34 E.g. pp. 4–5 and 54–5.

35 G. Aulén, *Jesus in Contemporary Historical Research* (SPCK, 1976), p. 145.

36 As in John 3, 14 or the great cry of triumph with which the Crucifixion ends in 19, 30.

37 P. Tillich, *Systematic Theology* (Nisbet, 1953), vol. I, pp. 149 and 155.

38 O. Cullmann, *Christ and Time* (SCM, 1951), p. 84.

39 *Christus Victor*, p. 157.

40 Ibid., p. 156.

41 A. Ritschl, *Justification and Reconciliation* (T. & T. Clark, Edinburgh, 1900), p. 320.

42 Ibid., p. 85.

43 R. C. Moberly, *Atonement and Personality* (John Murray, 1900); H. Rashdall, *The Idea of Atonement in Christian Theology* (Macmillan, 1919).

44 Moberly, *Atonement and Personality*, pp. 372–82; Rashdall, *The Idea of Atonement*, pp. 358–62; Ritschl, *Justification and Reconciliation*, pp. 48–54.

45 R. Weingart, *The Logic of Divine Love* (Oxford University Press, 1970).

46 *Tractatus ad Innocentium* II; Ep. 190, 7. I have adopted L. W. Grensted's translation in *A Short History of the Doctrine of the Atonement* (Manchester University Press, Manchester, 1920), p. 106.

47 Sermo XII, 484ab; quoted in Weingart, *The Logic of Divine Love*, p. 123.

48 My translation. I have used Buytaert's edition in *Corpus Christianorum* (Continuatio Mediaevalis, vol. XI, 1969), p. 211.

49 Ibid., vs. 6 and 5; p. 155.

49 Ibid., vs. 6 and 5; p. 155.

50 Ibid., pp. 113–18. The digression occurs after his commentary on 3, 26.

51 Ibid., p. 117.

52 *The Logic of Divine Love*, p. 186.

53 *Peter Abelard's Ethics*, ed. D. E. Luscombe (Oxford University Press, 1971), pp. 113ff.

54 Cf. esp. ibid., pp. 5–37.

55 *The Logic of Divine Love*, p. 176.

56 I seem to have been somewhat anticipated by J. McLeod Campbell in *The Nature of the Atonement* (1856) who also tries to give Anselm's notion of satisfaction a more modern sense. But intriguingly Grensted

treats him as 'the classical English exposition of the Moral theory' (*A Short History*, p. 349), and in any case he treats Christ's life as essentially an expression of sorrow for sin rather than as an attempt to make amends.

57 'Necessary and fitting reasons in Christian theology', in *The Rationality of Religious Belief: essays in honour of Basil G. Mitchell*, ed. W. J. Abraham and S. W. Holtzer (Oxford University Press, Oxford, 1987).

58 *Christus Victor*, e.g. p. 129.

59 F. W. Dillistone, *The Christian Understanding of Atonement* (James Nisbet, 1968), p. 195.

60 I, XI. I have adapted S. N. Dean's translation in *St. Anselm's Basic Writings*, 2nd edn (Open Court, La Salle, Ill., 1979), p. 202.

61 *Anselm of Canterbury*, ed. J. Hopkins and H. W. Richardson (SCM, 1974), vol. I, p. 144.

62 Ibid., pp. 141–2.

63 *Justification and Reconciliation*, p. 578.

64 For Paul cf. his frequent use of the expression 'in Christ' and esp. 1 Corinthians 15, 22–3; for Irenaeus, e.g. *Adversus Haereses* V, 21 and III, 22.

65 Edited by E. Carcacciolo-Trejo, *The Penguin Book of Latin American Verse* (Penguin, Harmondsworth, 1971). Practically all the poets whose works are quoted are twentieth century.

66 Most of their works are available in English, e.g. J. Amado, *Tieta* (Abacus, Sphere Books, 1982); M. V. Llosa, *Aunt Julia and the Scriptwriter* (Picador, Pan Books, 1984); C. Fuentes, *The Death of Artemio Cruz* (Penguin, Harmondsworth, 1978); G. G. Marquez, *The Autumn of the Patriarch* (Picador, Pan Books, 1978); J. L. Borges, *Labyrinths* (Penguin, Harmondsworth, 1970); G. Cabrera Infante, *Three Trapped Tigers* (Picador, Pan Books, 1980).

67 H. Assmann, *Practical Theology of Liberation* (Search Press, 1975), p. 37.

68 G. Guiterrez, *A Theology of Liberation* (SCM, 1974), ch. 2, esp. pp. 27ff.

69 Ibid., pp. 175–6.

70 Ibid., p. 155.

71 Ibid., p. 159.

72 A. A. Boesak, *Black Theology – Black Power* (Mowbrays, 1978), p. 17.

73 E.g. Isaiah 5, 1–9; Jeremiah 22, 13–19; Hosea 10, 12–13; Amos 4, 1–3; Micah 3, 8–12.

74 E. Norman, *Christianity and the World Order* (Oxford University Press, Oxford, 1979), p. 80.

75 Luke 6, 20. Matthew 5, 1 has 'Blessed are the poor in spirit.'

76 *A Theology of Liberation*, p. 298.

77 J. P. Miranda, *Marx and the Bible* (SCM, 1977), p. 18.

78 Ibid., p. 104.

79 Ibid., p. 63.

80 L. Boff, *Jesus Christ Liberator* (SPCK, 1980), pp. 51ff, esp. p. 53.

81 Ibid., p. 105 and pp. 289 and 290.

82 Ibid., p. 171.
83 J. Sobrino, *Christology at the Crossroads* (SCM, 1978), p. 367.
84 Ibid., pp. 120–1.
85 J. Ratzinger, *Libertatis Nuntius* (Catholic Truth Society, 1984), pp. 5 and 4.
86 Ibid., p. 12.
87 Ibid., p. 18.
88 Ibid., p. 26.
89 *Jesus Christ Liberator*, pp. 46 and 266.
90 Cf. *A Theology of Liberation*, p. 10.
91 J. L. Segundo, *The Liberation of Theology* (Gill & MacMillan, Dublin, 1977), p. 13. Cf. pp. 33–4.
92 Ibid., pp. 75ff.
93 Ibid., p. 101.
94 Cf. p. 116.
95 E. Cardinal, *The Gospel in Solentiname* (Orbis Books, Maryknoll, NY, 1976–82). There is an excellent summary of what took place in the first chapter of P. Berryman, *The Religious Roots of Rebellion* (SCM, 1984). These two quotations are taken from pp. 20 and 19.
96 If one can get beyond that first chapter, Berryman offers a good analysis of the appalling conditions prevailing in Central America. Nicaragua is discussed in chapters 4, 7 and 8.
97 *Christology at the Crossroads*, p. 36.
98 Ibid., p. 330. One might compare here his endorsement of Moltmann's attack on the traditional understanding of God as impassible, cf. pp. 194ff.
99 Preface to 2nd edition of *Das Capital*.
100 Thesis IV; *Marx and Engels on Religion*, ed. R. Niebuhr (Schocken Books, New York, 1964), p. 70.
101 Thesis XI; ibid, p. 72.
102 K. Marx and F. Engels, *Collected Works* (Lawrence & Wishart, 1975), vol. II, p. 555.
103 V. Lenin, F. Engels and K. Marx, *On Historical Materialism* (Progress Publishers, Moscow, 1972), p. 411.
104 Niebuhr (ed.), *Marx and Engels on Religion*, p. 42; from *Contribution to the Critique of Hegel's Philosophy of Right*.
105 Ibid., p. 51.
106 As N. Lash does in *A Matter of Hope* (Darton, Longman & Todd, 1981), ch. 2.
107 Miranda, *Marx and the Bible*, p. 258.
108 M. Machoveč, *A Marxist Looks at Jesus* (Darton, Longman & Todd, 1976), p. 31.
109 Ibid., p. 95.
110 R. Garaudy, *The Alternative Future* (Penguin, Harmondworth, 1976), p. 88.
111 Ibid., p. 85. Ironically Garaudy, having moved from Marxism to Christianity has now become a Muslim in his desire to identity closely with the oppressed in France.

112 L. Boff, *Church, Charism and Power* (SCM, 1985), p. 40.

113 D. Turner, *Marxism and Christianity* (Basil Blackwell, Oxford, 1983), pp. 25, 30, 38ff, 67ff.

114 Ibid., p. 92.

115 Ibid., p. 118.

116 Ibid., p. 124.

117 Ibid., p. 219. Cf. what Alfredo Fierro says of theology in *The Militant Gospel* (SCM, 1977), p. 354: 'Its only contribution is to say no to the closing in of the world, society and history upon themselves; and it attempts to express this no in symbols.'

118 *A Matter of Hope*, p. 284.

119 Niebuhr (ed.), *Marx and Engels on Religion*, pp. 74–5.

120 Lash, *A Matter of Hope*, chs 8 and 10.

121 Ibid., p. 63.

122 Ibid., p. 75.

123 Ibid., p. 158.

124 M. Horkheimer, *Critical Theory* (Seabury, NY, 1972), p. 129.

125 For an excellent survey of the history of the School, see M. Jay, *The Dialectical Imagination: a history of the Frankfurt School and the Institute of Social Research, 1923–50* (London, 1973).

126 T. Adorno, *Negative Dialectics* (Routledge and Kegan Paul, 1973), p. 144.

127 As indicated for example in a 1981 interview, quoted in R. J. Bernstein, *Beyond Objectivism and Relativism* (Basil Blackwell, Oxford, 1983), p. 178. Cf. also J. Habermas, *The Theory of Communicative Action* (Heinemann, 1984), vol. I, pp. 339ff, where a complex history, eventually through Adorno and Horkheimer, is given for one of his leading ideas.

128 J. Habermas, *Knowledge and Human Interests*, 2nd edn (Heinemann, 1978), pp. 3 and 4.

129 Significantly, he finds his ideas anticipated by a philosopher not much read in England, namely Fichte (d. 1814), for whom 'interested self-reflection' were 'constitutive likewise for knowing and acting'. So ibid., p. 210.

130 Ibid., p. 266.

131 Ibid., p. 371.

132 J. Habermas, *Theory and Practice* (Heinemann, 1974), p. 9, though the term 'emancipatory cognitive interest' in already found in *Knowledge and Human Interests* (e.g. p. 198).

133 J. Habermas, *Communication and the Evolution of Society* (Heinemann, 1979), p. 3.

134 Ibid., p. 64.

135 Ibid., ch. 2, esp. pp. 91–2. Cf. also *Moralbewusstsein und kommunikatives Handeln* (Suhrkamp, Frankfurt, 1983), esp. ch. 4.

136 'A reply to my critics', in *Habermas: Critical Debates*, ed. J. B. Thompson and D. Held (Macmillan, 1982), pp. 258–9.

137 *Communication and the Evolution of Society*, pp. 8–25.

138 J. Habermas, *Legitimation Crisis* (Heinemann, 1975), p. 7.

139 *Communication and the Evolution of Society*, p. 188.
140 *Theory and Practice*, p. 168.
141 *Legitimation Crisis*, p. 111.
142 *Communication and the Evolution of Society*, pp. 134–5.
143 The first quotation is from 'A reply to my critics', in *Habermas: Critical Debates*, p. 221; the second from *Towards a Rational Society* (Heinemann, 1971), p. 109.
144 'A reply to my critics, p. 221.
145 W. Pannenberg, *Theology and the Philosophy of Science* (Darton, Longman & Todd, 1976), p. 89.
146 Ibid., p. 41 n. 62.
147 'Wahrheitstheorien', in H. Fahrenbach (ed.), *Wirklichkeit und Reflexion: Festschrift für Walter Schulz* (Pfullingen, 1973), p. 216; T. McCarthy's translation in *The Critical Theory of Jürgen Habermas* (Polity Press, Oxford, 1984), p. 302.
148 R. J. Bernstein, *Beyond Objectivism and Relativism* (Basil Blackwell, Oxford, 1983), p. 204.
149 E. Schillebeeckx, *The Understanding of Faith* (Sheed & Ward, 1981 edn), pp. xi-xii.
150 Ibid., cf. esp. pp. 134 and 148.
151 H. Peukert, *Science, Action and Fundamental Theology* (MIT Press, Cambridge, Mass., 1984), pp. 241 and 38–9 and ch. 2 passim.
152 Ibid., p. 209.
153 Ibid., pp. 206–8.
154 Habermas notes that similar objections could be raised by vegetarians against his treatment of the animal world. Cf. 'A reply to my critics', pp. 246–8.
155 Cf. esp. J. Habermas, *Theorie des kommunikativen Handelns* (Suhrkamp, Frankfurt, 1981), vol. II, v, 3. This second volume is still untranslated.
156 *The Theory of Communicative Action*, vol. I, p. 68.
157 Ibid., p. 214. Cf. also p. 70.
158 McCarthy, *The Critical Theory of Jürgen Habermas*, p. 67.
159 R. Geuss, *The Idea of a Critical Theory* (Cambridge University Press, Cambridge, 1981), p. 66.
160 Quoted in McCarthy, *The Critical Theory of Jürgen Habermas*, pp. 206 & 106–7.
161 Peukert, *Science, Action and Fundamental Theology*, p. 224.
162 This way of putting it was suggested to me by Rüdiger Bender.

Chapter 5   The Church

1 E. Schillebeeckx, *Jesus: An Experiment in Christology* (Fount Paperback, London, 1983). Cf. e.g. the following: 'There is not such a big difference between the way we are able, after Jesus' death, to come to faith in the crucified-and-risen One and the way in which the disciples of Jesus arrived at the same faith' (p. 346). Marxsen similarly discounts the

Resurrection Appearances in *The Resurrection of Jesus of Nazareth* (SCM, 1970), pp. 79ff.

2 H. Küng, *The Church* (Search Press, 1968), p. 451.
3 Quoted in E. Schillebeeckx, *Ministry: a case for change* (SCM, 1981), p. 38.
4 Ibid., pp. 47 and 49.
5 Ibid., p. 52.
6 Ibid., p. 55.
7 Ibid., p. 67.
8 Ibid., p. 79.
9 Ibid., p. 139. Cf. pp. 82–3.
10 P. Grelot, *Église et ministères* (Cerf, Paris, 1983), pp. 42ff, esp. p. 54ff.
11 Y. Congar, *I Believe in the Holy Spirit* (Geoffrey Chapman, 1983), vol. II, p. 16.
12 Ibid., pp. 145ff, esp. pp. 153–4.
13 Ibid., vol. III, pp. 155ff.
14 R. Hanson, *Christian Priesthood Examined* (Lutterworth Press, 1979), pp. 41ff. He blames three factors for this, the lack of influence in the patristic period of Hebrews (which he interprets as arguing for the abolition of all priesthood with Christ), the attempt to give the Old Testament permanent symbolic significance, and the need to give more status to Christian leaders vis-à-vis paganism than seems implied by a literal translation of the threefold ministry of bishops, presbyters and deacons (literally 'inspectors, older men and helpers').
15 So Küng, *The Church*, pp. 377–8, 336 and 431.
16 Ibid., pp. 389 and 428.
17 Cf. Ephesians 4, 11, and 1 Corinthians 12, 8–10.
18 H. Küng, *Infallible?* (Collins, 1971), pp. 175–7 and 168.
19 Ibid., p. 153. For Congar, pp. 150–1.
20 P. Chirico, *Infallibility* (Sheed & Ward, 1977), p. xiii. Cf. p. x.
21 Ibid., pp. xviii and 57.
22 Ibid., p. 121.
23 Ibid., pp. 216 and 224.
24 Ibid., cf. pp. 191 and 188.
25 Ibid., p. 237.
26 J. Tillard, *The Bishop of Rome* (SPCK, 1983), pp. 174, 176 and 177.
27 Quoted in ibid., p. 24.
28 Ibid., p. 151.
29 I do not of course mean that this is all they are to be seen as, still less do I intend a definition. My purpose has been solely to contrast this model with the traditional authoritarian pattern of leadership.
30 John Taylor et al., *Believing in the Church* (SPCK, 1981), pp. 111ff and 206.
31 The joint contribution from Barton and Halliburton, ibid., p. 79.
32 Ibid., pp. 31–2.
33 S. Sykes, *The Identity of Christianity* (SPCK, 1984), p. 256.
34 Ibid., p. 284.
35 Ibid., p. 285.

36 Y. Congar, *Diversity and Communion* (SCM, 1984), p. 145.
37 It was apparently once widely accepted in both Orthodoxy and Lutheranism and was even employed at one stage in the English Reformation. So, ibid., p. 115.
38 Ibid., p. 76.
39 G. A. Lindbeck, *The Nature of Doctrine* (SPCK, 1984), p. 48. Lindbeck has been heavily influenced by the distinguished American anthropologist Clifford Geertz. Cf. esp. his 'Ideology as a cultural system', in *The Interpretation of Cultures* (Basic Books, Harper, New York, 1973), pp. 193–233.
40 Ibid., pp. 77–8.
41 As in the contrast between prophet and priest in the Old Testament, with the latter guarding the tradition and the former seeking to advance it in various ways. One needs to recall that there were numerous false prophets (with warnings against them, e.g. Deuteronomy 13, 1–5), as well as those who eventually achieved canonical status and so became part of the tradition.
42 If this is regarded as too intellectual an account, recall the ancient word for a creed, *symbolon*, with its suggestion of participation in much more than mere formal belief.
43 As indeed it is on me, in respect of my unorthodox views on Christ's Second Coming. See further, ch. 6.
44 Briefly recounted in M. Stanton, *Outside the Dream* (Routledge and Kegan Paul, 1983), pp. 43–5.
45 'The function and field of speech and language in psychoanalysis', in J. Lacan, *Écrits: a selection* (Tavistock, 1977), pp. 30–113, esp. pp. 31 and 34.
46 Cf. C. Clément, *The Lives and Legends of Jacques Lacan* (Columbia University Press, New York, 1983), pp. 103–6, for further details.
47 Ibid., p. 2. Cf. also ch. 1 passim, but esp. pp. 11 and 15.
48 *Écrits*, p. 79. Cf. pp. 53–4 and 285.
49 R. Georgin, *De Lévi-Strauss à Lacan* (Cistre, Paris, 1983), p. 90.
50 Lacan, *Écrits*, p. 73.
51 In Lacan's Preface to A. Lemaire, *Jacques Lacan* (Routledge and Kegan Paul, 1979), p. xiii. In some of the references that follow I have given a reference to Lemaire rather than Lacan's original text, as unlike the original thinker she is a model of clarity.
52 Cf. Lemaire, *Jacques Lacan*, pp. 230 and 234.
53 Ibid., p. 7.
54 Lemaire's way of putting it, ibid., p. 82.
55 Cf. ibid., pp. 176ff.
56 Cf. ibid., p. 88; Lacan, *Écrits*, p. 320.
57 Lacan, *Écrits*, p. 84; cf. p. 305.
58 Cf. Lemaire, *Jacques Lacan*, pp. 54 and 227.
59 Cf. ibid., pp. 32–4 and 200–5.
60 Two typical examples in Clément, *Lives and Legends*, pp. 9 and 42.
61 Lacan, *Écrits*, p. 72. Cf. also French selection, *Écrits* (Éditions de Seuil, 1971), vol. II, p. 27.

62 Lacan, English selection, p. 49.
63 Quoted without reference in Clément, *Lives and Legends*, p. 131.
64 *Jaques Lacan*, p. 68.
65 Explained by Clément, *Lives and Legends*, pp. 22–5.
66 Georgin, *De Lévi-Strauss à Lacan*, pp. 149ff, esp. p. 154.
67 Stanton, *Outside the Dream*, p. 63; Clément, *Lives and Legends*, p. 156.
68 G. Deleuze and F. Guattari, *Anti-Oedipus: capitalism and schizophrenia* (Athlone Press, 1984), e.g. p. 186.
69 Ibid., p. 257.
70 Ibid., p. 34.
71 Ibid., p. xvi.
72 Ibid., e.g. pp. 193, 222, 82.
73 Ibid., pp. 52–3 and 191.
74 Ibid., p. 50.
75 Ibid., p. 178.
76 Ibid., pp. 42ff.
77 Ibid., p. 47.
78 Ibid., quoted on pp. 131–2.
79 Ibid., p. 15.
80 Ibid., p. 271.
81 For an excellent survey of the extensive use of Délire in modern European thought, including Deleuze, cf. J.-J. Lecercle, *Philosophy through the Looking-Glass* (Hutchinson, 1985).
82 *Anti-Oedipus*, p. 360. Cf. p. 23.
83 Ibid., p. 322.
84 A minor exception occurs on p. 381.
85 G. Deleuze and C. Parnet, *Dialogues* (Flammarion, Paris, 1977), p. 96.
86 Ibid., pp. 173–6.
87 Derrida has also attacked Lacan's views. For his general position on psychoanalysis cf. esp. *La carte postale: de Socrate à Freud et au-delà* (Flammarion, Paris, 1980).
88 Deleuze has written a major work on Nietzsche: *Nietzsche and Philosophy* (Athlone Press, 1983).
89 Cf. 'Le desir nommé Marx', in J.-F. Lyotard, *Economie libidinale* (Minuit, Paris, 1974). In a more recent book, *Le différend* (Minuit, Paris, 1983), he argues that none of our categories are adequate (cf. e.g. p. 29), and just where we might feel most certain, uses Auschwitz to drive home his agnostic theme (pp. 90ff, 145ff and 159–62).
90 E.g. Deleuze and Parnet, *Dialogues*, pp. 168 and 76.
91 P. Virilio, *Pure War* (Columbia University Press, New York 1983), pp. 35.
92 Ibid., p. 142.
93 Ibid., pp. 43–4.
94 Ibid., p. 46.
95 Ibid., pp. 58–61.
96 Ibid., p. 73.
97 Mark 10, 43–4 (*Jerusalem Bible*).
98 L. Boff, *Church, Charism and Power* (SCM, 1985), p. 40.

99 Hebrews 13, 14 (A.V.)
100 Luke 14, 26 (A.V.)
101 Galatians 2, 20. Cf. 1 Corinthians 15, 10.
102 Matthew 25, 40.
103 J. D. Zizioulas, *Being as Communion* (Darton, Longman & Todd, 1985), p. 17.
104 Ibid., pp. 109–10.
105 Ibid., p. 182.
106 Ibid., p. 56.
107 Ibid., p. 139.
108 Ibid., pp. 215–16 and 226.
109 Ibid., pp. 137, 165 and 218.
110 Ibid., p. 166.
111 Y. Brilioth, *Eucharistic Faith and Practice: Evangelical and Catholic* (SPCK, 1930), ch. 8, esp. p. 288.
112 G. Wainwright, *Eucharist and Eschatology*, 2nd edn (Epworth Press, 1978).
113 Ibid., pp. 104–6; cf. also p. 112.
114 J. Martos, *Doors to the Sacred* (SCM, 1981), p. 141.
115 E. Schillebeeckx, *The Eucharist* (Sheed & Ward, 1977 edn), pp. 94ff.
116 Ibid., p. 101.
117 Ibid., pp. 108ff.
118 M. Gesteira Garza, *La eucarista, misterio de comunion* (Ediciones Cristiandad, Madrid, 1983), pp. 524ff.
119 F. J. Leenhardt, *Le sacrement de la sainte cène* (Delachaux & Niestlé Neuchâtel-Paris, 1948); ibid., *Ceci est mon corps* (Delachaux & Niestlé Neuchâtel-Paris, 1955).
120 *The Eucharist*, p. 113.
121 *La eucarista*, pp. 553ff.
122 Ibid., p. 555.
123 Ibid., p. 563.
124 *The Eucharist*, p. 113.
125 M. Thurian, *The Eucharistic Memorial* (Lutterworth Press, 1961), part II, p. 109. Cf. also p. 127.
126 A. Heron, *Table and Tradition* (The Handsel Press, Edinburgh, 1983), p. 98.
127 Ibid., p. 164.
128 Ibid., p. 166.
129 *The Eucharist*, p. 135 n. 52.
130 J.-H. Nicolas, *Synthèse dogmatique* (Éditions Universitaires, Fribourg, 1985; Éditions Beauchesne, Paris, 1985), p. 951.
131 Quoted in Latin without reference in Thurian, *The Eucharistic Memorial*, p. 115. Similar sentiments are also expressed in the *Consensus Tigurinus* of 1549, sections 21 and 25.
132 J. Calvin, *The Institutes of the Christian Religion* (Westminster Press, Philadelphia, Pa, 1960), IV, xvii, 31 (vol. II, p. 1403).
133 *Short Treatise on the Lord's Supper*, in *Calvin: Theological Treatises* (SCM Library of Christian Classics, vol. 22, 1954), p. 166.

134 *The Eucharistic Memorial*, p. 117.
135 *La eucarista*, p. 466.
136 J. Jeremias, *The Eucharistic Words of Jesus* (SCM, 1966), p. 233.
137 Most obviously John 6, which Jeremias, unlike Bultmann, not only treats as part of the original text but regards as containing a primitive version of the original institutional formula. Cf. *Eucharistic Words*, pp. 107–8, 125 and 170.
138 But this judgement is of course heavily conditioned by the fact that Aristotle's more literary works have been lost. For these, see further W. Jaeger, *Aristotle*, 2nd edn (Oxford University Press, 1948), chs 2–4.
139 Quoted in G. Macy, *The Theologies of the Eucharist in the Early Scholastic Period* (Oxford University Press, 1984), p. 33 (Migne, *Patrologia Latina* 139, 383C). Cf. also pp. 27–8, 34, 35, 47, 108, 124 and also his remarks about the overlapping between his three models, p. 139.
140 *Summa Theologiae* 3a, 73–8, (Blackfriars translation, Eyre & Spottiswoode, vol. 58, 1965).
141 3a, 75, 3 (p. 63).
142 3a, 75, 6 (p. 77).
143 3a, 75, 6 (p. 79).
144 3a, 76, 1 (p. 95).
145 3a, 76, 4 (pp. 105–7).
146 3a, 76, 5 (p. 109).
147 3a, 76, 5 (p. 111).
148 3a, 77, 5 (p. 147).
149 3a, 76, 3 (p. 103).
150 F. W. Dillistone, *Christianity and Symbolism* (SCM, 1955; reissued 1985), cf. pp. 22 and 36.
151 S. McFague, *Metaphorical Theology* (SCM, 1983), pp. 15–16.
152 Ibid., p. 48.
153 Ibid., pp. 59 and 18.
154 Ibid., p. 41.
155 Ibid., p. 6.
156 Ibid., p. 109.
157 Ibid., p. 53. Quoted from M. Wiles, *Faith and the Mystery of God* (SCM, 1982), p. 72.
158 J. M. Soskice, *Metaphor and Religious Language* (Oxford University Press, Oxford, 1985), p. 110.
159 Ibid., p. 90.
160 *Metaphorical Theology*, p. 12.
161 Her remarks on 'a profound questioning of the symbolic mentality' on p. 12 are unqualified.
162 M. Blonsky (ed.), *On Signs* (Basil Blackwell, Oxford, 1985). The relevant articles are on pp. 12–15, 16–32, 365–72, 414–20 and 475–80.
163 M. Eliade, *Symbolism, the Sacred, and the Arts* (Crossroad, New York, 1985), pp. 82 and 46. One might also compare Roland Barthes' comments on the religious significance of a wrestling match in *Mythologies* (Granada, 1973), pp. 15–25.
164 *Metaphorical Theology*, p. 63.

165 P. Ricoeur, *The Conflict of Interpretations* (Northwestern University Press, Evanston, Ill., 1974), p. 288.
166 P. Ricoeur, *Hermeneutics and the Human Sciences* (Cambridge University Press, Cambridge, 1981), p. 33.
167 P. Ricoeur, *The Rule of Metaphor* (Routledge & Kegan Paul, 1975), p. 254.
168 *Interpretation Theory* (Christian University Press, Fort Worth, Tex., 1976), p. 58.
169 In *Revue d'histoire et de philosophie religieuse*, 1975, p. 14.
170 T. M. Van Leeuwen, *The Surplus of Meaning* (Rodolpi, Amsterdam, 1981). He draws the contrast with Heidegger on pp. 63–4.
171 *The Conflict of Interpretations*, p. 51.
172 Ibid., pp. 333–4.
173 M. Eliade, *The Sacred and the Profane* (Harvest/HBJ, San Diego, 1959), p. 118. Cf. also p. 34.
174 *The Conflict of Interpretations*, p. 319.
175 'God and symbolic action', in E. Henderson and B. Hebblethwaite (ed.), *God's Action in the World* (Cambridge University Press, New York, forthcoming).
176 Cf. Dillistone, *Christianity and Symbolism*, pp. 183ff.
177 For attitudes to drinking blood, cf. e.g. Leviticius 17, 10. For the rules about what is to be done with the blood, Leviticus 3.
178 J. Jeremias, *The Eucharistic Words of Jesus* (SCM, 1966), pp. 170 and 225ff.
179 1 Corinthians 11, 25. The same formula occurs in Luke 22, 20.
180 Mark 14, 24–5; Matthew 26, 27–9.
181 John 6, 53–6.
182 D. Dayan and E. Katz, 'Electronic ceremonies: television performs a royal wedding', in Blonsky (ed.), *On Signs*.
183 M. Eliade, *Ordeal by Labyrinth* (University of Chicago Press, Chicago, 1982), p. 55.
184 Quoted in Macy, *Theologies of the Eucharist*, p. 70.
185 P. Ricoeur, *Time and Narrative* (University of Chicago Press, Chicago, 1984), vol. I, p. 3.
186 Ibid., p. 214; cf. also p. 101.
187 M. Tournier, *Le vent Paraclet* (Gallimard, Paris, 1977), p. 193.

Chapter 6   The Last Things

1 A. Schweitzer, *The Quest of the Historical Jesus* (A. & C. Black, 1910); E. P. Sanders, *Jesus and Judaism* (SCM, 1985), esp. pp. 61ff; C. H. Dodd, *The Parables of the Kingdom* (Nisbet, 1935); idem, *The Apostle Preaching and Its Development* (Hodder & Stoughton, 1936); G. B. Caird, *The Language and Imagery of the Bible* (Duckworth, 1980), pp. 243ff.
2 The incident is recalled in C. E. Raven, *Teilhard de Chardin: Scientist and Seer* (Collins, 1962), pp. 54–60.

3 *Mind*, 70 (1961), pp. 99–106.

4 H. de Lubac, *The Religion of Teilhard de Chardin* (Collins, 1967), pp. 84–7.

5 Ibid., pp. 71–2. The phrase occurs in the first paragraph of the Preface to *The Phenomenon of Man* (Fontana, 1965), p. 31.

6 A fact stressed by de Lubac, *The Religion of Teilhard de Chardin*, pp. 108–20 and 137–8.

7 *The Phenomenon of Man*, pp. 277 and 279.

8 G. Baum, *Man Becoming* (Seabury Press, New York, 1979), ch. 1.

9 *The Phenomenon of Man*, p. 294.

10 Both quotations from ibid., p. 288.

11 *Le milieu divin* (Fontana, 1964), p. 143.

12 In *Hymn of the Universe* (Fontana, 1970), p. 28.

13 *Teilhard de Chardin*, ch. 8.

14 *The Phenomenon of Man*, p. 256.

15 Ibid., p. 341.

16 J. B. Metz, *Faith in History and Society* (Burns & Oates, 1980), p. 107; J. Monod, *Chance and Necessity* (Fontana, 1974).

17 *Hearers of the Word*. For a comparison of the extent of the differences between the original and revised edition, cf. R. D. Johns, *Man in the World: the political theology of Johannes Baptist Metz* (Scholars Press, Missoula, Mont., 1976), pp. 73–8.

18 G. Vass, *Understanding Karl Rahner* (Sheed & Ward, 1985), vol. II, p. 48.

19 J. B. Metz, *Theology of the World* (Burns & Oates, 1969), p. 26.

20 Ibid., p. 17.

21 Ibid., p. 49.

22 Ibid., p. 142.

23 *Faith in History and Society*, p. 25; *Theology of the World*, p. 25.

24 *Faith in History and Society*, p. 90.

25 Ibid., p. 108.

26 Ibid., pp. 112–13.

27 *Theology of the World*, p. 146.

28 Best illustrated by the quotation given in R. D. Johns, *Man in the World*, p. 93.

29 R. Schaeffler, *Was dürfen wir hoffen?* (Wissenschaftliche Buchgesell-schaft, Darmstadt, 1979), pp. 50ff.

30 Ibid., p. 324.

31 *Faith in History and Society*, p. 165; idem, *Followers of Christ* (Burns & Oates, 1978), pp. 50ff. For an interesting comparison of the work of Metz with that of H. Wenrich on narrative theology, cf. D. Mieth, *Dichtung, Glaube und Moral* (Matthias-Grünwald, Mainz, 1976), pp. 41ff.

32 *Faith in History and Society*, p. 207.

33 'Topos Utopia', in *Abschied von der Utopie?* (Suhrkamp, Frankfurt, 1980), p. 43.

34 E. Bloch, *The Principle of Hope* (Basil Blackwell, Oxford, 1986), 3 vols.

35 H. Kimmerle, 'Spuren der Hoffnung', in H. Deuser and P. Steinacker (eds), *Ernst Blochs Vermittlungen zur Theologie* (Kaiser, Munich, 1983), p. 17.

36 For the complete version of Marx's statement, see the Introduction to his *Critique of Hegel's Philosophy of Right*. For Bloch's interpretation, *Atheismus im Christentum* (Suhrkamp taschenbuch, Frankfurt, 1985), pp. 90–2.

37 Ibid., pp. 316–17. Cf. also *Das Prinzip Hoffnung*, in *Gesamtausgabe* (Suhrkamp, Frankfurt, 1959–77), vol. V, pp. 1405–17 and 1515–24.

38 J. Moltmann, *Im Gespräch mit Ernst Bloch* (Kaiser, Munich, 1976), pp. 80–1.

39 *Atheismus in Christentum*, pp. 98–111, esp. p. 111.

40 Luke 16, 19–31.

41 E. Bloch, *Essays on the Philosophy of Music* (Cambridge University Press, Cambridge, 1985), pp. 131 and 89. The extent of Bloch's interest in music is well illustrated by the fact that he had originally intended to entitle *Der Geist der Utopie* 'Musik und Apocalypse'. So G. Scholem, *Walter Benjamin* (Faber, 1982), p. 79.

42 Ibid., p. 239.

43 Hebrews, 10, 31.

44 K. Barth, *Church Dogmatics* (T. & T. Clark, Edinburgh, 1961), vol. III, 3, p. 297.

45 *Atheismus in Christentum*, p. 111.

46 'Erbe der Mystik im Werk von Ernst Bloch', in Deuser and Steinacker (eds), *Ernst Blochs Vermittlungen zur Theologie*, p. 120.

47 L. Kolakowski, *Main Currents of Marxism* (Oxford University Press, Oxford, 1981), vol. III, pp. 421–49, esp. p. 437.

48 *Das Materialismusproblem*, in *Gesamtausgabe*, vol. VII, pp. 389–401 and 464.

49 W. Hudson, *The Marxist Philosophy of Ernst Bloch* (Macmillan, 1982), p. 208.

50 *Im Gespräch mit Ernst Bloch*, pp. 57–8.

51 J. Moltmann, *The Crucified God* (SCM, 1974), p. 5.

52 T. W. Adorno, *The Jargon of Authenticity* (Routledge and Kegan Paul, 1973), pp. 131–2.

53 Ibid., p. 138.

54 Ibid., p. 152.

55 Ibid., p. 156.

56 *The Crucified God*, p. 227.

57 Ibid., pp. 219ff. Cf. also S. Sutherland, *Atheism and the Rejection of God* (Basil Blackwell, Oxford, 1977).

58 Plato, *Republic* X, 617e.

59 Thesis presented to German university as a university teaching qualification. In Adorno's case for Frankfurt in 1931 after a previous unsuccessful attempt on a different theme.

60 'On Kierkegaard's doctrine of love', in *Zeitschrift fur Sozialforschung*, 8 (1940), pp. 413–29.

61 *The Jargon of Authenticity*, p. 162.

62 G. Rose, *The Melancholy Science*, (Macmillan, 1978), cf. esp. pp. 24 and 30.
63 T. W. Adorno, *Against Epistemology* (Basil Blackwell, Oxford, 1982), p. 212.
64 Idem, *Minima Moralia* (Verso, 1974), pp. 131–2. Even more derogatorily he qualifies this kind of totality as one 'which the National Socialists have realised'. For further remarks on religion, cf. also 'Vernunft und Offenbarung', in *Stichworte* (Suhrkamp, Frankfurt, 1969), pp. 20–8.
65 T. W. Adorno, *Negative Dialektik* (Suhrkamp taschenbuch, Frankfurt, 1982), p. 205.
66 'Reconciliation under duress', in R. Taylor (ed.), *Aesthetics and Politics* (Verso, 1980), pp. 151–76, esp. pp. 161–2 and 171–2.
67 In 'Commitment', in ibid., pp. 177–95, esp. p. 194.
68 *Negative Dialektik*, p. 394.
69 *Essays on the Philosophy of Music*, p. 68.
70 Available for example in bilingual edition in M. Hamburger (ed.), *Paul Celan: poems* (Carcanet, Manchester, 1980), pp. 50–3.
71 E. Jüngel, *The Doctrine of the Trinity* (Scottish Academic Press, Edinburgh, 1976), p. viii.
72 E. Jüngel, *God as the Mystery of the World* (T. & T. Clark, Edinburgh, 1983), p. 13.
73 Ibid., e.g. p. 103, sec. 13, esp. pp. 213–14 and p. 373.
74 E. Jüngel, *Death: the riddle and the mystery* (Saint Andrew Press, Edinburgh, 1975), pp. 41ff, esp. p. 44.
75 Ibid., p. 69.
76 Ibid., p. 72.
77 Ibid., e.g. p. 115.
78 Ibid., p. 83.
79 Ibid., p. 90.
80 Ibid., p. 92.
81 E.g. Romans 6, 3ff; John 17, 3.
82 Cf. e.g. P. T. Geach, *God and the Soul* (Routledge and Kegan Paul, 1969), ch. 2.
83 *God as the Mystery of the World*, p. 43.
84 Ibid., p. 16. Cf. also pp. 109 and 194–5.
85 Ibid., pp. 118 and 39.
86 Ibid., p. 122.
87 Ibid., pp. 63ff. Note esp. p. 75 n. 74. Though to be fair to him it needs to be noted that others also interpret Hegel's use of death of God language as offering an orthodox alternative to Nietzsche's challenge. Cf. e.g. J. Salaquarda's Introduction to the collection of essays he edited on the Nietzschean theme: *Philosophische Theologie im Schatten des Nihilismus* (Gruyter, Berlin, 1971), esp. pp. 5ff.
88 Ibid., pp. 55ff and pp. 199ff, esp. p. 219.
89 J. B. Webster, *Eberhard Jüngel* (Cambridge University Press, Cambridge, 1986), p. 54. His italics.
90 Contrast Mark 15, 34 and John 19, 30 (the Greek perfect tense of 'It is finished' is normally interpreted as a cry of triumph).

91 *Death: the riddle and the mystery*, p. 119.
92 The title of section 19 (pp. 299ff) of *God as the Mystery of the World*.
93 Quoted on back cover of W. Benjamin, *One Way Streets and Other Writings* (Verso, 1985).
94 In the Introduction to W. Benjamin, *The Origin of German Tragic Drama* (Verso, 1985), p. 13. Steiner is referring to the theoretical preface, 'Epistemolo-Critical Prologue', pp. 27–56.
95 W. Benjamin, *Illuminations* (Fontana, 1973), pp. 83–109, esp. p. 83.
96 Ibid., p. 87.
97 Ibid., pp. 90–1.
98 Ibid., p. 94.
99 'The image of Proust', in ibid., pp. 203ff.
100 H. W. Frei, *The Eclipse of Biblical Narrative* (Yale University Press, New Haven, Conn., 1974), pp. 86–7.
101 Ibid., pp. 307ff, esp. pp. 311–12.
102 Ibid., p. 130.
103 Quoted without reference in G. W. Stroup, *The Promise of Narrative Theology* (SCM, 1984), p. 69.
104 Ibid., pp. 174ff, esp. p. 179.
105 Ibid., pp. 116 and 127.
106 Ibid., p. 36.
107 Ibid., p. 157. Cf. also p. 163.
108 *The Origin of German Tragic Drama*, p. 54.
109 Ibid., pp. 65–9. I have retained the German title in the text because the English translation is very misleading.
110 Ibid., p. 79. For the absence of 'eschatology' and 'apocalyptic', cf. pp. 66 and 80.
111 Ibid., e.g. pp. 83–4.
112 Ibid., p. 138.
113 For Surrealism, *One Way Street*, pp. 225ff. For Brecht, *Illuminations*, pp. 149ff.
114 *The Origin of German Tragic Drama*, p. 182.
115 K. Kesey, *One Flew over the Cuckoo's Nest* (Picador, 1973); M. Tournier, *The Four Wise Men* (Methuen, 1982).
116 Cf. 1 Kings 16, 23–8. Assyrian records described Israel as 'the House of Omri'.
117 Cf. e.g. Thesis XIII in *Illuminations*, pp. 262–3.
118 Thesis XIV in *Illuminationen* (Suhrkamp taschenbuch, Frankfurt, 1977), p. 258. The German edition has additional material not available in the English translation.
119 For the notion of 'aura', cf. e.g. *Illuminations*, pp. 109, 188, 223–7 and 245 n. 5.
120 Ibid., pp. 134–5.
121 For additional reasons for believing in Purgatory, cf. my article 'No Heaven without Purgatory', in *Religious Studies*, 1985, pp. 447–56.
122 J. Roberts, *Walter Benjamin* (Macmillan, 1982), esp. pp. 134–5 and 196–9; T. Eagleton, *Walter Benjamin* (Verso, 1981), esp. p. 81 n. 2; G. Scholem, *Walter Benjamin: the story of a friendship* (Faber, 1982), passim.

123 Thesis I in *Illuminations*, p. 255.
124 R. Wolin, *Walter Benjamin: an aesthetic of redemption* (Columbia University Press, New York, 1982), p. 260. This is the best book on Benjamin's thought currently available.
125 Thesis IX in *Illuminations*, pp. 259–60.
126 Scholem, *Walter Benjamin*, p. 56.
127 *God as the Mystery of the World*, e.g. pp. 316 and 345–6.
128 Ibid., pp. 260, 140 and 298.

Index